W9-BXZ-456

The Feeling of History

∴

The Feeling of History

∴

ISLAM, ROMANTICISM, AND ANDALUSIA

Charles Hirschkind

THE UNIVERSITY OF CHICAGO PRESS

CHICAGO AND LONDON

The University of Chicago Press, Chicago 60637
The University of Chicago Press, Ltd., London
© 2021 by The University of Chicago
All rights reserved. No part of this book may be used or reproduced
in any manner whatsoever without written permission, except in
the case of brief quotations in critical articles and reviews. For more
information, contact the University of Chicago Press, 1427 E. 60th St.,
Chicago, IL 60637.
Published 2021
Printed in the United States of America

29 28 27 26 25 24 23 22 21 20   1 2 3 4 5

ISBN-13: 978-0-226-74681-4 (cloth)
ISBN-13: 978-0-226-74695-1 (paper)
ISBN-13: 978-0-226-74700-2 (e-book)
DOI: https://doi.org/10.7208/chicago/9780226747002.001.0001

Library of Congress Cataloging-in-Publication Data

Names: Hirschkind, Charles, author.
Title: The feeling of history : Islam, romanticism, and Andalusia /
Charles Hirschkind.
Other titles: Islam, romanticism, and Andalusia
Description: Chicago : The University of Chicago Press, 2021. |
Includes bibliographical references and index.
Identifiers: LCCN 2020022829 | ISBN 9780226746814 (cloth) |
ISBN 9780226746951 (paperback) | ISBN 9780226747002 (ebook)
Subjects: LCSH: Collective memory—Spain—Andalusia. |
Orientalism—Spain—Andalusia. | Andalusia (Spain)—Civilization. |
Andalusia (Spain)—Civilization—Islamic influences. | Andalusia
(Spain)—Historiography.
Classification: LCC DP302.A467 H56 2020 | DDC 946/.02—dc23
LC record available at https://lccn.loc.gov/2020022829

♾ This paper meets the requirements of ANSI/NISO Z39.48-1992
(Permanence of Paper).

For Saba

Contents

Introduction

The argument I explore here can be simply stated: medieval Muslim Iberia did not disappear from history with the seizure of Granada in 1492 by Christian armies, as our history books have it. Rather, forced into hiding, it continued on as an invisible warp within the fabric of Spanish society. The medieval realm of al-Andalus and contemporary Spain and Portugal, in other words, do not belong to two distant historical periods, one medieval and one modern, but cohere in a single continuous development, unbroken by the periodicities imposed by modern historiography. Signs of this anachronistic Mediterranean world are today ubiquitous—evident in the expressive gestures of contemporary Andalusians, in the imprint of Arabic left on the Spanish language, in architectural and musical motifs binding one side of the sea to the other. These cultural features articulate a place and time that intersects with modern Spain and Europe but also exceeds the historical geography defined by these names, incorporating pasts and regions beyond the boundaries these names secure.

To explore this heterotopia at the edge of Europe, however, to uncover its political and philosophical traditions, its cultural and aesthetic forms, turns out to be incredibly difficult. Curiosity about it, experts in the field caution, is misguided, really just a bit of nostalgic whimsy. She who insists otherwise has caught the Romantic bug. The medieval Arabic embedded in her contemporary Spanish turns out not to be evidence of a complex inheritance but, she will be told, only an unremarkable linguistic relic, one no more significant than the linguistic fusions common in other modern languages. Her discovery that the gestural vocabulary of her hands is mirrored back to her from the other side of the Mediterranean in present-day Morocco is not evidence of an ongoing history of exchange and circulation but simply her indulgence in a well-worn Orientalist practice, that of holding up a southern mirror to Europe's northern face. And when she hears medieval fusions of Arabic, Jewish, and Roma musics resonating in the cry of the flamenco singer, she has not finally moved beyond the narrow walls of European nationalisms but is instead unwittingly seized by a most nationalist of emotions, one forged by the early twentieth-century Andalusians who invented a musical past to legitimate their claims for regional autonomy. At each step away from Spain and its conceptual and genealogical anchorage in Europe, she winds up back where she started, chastised as another naïf, spellbound by the fantastical images produced by the play of mirrors between East and West, North and South. This lifeworld, she will be taught by the leading experts on the topic, was only and ever the fictive product of a Romantic imagination, an Orientalist fantasy sold like a trinket to tourists and nostalgists.

Despite these obstacles, a small number of men and women, a society of *appassionati*, train themselves to recognize the subtle outlines of this shifting lifeworld. To do so they cultivate and promote new perceptual habits, often through a sustained engagement with medieval Iberian history, with Andalusi aesthetic traditions, and with the cultures of the modern Middle East, with which they find a deep kinship. Scavengers of a weathered and damaged text, they assemble the shards of sense they find in ancient monuments, in etymologies, in gestures, in names, and in music, drawing these fragments of the past into a lived inheritance so as to mend the fabric that binds al-Andalus to Andalusia. The Alhambra, Granada's famed Nasrid Fort, forms a powerful material anchor. In its mystical arabesques they intuit the lineaments and underlying principles of an aesthetic regime that suffuses and conjoins past and present. It is music, however, more than any other genre, that equips them to navigate the divide between medieval and modern, to hear and feel the resonances that give unity to this territory. And though they will often approach this anachronistic world along a route paved by the idealized images of Spain's Romantic poets and Orientalist artists, they attune themselves to not be lured into the dead ends to which these roads have so often led.

For those equipped with the requisite sensibilities to inhabit this world, it is not some aesthetic vacationland but a historical fact illuminated by and corresponding to the challenges of our present political moment, particularly the hardening of lines between Europe and the Middle East and between Europeans and the North African immigrants in their midst. They are confronted daily with countless editorials comparing the arrival of Muslim immigrants into the country with the "Muslim conquest of 711" and warning that Spaniards once again are being called on to defend Europe's southern border. The violence and paranoia of the Inquisition, they find, are alive and well in fortress Europe.

A THIRD SPAIN

In this book I examine the lives of some of those who have explored this lifeworld—forged at the hinge of the medieval Muslim kingdoms of al-Andalus and present-day Andalusia—and who have advocated on its behalf, a group I will refer to as *andalucistas*.[1] Andalucismo, as I interpret it here, is a modern tradition of critical reflection on the norms of European politics and culture based on a cultivated appreciation for the histories and legacies of southern Iberia's Muslim and Jewish societies.[2] This tradition is founded on a seemingly simple principle: that contemporary Andalusia is linked in vitally important ways with al-Andalus (medieval Islamic Iberia) and that the challenges faced by Andalusians today—and by Europeans more broadly—require a recognition of that historical identity and continuity. Al-Andalus, in this formulation, is not a distant mirror from which to reflect on contemporary challenges, a beautiful image to inspire, but a critical dimension of our contemporary existence. The continuous erasure of this inheritance, its transformation into a museum piece by modern historical discourse, are ideological procedures designed to shore up Europe's temporal and geographic borders. The task of the *andalucistas* can thus be described as a kind of historical therapeutics, a reorientation of cultural and political subjectivity through an excavation of a buried past. This task is not simply an intellectual exercise, a project of historical research. It is carried out in the multiple ways people seek to accommodate their lives to the demands of an inheritance only partially available to knowledge and thus often more felt than known. While historical narrative takes a prominent role within the discourse of Andalucismo, *andalucistas* count few professional historians among their ranks; journalists, political activists, writers, artists, and musicians make up most of their number.

Al-Andalus is a term frequently used by historians to refer to the period when Muslim sovereigns ruled over parts of the Iberian Peninsula.[3] As historical periods go, it is one of the most precisely defined and bordered, beginning in 711 with the arrival on the peninsula of a small Muslim force led by the Umayyad general Tariq Ibn-Ziyad and ending in 1492 with the conquest of Granada, the last Iberian Muslim kingdom, by the armies of the Catholic monarchs Ferdinand and Isabella. Of course historians of Spain will complexify this chronology, noting on one hand that most of the Iberian territories that were at one time under Muslim rule had been lost to Christian armies almost two and a half centuries before 1492 and on the other that the final expulsion of the descendants of Iberian Muslims (referred to as Moriscos) from the peninsula did not occur until the early seventeenth century. These qualifications notwithstanding, al-Andalus, to all intents and purposes, will by most accounts belong only to the past, interred behind that most fateful of years, 1492.

Within *andalucista* narratives, however, the historical career of al-Andalus does not abruptly conclude with the defeat of the Nasrid rulers of Granada but continues to exert its presence in subterranean forms largely unrecognizable within the dominant epistemes of post-1492 Europe. More precisely, with the collapse of Muslim rule, the history of the peninsula proceeds along three discrete pathways. The first is the path of exile, of generations, Muslim and Jewish, compelled to an elsewhere, many to permanent residence in North Africa, where still today the descendants of the Iberian Muslims are known as Andalusians.[4] The second (culminating in Spain's dominant political order) is that defined by the country's simultaneously Christian and European trajectory, both of these elements converging in different moments of their early-modern and contemporary development around a shared opposition to an Islamic (and until recently, Jewish) Other. Finally, the third historical pathway, Andalucismo affirms, is that of a Mediterranean society, one constitutively entwined with Islamic and Jewish cultural forms and bound, therefore, in a familial relation to the peoples and nations across the sea. This third historical arc, *andalucistas* assert, has been systematically denied across Spanish history, forced into silence and obscurity by the dominant arbiters of public memory beginning with the Catholic Inquisitors themselves in the sixteenth and seventeenth centuries. Over the subsequent years, the perceptual infrastructure installed by this campaign became a durable and abiding inheritance, immunizing Spain's national, Catholic soul from any attachments rooted in its Muslim and Jewish past.[5]

As many scholars have noted, the religious, political, and epistemological rupture of 1492 was decisive both for Spain and for the career of European modernity more broadly. As the literary historian Edwige Tamalet Talbayev has recently observed, "In the enduring post-Andalusian, divisive world order of Western modernity born of the rubble of Mediterranean shared history, Spain's identity emerged from the eradication of cross-confessional contact. It materialized in the form of anti-Jewish and anti-Muslim violence, mass conversions, and the establishment of the Inquisition, until very recent revaluations of its Muslim past fractured the monolithic narrative of the Catholic monarchs' history" (Talbayev 2017, 88). Today the political correlate of this prevailing sensory regime is manifest in the plethora of border controls separating Spain from North Africa and in the political, religious, and cultural divides setting Europe and the United States in anxious opposition to the Middle East. Andalucismo puts into question the discursive protocols and sensory epistemology that secure these oppositions and that produce the historical closure of al-Andalus and its noncontemporaneity with our time.

Over the following chapters I follow the threads of Andalucismo as it unfolds across the lives of a number of the tradition's proponents, some contemporary, others founding figures. I focus on individual lives because the tradition I wish to articulate only acquires a discernable pattern when traced on a biographical image. *Andalucista* arguments, performances, and ideas, when taken individually, disappear into a terrain dominated by such familiar terms as *Romanticism, Orientalism, nationalism,* and *nostalgia.* The perspectives and commitments that undergird these terms, I argue, are an obstacle when it comes to exploring the inquiries and insights of Andalucismo. At the same time, this tradition is anchored less in a subject than in a sensibility, one that traverses people and practices. In this book I pursue this sensibility across a heterogeneous set of trajectories, movements across geographic, moral, social, aesthetic, and technical registers that in different ways open up the historical borders of al-Andalus onto our present and in so doing so proffer a different historical geography from which to think about contemporary Spain and Europe and their relation to Islam and the Middle East.

Importantly, there is no single political perspective authorized by this tradition. For example, while the Granadan poet Federico García Lorca was murdered by right-wing military forces in Granada at the beginning of the civil war in 1936, his fellow *andalucista* and occasional interlocutor Rudolfo Gil Benumeya remained a colonial official within the Franco regime throughout most of his career (I discuss the lives of these two men below, Lorca in chap. 4 and Gil Benumeya in chap. 1). What unites thinkers within this tradition is not a political prescription but the sense of a shared Andalusian historical legacy as the ground from which the present must be encountered, interrogated, and lived. A sustained suspicion of Spain's Europeanizing ambitions can be traced across the career of the tradition, especially toward the rationalizing and centralizing impulses that have accompanied these ambitions and their destructive impact on regional traditions and cultural forms. While this impetus has led many scholars to dismiss Andalucismo for its Romantic pedigree, I argue that the unique historical horizon it articulates distinguishes this tradition from Romanticism as it is commonly understood—or rather, it demands that we recognize its distinct trajectory within the broader movement defined by this term and particularly the friction it exerts on projects of Spanish and European identity.

For this reason, and contrary to most interpreters of this tradition, I do not conceive of Andalucismo as a species of Romantic nationalism nor as a project that constructs a past to serve as support for a more capacious form of national identity. This is not to say the tradition has not been recruited for nationalist and regionalist ends. But the past that *andalucistas* find themselves to inhabit, feel themselves passionately compelled to acknowledge, does not anchor a pregiven identity so much as unsettle the grounds on which existing identity formations rest. Surrounded by the material, artifactual, and linguistic remnants of al-Andalus, the followers of this tradition discover themselves to be inheritors of a past that, while elusive and inaccessible in some aspects, nonetheless demands to be listened to openly—even if this listening disturbs or unravels their sense of identity as Europeans, Spaniards, or Andalusians.

This style of historical reflection—one that recounts not who we are but why we are other than what we have been told—owes to a form of discourse whose emergence Foucault traces to the late sixteenth century. Before this moment, indeed, from the Romans up through the Middle Ages, history was the story of sovereign right, a testament to the glorious victories of the king and the unbroken continuity of the ancestral chain he represented. Like other rituals of sovereignty, the function of history was "to speak the right of power and to intensify the luster of power" (Foucault 2003, 66). In the late sixteenth century, however, a new form of historical discourse emerges, a "counterhistory," Foucault observes, one "closer to the mythico-religious discourse of the Jews than to the politico-legendary history of the Romans" (2003, 71). Instead of intensifying the glory and right of the sovereign, this new history takes the side of those defeated and silenced by sovereign power, those whose historical experience and identity have been left in darkness by the victors. "The new history," Foucault writes, in a formulation that reappears almost to the letter across the texts of Andalucismo, "has to disinter something that has been hidden, and which has been hidden not only because it has been neglected, but because it has been carefully, deliberately, and wickedly misrepresented. . . . This will not, then, be a history of continuity, but a history of the deciphering, the detection of the secret, of the outwitting of the ruse, and of the reappropriation of a knowledge that has been distorted or buried" (2003, 72). This narrative form, more prophetic than documentary, will provide the scaffolding for *andalucista* historical reflection, shaping its central claims about a people forced to live a lie of racial and religious purity and only now beginning to decipher the truth about themselves and about the past hidden within them.

FORMATION OF A TRADITION

While Andalucismo begins to acquire its recognizable form around the late nineteenth century, antecedents to the tradition can be traced back much farther. An early moment in the prehistory of Andalucismo occurs during the sixteenth century with the emergence of a popular literary form centered on the chivalric exploits of the knights and noblemen of al-Andalus (see Carrasco Urgoiti 1989, 2005). For many of its modern interpreters, this literary tradition is to be understood as an early version of the contemporary mythology of the noble Moor, an idealizing portrait of a vanquished enemy with little or no relation to the historical realities of Muslims in Spain. This judgment, however, does not do justice to the way this tradition—and the attention and fascination given at the time to things *árabe* more generally—directly responded to pressing contemporary questions about the status of the Moriscos (Muslims who had been forced to convert to Christianity) and their relation to Spanish culture and society more broadly. As the literary historian Barbara Fuchs has noted, "Far from idealizing fantasies, the [Maurophilic] texts participate fully in the urgent negotiation of a Moorishness that is not only a historiographical relic but a vivid presence in quotidian Spanish culture" (Fuchs 2009, 5). The negotiation that Fuchs refers to here concerns "the Moorish question" (not unlike "the Muslim question" of today), namely, the place of the large number of assimilated Muslims within a Spanish society and polity that was adopting steadily more homogenizing and exclusively Christian versions of identity.[6] Within this context of political and cultural upheaval, the positive, "idealizing" valuation given to Muslims was one factor in a broader movement to counter such exclusivist versions of identity and thus create a space hospitable to the Moriscos and the Muslim culture that marked them. A second literary precursor to Andalucismo occurs within Spanish Golden Age literature (sixteenth to eighteenth centuries), where one finds a significant number of works examining the tensions between increasingly dominant monocultural constructions of identity and the region's Semitic genealogy, then in the process of being erased or rendered illegible (see, e.g., Fuchs 2003; Menocal 2002; Quinn 2013; Castro 1967).

While these early literary trends are integral to the tradition this book explores, it is only in the nineteenth century that Andalucismo acquires its name and the contours of a distinct cultural and political movement. The encounter of cultural and historical horizons articulated by the nineteenth-century Spanish scholars that gave birth to this movement was conditioned by the Orientalization of southern Europe then taking place across a range of European popular and scholarly discourses. According to the literary scholar Roberto Dainotto, as European Orientalism was reaching its apogee in the mid-eighteenth century, a new logic of European self-definition emerged in which the Oriental Other was internalized, translated, and relocated into Europe's own south (see Dainotto 2000, 2006, 2007). Europe's antithesis—its "Orient"—was now incorporated within its own heterogeneous topography. Commenting on Hegel's characterization of this process, Dainotto observes,

> The "infinite process of civilization"—the teleological movement from what was to what is now—institutes then a geographical past of Europe, an "origin" that is no longer elsewhere—in the wilderness of Africa or in the flatlands of Asia—but right in the middle of the "liquid" and "centerless" *mare nostrum*. Europe, in order to become a totality, invents its own south, the place, namely, where the "other" civilizations are translated into, and internalized as, a past moment in the giddy progress of Europe. (Dainotto 2000, 380–81)

Not surprisingly, it is at this historical juncture that the question of Iberia's Muslim and Jewish past emerges as a concern within Spanish historiography.

Forced to inhabit the role of the nobly savage past within the total system that was gradually consolidating Europe's modern identity, Spaniards reacted in two broad directions. The first, evident in much historical writing up through the present, was to insist on the nation's essential Europeanness, often through the erasure, denial, or denigration of its own African and Middle Eastern genealogy. A second direction, pioneered initially by scholars within the emerging field of Arabism, was to exploit the gaps opened up within Spain's historical experience by its very peripheralization so as to assert a unique role for the country within the story of modern Europe, one based on a positive valorization of its Muslim and Jewish legacies.[7] While many advocates of this view argued that Spain's Andalusian heritage positioned the country at the origin of modern Europe, others rejected the idea that Europe should be seen as the telos of this heritage. Europe did indeed begin at the Pyrenees, as Montesquieu had asserted disparagingly, and there was no reason why Spaniards shouldn't embrace and celebrate this fact.

Drawing sustenance from this latter historiographical current, Andalucismo first emerges in the late nineteenth century as a movement among a small group of intellectuals who, confronted with the sense of national malaise provoked by the loss of Spain's overseas empire and the country's state of economic and political weakness, began to seek out resources of national renewal in the nation's past and in the folkloric traditions where that past, in their view, still lived on.[8] For some of these thinkers, including Ángel Ganivet, a nineteenth-century pioneer of *andalucista* thinking, a reflection on Andalusian traditions led directly to a reconsideration of the Muslim and Jewish inheritance within contemporary Andalusia and an acknowledgment of its imprint across the human and material physiognomy of the region. The Andalucismo of Ganivet and his successors found important resources for this exercise in the country's rich literary traditions, including nineteenth-century Spanish Romanticism as well as in the growing corpus of Spanish Arabism and Orientalism.[9] By the second decade of the twentieth century, this movement of cultural recuperation pioneered by fin de siècle intellectuals became directly linked to a politics of regional autonomy, an ambition that was already well developed in other parts of Spain, notably Catalonia and the Basque country. In common usage Andalucismo refers primarily to this regional-nationalist movement, though today the goal of complete political independence has been largely abandoned, and the movement's concerns have come to focus on the cultural and educational policies of the Andalusian state. Indeed, as the economy of the province has come to depend ever more on a tourist trade centered around the region's Muslim and Jewish architectural legacy, this project has been pursued with greater urgency and investment.[10]

Andalucismo also has a career in another ideological context outside the regional-nationalist movement as one line of thought within Spanish Africanism, a discourse that served to promote and legitimate Spanish colonial ambitions in North Africa and that was embodied most directly in the Spanish Protectorate in Morocco (1912–1956). Andalucismo provided the Africanists with an image of Spain and Morocco bound harmoniously together by a common culture and history, a trans-Mediterranean "brotherhood" (*hermandad*), thus enabling Spanish state propaganda to portray the country's military occupation as an act of fraternal beneficence (see chap. 1). Composed primarily of men affiliated with the administration of the Protectorate, Africanism thrived within its own network of journals and institutional fora throughout the duration of the occupation.[11] While these diverse political currents and institutions of the Spanish state gave momentum to Andalucismo across the first half of the twentieth century, the center of gravity of the tradition, the impetus from which its coherence derives, has always placed it in critical tension with the goals and bureaucratic imperatives of these institutions, a tension that I trace across the chapters of this book.

The most provocative and influential interpretation of the Muslim and

Jewish contributions to the formation of Spain written during the twentieth century is that of Américo Castro, a scholar whose work had a decisive
impact on the tradition of Andalucismo.[12] Writing from exile in the United
States in the early years of the Franco regime, Castro came to formulate an
understanding of Spanish history that posited a direct link between "the
enthronement of mental ineptitude and paralysis" (Castro 1948, 597–98)
exemplified in the Franco dictatorship and the institutions of the Spanish
Inquisition, the two united in their concerns over Spanish racial purity.[13]
Castro rejected a long tradition of Spanish historiography that posited the
origins of the nation in the Visigothic Empire (fifth to eighth centuries) and
which viewed the eight hundred years of Muslim presence as a national
parenthesis finally to be overcome by the Reconquista and the return to
religious and territorial unity. Rather, Spanish identity, he argued, was the
product of a creative symbiosis among Muslims, Jews, and Christians set in
motion by the Muslim entry into Spain in 711. In a characteristic statement
he notes, "That which made possible such great works as the Celestina and
the Quijote, and hence the European novel and drama, was a certain vision
of man in which were woven—as in an ideal and precious tapestry—the Islamic, Christian, and Judaic conceptions of man" (Castro 1961, 13).[14] Castro
was not a historian by training but rather a literary scholar, and his Romantic and existentialist vision of history took language and literary works as
its primary material. Through a brilliant and original reading of medieval
and early-modern Spanish literary forms, Castro sought to elucidate how
this conjunction of the three "castes" (*castas*) had produced a unique form
of life, or what, in his existentialist vocabulary, he termed a *morada vital*,
a dwelling place of life—namely, a weave of moral, aesthetic, and religious
values that conjoined to form a distinctly Spanish way of life. His inquiries
gave particular attention not only to grammatical and semantic hybrids but
to the way Spanish literary expression had incorporated a vision of human
life—of love, joy, pain, and death—directly from Muslim and Jewish traditions.

Influenced by German Romanticism, Castro understood the task of the
historian to include revivifying the dynamic relation between past and
present, thereby releasing the creative potential of historical events from
their temporal prison. Of particular significance for Andalucismo was
Castro's diagnosis of the disorder afflicting Spanish society and psychology
produced by the nation's compulsive rejection of its Muslim and Jewish legacies. He coined the term *vivir desviviéndose*—"living by denying the reality
of one's existence" (Sáenz 1997, 162), in one useful translation—precisely
to describe this aspect of Spanish life. One of the claims of this book is that
this is not just a Spanish malady but one that infects Europe as a whole.

ISLAM CONTRA EUROPE

From the viewpoint of Andalucismo, the historiography of al-Andalus has not done justice to the past it explores. The dispassionate gaze of the historians rests on a foundation of unacknowledged violence, a long-standing effort to immunize Spain and Europe against Jews and Muslims—viewed as a threat to its Christian/European identity—in an effort carried out earlier by the authorities of the Holy Inquisition and continuing today in the construction of camps encircled by electrified wire to detain immigrants coming from across the Mediterranean. The task assigned to medieval historiography within this enterprise is to sterilize Iberia against any lived connection to its past, to relegate any vestiges emanating from that past to the museum so to ensure that whatever imbrications one encounters between al-Andalus and contemporary Andalusia—and between one side of the Mediterranean and the other—they will not stir in the contemporary European reader any emotion or provoke any action that cannot be contained within, and made to serve, the existing European political order.[15] The primary lesson of Iberia's Muslim and Jewish history will be that it ended.

Within conventional histories of Europe, al-Andalus has most frequently been ascribed the role of a carrier society, a vehicle through which certain elements of Greek and Roman thought entered European civilization but one which contributed nothing of its own to that formation.[16] Thus, while contemporary Spain may be considered an integral component of the geographic imaginary of Europe—if more tenuously so, in light of recent economic indicators—the Muslim past has remained substantively outside the confines of that civilizational space. This effacement of Muslims from the processes giving form to Europe has a disciplinary correlate in the marginality of Arabic within the field of medieval studies despite the great importance of scholarship written in Arabic across this period.[17] The observations I make here are hardly new. For many decades, scholars have called attention to the rather distorted view of medieval society engendered by the relative exclusion of Arabo-Islamic sources from the academic purview of medieval studies. The fact that this remains largely unchanged despite years of scholarly criticism is indicative that what is at stake in defining Europe's historical parameters extends beyond a matter of academic institutional heritage, pointing to the exceptional status of Islam in relation to the historical operations that define and circumscribe the civilizational project of Europe.[18]

As scholars of early-modern Europe have persuasively argued, Europe's historical animosity toward Islam involved more than a natural antipathy felt for a rival empire, forming a significant factor in the emergence of the notion of Europe itself.[19] As the historian Tomaž Mastnak has noted, "Europe as a self-conscious collective entity emerged relatively late in the course of human events, and Western, Latin Christians' hostility toward the Muslims—anti-Muslim sentiments, ideas, calls for action, and action—played a key role in its formation" (Mastnak 2003, 205).[20] What is at stake here is not just an antagonism born of a shared border. The border itself, conceptually as well as practically, was the product of an exteriorization of Islam, its political and theological relegation to an outside, a point stressed by Gil Anidjar (2003) in his perceptive reading of the entwined figures of the Jew and the Arab within European political and philosophical thought. As Anidjar summarizes in an introductory comment,

> Islam thus becomes an "internal exteriority," an included exclusion, according to the structure of the exception formalized most famously by Carl Schmitt and that will occupy us throughout what follows: If the name of this exclusion, this exteriorization, is "Islam," then in naming itself as what faces Islam, "Europe" hides itself from itself by claiming to have a name and a face independently of Islam. (Anidjar 2003, xxii)

The Reconquista, a concept fully articulated only in the context of mid-nineteenth-century Spanish nationalism (see chap. 2), must be seen as one paradigmatic figure within the discourse on Islam's exteriority to Europe.

Over the years, this European tradition has lost little of its vitality, evident in the contemporary proliferation of discourse on the incompatibility of Muslim immigrants with "European values." During the war in Bosnia, it should be recalled, Serbs sought support for their assault on Bosnia by portraying their actions as a European crusade carried out by Europeans in the name of Europe. As Mastnak observes,

> It is not surprising that it was while this "European project" was making progress that the talk of Crusades resurfaced in Europe—most clearly in the war against Bosnia. The term crusade was used by both the perpetrators of the genocide, when they tried to make sense of their actions to themselves (and to their Euro-American accomplices), and by those against whom this crime of humanity had been directed, who were also struggling to understand what had befallen them. (Mastnak 2003, 231)

The argument did indeed make sense to many politicians in Europe and the United States who found their ability to take action against the slaughter constrained by a worry that their efforts might result in a Muslim country in the heart of Europe.[21]

The political stakes of this exclusionary stance toward Islam are today even more clear. For some years now, European political life has resolved to a significant extent around the question of whether and how Muslim immigrants are to be accorded a place within European societies. (This issue has also, of course, become hotly contested within American political debates, particularly under the Trump administration.) Many in Europe today view Muslim immigrants as representatives of an alien civilization, one incompatible with and a direct threat to modern European values and freedoms.[22] To proponents of this view, Europe is to be seen as the product of a unique historical trajectory, one whose moral and political virtues were grown from a Christian—and, increasingly, a Judeo-Christian—soil that Islam does not share. A comment by the German sociologist and philosopher Jürgen Habermas exemplifies this stance:

> Universalistic egalitarianism, from which sprang the ideals of freedom and a collective life in solidarity, the autonomous conduct of life and emancipation, the individual morality of conscience, human rights and democracy, is the direct legacy of the Judaic ethics of justice and the Christian ethic of love. This legacy, substantially unchanged, has been the object of continual critical appropriation and reinterpretation. To this day, there is no alternative to it. And in light of the current challenges of a postnational constellation, we continue to draw on the substance of this constellation. Everything else is just idle postmodern talk. (Habermas 2006, 150–51)

No direct reference to Europe is needed to anchor such a striking claim, as Habermas's readers will recognize that there is only one civilizational location whose celebrated heritage is universally recognizable in such terms as human rights, democracy, autonomy, and individual morality.

Habermas's claim is part of the intellectual scaffolding that sustains today's anti-Muslim polemics in Europe. Although this narrative is neither seamless nor uncontested, it has increasingly defined the broader ground on which opposing political viewpoints on the desirability of Muslim immigration devolves. Similar views abound in Spain as well. To take one example, Serafín Fanjul, professor of Arabic literature at Madrid's Complutense University and an important voice in public indictments of Islam, responds to invocation of the country's Islamic heritage by insisting on its European philosophical, cultural, religious, and racial pedigree:

Confronted with evidence of our belonging to the great civilization of Europe (the neo-Latin variety, with a background in Greek Philosophy, combined with Roman and Germanic legal traditions), with a Christian cultural and religious foundation, a Northern Mediterranean physical type (with some small regional variations, as in Galicia and Asturias), and with a historical trajectory parallel to and implicated with the rest of the continent (Feudalism, Renaissance, Enlightenment, etc.), [these denigrators of Spain] respond—first the travellers and then the local imitators—by blowing out of proportion trifles both inconsequential and of debatable significance, in order to claim an Arab or Moorish character. (Fanjul 2014)

Yet in Spain, an entity "constructed in its political, economic, cultural, and religious dimensions, on the ruins of al-Andalus" (Buresi 2009, 129), the historiographical operation that secures the nation's place within a European civilizational narrative remains brittle, its immunity from competing histories less secure than one would find in France, Germany, or England.

The historian David Nirenberg is among those who have challenged the claim that Europe has been consistently defined through its opposition to Islam. In his view, those who claim that Islam has no historical relation whatsoever to Europe (a view exemplified in his article by Pope Benedict) and those who, to the contrary, argue that Islam is profoundly entwined with European history but that this entwinement has been neglected or ignored because of bias (his example is the literary historian María Rosa Menocal),[23] are in fact advancing arguments that simply mirror each other, "equally fantastic" insomuch as they both portray the relation between Islam and Europe in polarizing terms (Nirenberg 2008, 5). In contrast to these two viewpoints, Nirenberg argues that European views of Islam and its relation to Europe have been both negative and positive:

Both exclusion and inclusion are inseparable faces of a debate over Islam that appears in tandem with the idea of Europe itself. The emergence of the one is cognitively related to the emergence of the other, so much so that we might even say that the debate about Europe's relationship to Islam is both a constitutive attribute of Europe, and a distinctively European product. (Nirenberg 2008, 24–25)

Nirenberg is certainly right that Herder (cited in his text) and other Romantic writers reflected extensively on the importance of Arab scholarship in the genealogy of European literature, the one field Nirenberg addresses in the article. Yet he fails to note how, almost without exception, their writings on the contribution of Arabs and Islam to the formation of Europe sought to emphasize its insubstantiality, a mere spark for a creation whose originality lay elsewhere.[24]

It is Nirenberg's suggestion, however, that Europe has been conceptually constituted as much by an overt embrace of the legacy of al-Andalus as by its rejection that strains comprehension. Extending on the argument cited above, he writes, "in the West that legacy [the legacy of al-Andalus] had been more or less constantly cultivated from the sixteenth century to the present by those who would include Islam in countless registers of European culture: art and architecture, literature and music, history, philology, philosophy and theology, to name a few" (Nirenberg 2008, 27–8). A quick perusal of the syllabi for introductory courses on "European culture" as exemplified in any of the academic fields mentioned here reveals Islam to be little more than a footnote, relegated to a week of study at best over the course of a semester. If we are to understand Europe as a concept constituted, to a significant degree, through an internal debate about the contribution of Arabo-Islamic tradition to its own formation, it is clear that contrary to Nirenberg's view, one party to this debate has consistently and repeatedly triumphed over the other.[25]

DANGEROUS HISTORIES

As a genre of critical historical discourse, Andalucismo has from its inception wandered along the border of academic respectability, a suspect mode of knowledge production, too passionately attached to its object of reflection on the one hand and too enmeshed in the political realities of its time on the other. For the majority of contemporary Spanish scholars, the discourses of Andalucismo remain mired in a Romantic fictionalization of the past, one encouraged and sustained by the ideological service it provides to a variety of commercial and political ambitions. Idealizing the medieval society of al-Andalus as a utopia of interconfessional harmony, of *convivencia*, the *andalucistas*, these critics complain, proffer a highly distorted, selective, and consequently false image of that society. The violence and inequality integral to medieval Iberian society and politics are sanitized and aestheticized, they argue, in order to fashion an image of a lost utopia useful to a contemporary politics of multiculturalism.

Such critical judgments are echoed throughout much of the scholarship on medieval Spain. One example will serve. In an article concerned precisely with the danger of idealization, the prominent Spanish medievalist Manuela Marín criticizes the enthusiastic attention given by some scholars to an Andalusian *art de vivre* that flourished, it is said, in Iberia during the tenth and eleventh centuries (Marín 1998). While such art forms may have been a preoccupation of a few, the vast majority of people, she reminds us, were far more concerned with the struggle to survive. The idealizing impulse of Andalucismo, she cautions, seizes on aesthetic marginalia while neglecting the true subject of (democratic) history: the masses and the political-economic determinants of their lives.[26] In short, *andalucistas* have selectively ignored this historical reality because, Marín suggests, "it would demolish the very foundation of the myth by which al-Andalus — a global and immutable essence — was extracted from history to become a representation for the nostalgic desire for paradise" (Marín 1998, 54).

Marín and other critics are right when they identify a sense of enthusiastic appreciation, even wonder, as integral to an *andalucista* sensibility, though it is telling that such critics show far less concern for the way attitudes of disapproval, skepticism, and often simple disdain have been taken as appropriate epistemic affects for much of European scholarship on Islam, as Edward Said (1978) argued some time ago.[27] But it is interesting to note how Marín's cautionary note seems far less plausible when applied to the study of ancient Greece than it does when discussing medieval Iberia. Scholars of Greek philosophy and aesthetics rarely face the criticism that their work, by neglecting the conditions of slavery and scarcity that weighed heavily on the lives of the vast majority of people at the time, distorts or idealizes the period it describes.[28] Why would studies of medieval Andalusi life and culture that leave aside questions of political economy not be similarly valuable?

As I examine in chapter 2, for many contemporary Spaniards, the problem with the *andalucistas* is not simply one of historical error. Despite its contemporary association with liberal and left-wing currents, Andalucismo carries with it echoes of Spanish fascism, echoes kept alive for many Spaniards by the still unresolved tensions left by the Spanish Civil War.[29] Specifically, its drive to cull a deep and abiding historical identity from the vagaries and discontinuities of the past joins this tradition to the Romantic nationalism of the early twentieth century that culminated in the National Catholicism of the Franco regime. Andalucismo, on this view, is yet another myth of national belonging, of a unique and immutable Spanish soul, a movement that threatens to subvert the project of liberal-democratic reform vigorously pursued since the end of the Franco regime in the mid-1970s.

Moreover, the vision of the *andalucistas* is felt by many to imperil the country's ongoing integration into the progressive project of Europe. One salient dimension of Spanish modernity has been the nation's quest for inclusion into the assembly of European nations, a quest undertaken against the backdrop of the country's historical relegation to an inferior (read "Oriental") status by other European nations. The discourse of Andalucismo, in this context, reawakens anxieties about the nation appearing, once again, as an Oriental Other, as Spain of the *Leyenda Negra* (Black Legend),[30] an exotic and forever backward society. For many of the Spaniards I spoke with and who viewed the country's hard-fought acceptance into the community of Europe as the primary bulwark against the reassertion of a reactionary provincialism, Andalucismo is a dangerous indulgence, especially in a moment when Europeans are increasingly invoking a Judeo-Christian heritage as the basis for civilizational unity in the face of a perceived Islamic threat. In short, contemporary political concerns about Spain's Christian and European identities weigh heavily on the production of historical discourse concerning the country's Islamic period.

A FEELING FOR THE PAST

Is Andalucismo rightly understood to be first and foremost a child of the Romantic imagination, an offshoot of this early nineteenth-century movement? Yes, though not in the way many of those who assert this charge intend. Critics of Andalucismo often write as if that tradition's Romantic pedigree told us all that was needed to know about it, about the variety of error to which its practitioners had succumbed, a judgment that de facto circumscribes any insights that it might yield.[31] This dismissive stance seems particularly unwarranted when one considers the extent to which the contributions of the Romantics anticipated so many of the most fertile trends within the contemporary theoretical landscape for thinking about language, culture, history, religion, and society (the works of Wittgenstein and Heidegger, to start).[32] Romanticism was not just a reactionary detour from the one true path as defined by the Enlightenment, as some critics of Andalucismo seem to assume. Rather, it was an incisive and philosophically profound critique of the highly limited and abstract view of human life and thought that underlay many of the central ideas of the Enlightenment and particularly its vision of a form of knowledge purified of its connections to tradition, language, and embodied experience.

Insomuch as we approach Romanticism as a particular attempt to rescue an imaginative faculty from its banishment to the realm of irreality, to give it broader authority within social and political life, then the *andalucistas* are rightly seen as inheritors of this project. It is worth recalling here that the sense of belonging articulated by the Romantics was not understood as something simply given; it was both real and imaginary, built on a dynamic and creative engagement with the past. As the historian Charles Larmore writes of this movement,

> The Romantic imagination in general aims to be creative and responsive at once, attuned to experience as it also enriches it. So it may well be true that the Romantic sense of belonging is inescapably an act of the imagination, transfiguring as it does its favored traditions in a traditionalist spirit that they themselves did not have before. But this does not mean that such forms of life do not really exist. And where they do exist and move our being, our imaginative identification of them can count as an expression of reason. (Larmore 1996, 63)

The Romantic imagination is not a vehicle of the Unreal (the dream, the hallucination) but, as Larmore's work attests, ought to be understood primarily as a honed faculty, intermediary between the sensible and the intelligible and mediating between them. Across the lives of the Andalusians whose biographical careers I explore below, there exists a distinct Romantic element evident in a shared emphasis on the recovery and valorization of sensory experience and aesthetic sensibility as necessary to the ethos—the form of life—they seek to uncover and to the historically rich landscape they seek practically and imaginatively to inhabit.

As mentioned above, moods of wonder and awe as well as melancholy are pervasive within the oeuvre of Andalucismo, a fact frequently cited by observers of the tradition to indicate its lack of adherence to standards of historical objectivity. But here I want to ask, do all pasts demand the same dispassionate attitude from us? Is there a singular affective tone appropriate to the heterogeneous pasts to which we find ourselves attached and by which they can be authoritatively disclosed? As the historian Constantin Fasolt has observed, the historical discipline's rhetoric of dispassion masks a particular ideological stance: "the dispassionate study of the past as such," he writes, "quite irrespective of the result to which research may lead, serves to confirm a certain view of what human beings and their relationships are like. To study history in order to produce an adequate account of the past is in and of itself to take a stand in favor of individual autonomy against all other possibilities including, but by no means limited to, providence and custom" (Fasolt 2005, 6). By establishing a firm boundary between past and present and by rejecting all anachronism on principle, history (the practice of historians) seeks to immunize us from the past and to thus leave us unfettered to shape our world as free individuals.[33] A historical perspective, in other words, is integral to a liberal political imaginary and a bulwark against "other possibilities."

Yet despite the authority commanded by historical narrative in modern society, in life we sometimes find ourselves tripped up by such other possibilities. Our way of life, for example, may passionately dispose us to certain pasts in ways that we may only dimly understand. A powerful example of this experience can be found in W. E. B. Du Bois's autobiography, *Dusk of Dawn*, at a juncture in his account where Du Bois is reflecting on his relation to Africa. Although he had almost no direct personal tie to the continent, it nonetheless played an immense role in the way he came to think about himself and interpret the events of his life. Among the members of his own extended family, he notes, no one had ever visited Africa or even expressed an interest in it. The one exception was his great grandmother, a woman who may have once been to the continent, Du Bois recalls, and who had taught him his "one direct cultural connection" to the place: a melody that "traveled down to us and we sing it to our children, knowing as little as our fathers what its words may mean, but knowing well the meaning of its music" (Du Bois [1988] 2007, 58). Despite having only this one simple melody linking him to Africa and its history, Du Bois gradually comes to recognize the immense significance the continent has for him "as a large determinant of my life and character" (58). Reflecting on this experience—one, he tells us, that "I can feel better than I can explain"—he writes,

> One thing is sure and that is the fact that since the fifteenth century these ancestors of mine and their other descendants have had a common history; have suffered a common disaster and have one long memory. The actual ties of heritage between the individuals of this group, vary with the ancestors that they have in common and many others: Europeans and Semites, perhaps Mongolians, certainly American Indians. But the physical bond is least and the badge of color relatively unimportant save as a badge; the real essence of this kinship is its social heritage of slavery; the discrimination and insult; and this heritage binds together not simply the children of Africa, but extends through yellow Asia and into the South Seas. It is this unity that draws me to Africa. (59)

As Du Bois relates, this heritage of slavery was one he only gradually came to recognize as his own, a process that involved both reflexive and unreflexive learning. It was his experience, and particularly the experiences of race and racial injustice in the United States, that inscribed his life into this temporality of suffering and that attuned him to his place within it.[34]

Du Bois's autobiographical ruminations on temporality and belonging pull us away from voluntarist accounts of history and toward a recognition of the place of experience, of our emotional attunements and sensibilities, within historical reflection. His observations find an unexpected echo in a text by Ludwig Wittgenstein in which the philosopher discusses Sir James Frazer's anthropological classic, *The Golden Bough* (Wittgenstein 1993 [1931]).[35] In this essay, Wittgenstein voices a strong dissatisfaction with Frazer's style of explicating "primitive" rituals by tracing them back to their origins and then constructing a causal history to account for their contemporary forms. This style of historical explanation diverts us, in Wittgenstein's view, from what really matters about such rituals: the feelings and sensibilities they elicit in us. For example, in his discussion of the rule of succession practiced among the priests of Diana at Nemi (a rule that required a new candidate for the position to slay the current occupant of the role), Frazer argues that the origins of the practice were to be found in ancient magical practices, what amounted to early attempts at scientific explanation in Frazer's evolutionary view. Wittgenstein's response is not to say that such an account is factually wrong but that it fails to address a more important dimension of the ritual, namely, the profound impression it makes on us. "Compared with the impression which the thing makes on us," he writes, "the explanation is too uncertain. Every explanation is after all a hypothesis. But a hypothetical explanation will be of little help to someone, say, who is upset because of love. It will not calm him" (Wittgenstein 1993, 123).[36]

Wittgenstein here invites us to attend to the way such rituals or practices resonate with our own experience, with our own passional makeup as fellow human beings. An account that leaves this unaddressed, that does not help us clarify our felt relation to these events, will not satisfy us, and indeed, may actually serve to alienate us from important dimensions of ourselves (an alienated state Castro found among his contemporaries in Spain and sought to capture with the term *vivir desviviéndose*). Again, this is not to say that an explanatory account of such a situation cannot be given but rather to recognize that we may seek, or need, something rather different and that these desires or needs should be given epistemic value in our forms of inquiry. In such cases, where a hypothetical explanation seems to violate our felt relation to the practices or events we are trying to understand, our feelingful thinking may be better served, Wittgenstein suggests, by what he calls a "perspicuous representation" (*übersichtliche Darstellung*), "a form of discourse that will bring these practices to the level of a certain type of representation and, as it were, hold them there, allowing them to be acknowledged for what they are, rather than letting them be 'explained' away in shifting the focus from *them* to their *causes*" (Redding 1987, 265).

While Wittgenstein's focus here is on Frazer's account of "primitive ritual," his point is equally important when thinking about our relation to the
past. Wittgenstein allows us to consider that the importance of the past to
our lives is not necessarily satisfied by the type of dispassionate reflection
undertaken by the discipline of history (or by Frazer's scientific anthropology). Our lives may be oriented to certain pasts, attached to them, in
ways that unsettle, disturb, captivate, or otherwise affect us not because of
some failure of disidentification, an inability to achieve a properly objective distance, but simply because of who we are as embodied, temporally
situated beings.[37] The past, thus conceived, is not merely a tool of our interests but—like the object of love—a point of our vulnerability where life
exceeds our reflexive grasp of it.[38] A certain past, in other words, may leave
us simultaneously captivated and radically displaced from our moorings.

The philosopher Cora Diamond has sought to elaborate this aspect of
Wittgenstein's thought in terms of what she calls "difficulties of reality":

> The phenomena with which I'm concerned [are] experiences in which
> we take something in reality to be resistant to our thinking it, or possibly
> to be painful in its inexplicability, difficult in that way, or perhaps awe-
> some and astonishing in its inexplicability. We take things so. And the
> things we take so may simply not, to others, present that kind of diffi-
> culty, of being hard or impossible or agonizing to get one's mind around.
> (Diamond 2003, 99)

While readers of Wittgenstein usually characterize his style of thought as
one of bringing words back from their philosophical and metaphysical uses
to their home in ordinary language (see Wittgenstein 1973, 116), Diamond
highlights a less often noted dimension of the philosopher's approach: that
the reality we encounter may not only resist expression in our available languages, leaving us feeling that our ways of speaking are inadequate, blunt
instruments, but that that resistance may forcefully impinge on us, may
compel us outside our familiar habits by the way it pains, astonishes, or
powerfully attracts us. As Stephen Mulhall notes in his reflections on Diamond's work, "difficulties of reality," in revealing reality to be resistant to
our ways of thinking, may at times "[make] us incomprehensible to others,
and even to ourselves" (Mulhall 2012, 20–21). It is this incomprehension,
I want to suggest, that we encounter in the rhetorics and poetics of Andalucismo. In such instances, what may be needed, Wittgenstein suggests, is not
explanation but something more like *presentation*—a way of allowing things
to be seen and grasped for what they are and mean to us. Not a hypothetical
account, but rather one that, say, "calms" us, consoles or braces us.

To speak of a form of life founded on a vulnerability to the past, on a passional attachment to it, takes us in a very different direction than the sort of instrumentalism or voluntarism implied in the idea of "the political use of history." This is not to say, however, that political concerns are not integral to such a perspective. Insomuch as the hold the past exercises on us is shaped by our wider experience, the political and institutional conditions within which our sensibilities are cultivated and attuned will play a decisive role in determining how we encounter and respond to our historical emplacement. The question becomes, how does power shape the sensibilities by which particular pasts articulate with the present? In an article focusing on Buddhism in South Asia, Ananda Abeysekara hones in on this question in a discussion focused on the temporality of traditions:

> The question of how one remembers the past is a question of how one encounters temporality within the sensibilities of the present. That encounter of temporality is not merely a subjective experience of history; it is an encounter with the conditions of power. . . . The shared sensibilities of memory depend on dispositions made possible by the circumstances of the present, which are not merely available to be appropriated within the realm of the "popular." The present is not a "homogenous time" within which the past, as an unchanging substance, can be inherited. The present is constituted by the altering conditions of sensibilities and dispositions—conditions that create particular modes of receptiveness, which may produce particular forms of sensibility. Sensibilities of temporality, of inhabiting different kinds of time—say, the memory of Dharmapala—in the shared life of a tradition are not quite like a "popular" fashion that one may easily appropriate. (Abeysekara 2019, 34)

Abeysekara invites us to attend to the processes by which particular regions of the past become integral to our lives, exercising a hold on us.[39] The sensibilities that dispose us toward certain pasts (sometimes passionately, as Wittgenstein reminds us) are not merely the artifact of "popular fashion" but rather are conditioned by heterogeneous forces that give shape to our practical existence. This is why my account of Andalucismo returns repeatedly to the discursive and institutional powers of nationalism, Spanish colonialism, Orientalism, and the contemporary heritage industry, each of which has affected the shape of this tradition and the sensibilities that sustain it.

Abeysekara's point about the relation between experience and historical inquiry can be usefully illuminated through a very different context.[40]

Take, for example, calls for the payment of reparations for the enslavement of African Americans in the United States and the forms of historical discourse that are marshaled to give force to such claims. What ethical and epistemic attitude toward the "evidence of history" or toward the temporality of suffering must one adopt in order to be persuaded by the reasonableness of such claims, in order to see the continuities of identity binding present generations to those long past and to recognize in reparations a way of doing justice to that history? Or, for that matter, to *not* see the reasonableness of these claims? Can we make sense of either historical viewpoint without considering the epistemic value of the emotions and without addressing the political investments that nourish the attitudes and anxieties that shape American racial divides?[41]

In sum, Du Bois, Wittgenstein, and Abeysekara, if in different ways, encourage us to consider the fact that our relation to a given past may not be one of indifference or neutrality, that it may rather be affectively structured in a way that asks of us a unique attunement and response. For the *andalucistas*, medieval Iberia exerts just such a power due both to the decisive imprint it bestowed on Spanish culture and to the violent means by which that imprint, and the people who made it, were extirpated from the country's soil and psyche. Notably, in my conversations with Spanish historians and Arabists, many of them spoke of the impression made on them during a first visit to the Alhambra or to Córdoba's Red Mosque, how moved they felt at the time, and how, for a few of them, this early experience had provided the spark that led them to pursue their particular career path. Yet while they recognized the emotions evoked by the Muslim and Jewish monuments of Andalusia as important to the subsequent direction their lives had taken, they insisted that such emotions, when allowed a place within one's historical thinking (as with the *andalucistas*), could only corrupt the purity of one's analytical gaze.

This sterilization of the sensa of the Iberian past, however, comes at a price. In divesting the medieval past of its emotional and ethical hold on the present, of the profound impressions this period makes on many today in Andalusia and beyond, the discipline of history relegates these impressions to the status of nostalgic longings or Romantic fancies, feelings exemplary of a particular modern European experience but incapable of providing a reasoned ethical and political orientation to the present. A geography of thought and experience is thereby removed from consideration. This loss comes with a political cost, including the diminishment of our capacity to think about, or engage with, the Middle East in other than conflictual terms.

EXPERIENCE LOST

The positive valorization of the sensorium in relation to historical ways of knowing, a cornerstone of Andalucismo, finds an early and instructive elaboration in a text by one of the tradition's founding figures, Ángel Ganivet (d. 1899). In his paean to the city of Granada (*Granada la bella* [Granada the beautiful], 1896), Ganivet stresses the primacy of sensory life for his understanding of knowledge and experience: "to see, hear, smell, taste, and even touch—that is, to live—is my exclusive method; afterward, these sensations organize themselves, and from that organization arise my ideas" ([1896] 2003, 19). Ganivet was an admirer of the works of Théodule-Armand Ribot and Pierre Janet, two late nineteenth-century French psychologists known for their investigations into disorders of alienation and dissociation.[42] He took a particular interest in these scholars' interpretations of dissociative experience in terms of a failure or weakening of "the synthetic sense"—namely that sensory mode, operating outside and before consciousness, by which sentient beings sense they are alive, what Ribot characterized as "organic awareness."[43] Dissociatives, in their view, suffered from a kind of hyper-Cartesianism wherein cognitive activity was cut off from the perceptual substrate that gave it unity and order, including the perception of one's own existence. Detached from any felt sense of their own sensory activity, their thoughts and affects floated free, unmoored from any anchor in the experience of a determinate living being.[44]

Engaging the work of these scholars, Ganivet diagnosed the Spanish decline that so preoccupied his contemporaries in terms of a loss of the synthetic sense—that by means of which "sensations organize themselves" so as to enable ideas to "arise"—a condition that had, in his view, produced a state of "*abulia*," a listlessness characterized by a weakening of the will (Ganivet 1906, 165–69; see also Ginsberg 1985, 32–33). In this state, modern Spanish society could only engage the past in a static way, mechanically reproducing its traces but unable to vivify them in relation to a changing present. The processes of abstraction and generalization that characterized modernity, in Ganivet's view, thus resulted in a fixed, deanimated past.[45] In these reflections Ganivet anticipated Wittgenstein, for whom the contemporary demand to purify historical and anthropological writing of its sensory elements was evidence of "the narrowness of our spiritual life" (Wittgenstein [1931] 1993, 133).

Ganivet may be read as yet another witness to the modern experience of sensory loss, an experience whose psychological contours were delineated by Ribot and Janet and whose historical and political significance found a decisive interpretation in Walter Benjamin.[46] An outspoken critic of European modernity, Ganivet saw the withering of a lived relation to the past as one consequence of the homogenizing force of centralized state power—with its *funesta simetría* (terrible symmetry)—and its destruction of local traditions, particular those of his natal city of Granada ([1896] 2003, 25). In its unrelenting application of a commercial and utilitarian calculus to all matters of urban renewal, the modern capitalist system had, in his view, largely effaced the spiritual and historical foundations that underlay Granada's unique form of life. That form, one he sought to excavate with his "exclusive method" of relying on the five senses, was the result of a historical sedimentation left by Muslims and Jews on the social, aesthetic, and spiritual traditions of Andalusia. In Ganivet's critique of modernity, in other words, we can read two intersecting themes, each central to the modern itinerary and self-definition of Europe: the decline in the value of sensory experience, epitomized in the purity of the cogito effected within Cartesian philosophy, on one hand, and the evacuation of Islam and Judaism from the European continent, an event formulated in the Spanish context in terms of a purity of blood (*limpieza de sangre*). I read Ganivet's work, an essential reference for the tradition this book examines, as an invitation to think about the overlaps and intersections occurring across these two histories of erasure that inaugurate European modernity.

Ganivet's intellectual itinerary is a markedly Spanish one (or more precisely, Granadan, as I discuss in chap. 4). The fact that his antimodernism led him to a reassessment of Iberia's Muslim and Jewish past and its significance for modern Spain bears witness to the unique history of Iberia in relation to Islam and the Middle East. Yet while it is important to acknowledge the singularity of the Iberian historical experience, its medieval past is also implicated in broader historical processes that have shaped European modernity. Because of the relative omission of the peninsula's Islamic legacy within accounts of European modernity, this legacy often arrives in disguise, evidenced for instance in the parodic games of Muslim cross-dressing that have a long tradition within Spain (see Fuchs 2007). More often, and to adapt an insight from Juan Goytisolo, this legacy appears as a "shadow" accompanying Europe along its trajectory of modern progress.

One can observe this shadow, the histories and legacies it both reveals and hides, in a text by the Italian philosopher Giorgio Agamben. In *Infancy and History*, Agamben engages Benjamin's reflections on the waning of experience in modern life, focusing on the contrast between experience, imagination, and authority in antiquity and the conceptual transformation in the use of these terms during the modern period. In Agamben's reading, a decisive shift in the grammar of these concepts took place during the sixteenth and seventeenth centuries. Within an earlier tradition, one stretching from Aristotle up through Montaigne, the subject of experience remained distinct from the subject of knowledge: while the former was transmitted though proverbs and maxims (hence, Benjamin's storyteller) and was predicated on the activity of the entire human sensorium, the latter referred to the active intelligence (or nous), something separate from experience, both individuated and impassive (Agamben 1993, 17–18). Within the framework of this tradition, the subject both *underwent* experience in the course of everyday life and *had* experience in the sense that he accumulated experience as he became what life made him to be. Subsequently, with the scientific tradition inaugurated by Bacon and Kepler, experience and knowledge come to refer to a single subject conjoined, Agamben notes, "at an abstract Archimedean point: the Cartesian cogito, consciousness" (19). Recast as a servant of knowledge and stripped of its grounding in everyday sensorial life, experience would no longer anchor the slow, absorptive processes through which Benjamin's storyteller acceded to the collective wisdom of a community, to common sense. It is at this historical juncture, Agamben tells us, that the old subject of experience splits in two, a split that finds it first literary expression in a novel written at the beginning of the seventeenth century: Cervantes's *Don Quixote*. "Don Quixote, the old subject of knowledge," Agamben writes, "has been befuddled by a spell and can only undergo experience without ever having it. By his side, Sancho Panza, the old subject of experience, can only have it, without ever undergoing it" (24).[47]

There is another vanishing subject, however, that organizes Cervantes's narrative, side by side with what Agamben identifies as "the old subject of experience": the Muslim, or the Morisco. The literary innovations that led scholars to designate *Don Quixote* as "the first novel" involved precisely an attempt to craft a form of literary expression adequate to the emerging social reality of late sixteenth-century Iberia, one key dimension of which was the exclusion of the Moriscos (the "New Christians") and their culture from Iberian society.[48] First published in 1605, just four years before the final expulsion of the Moriscos from the Iberian Peninsula, Cervantes rejected the idealized images at the heart of the popular tradition of "frontier ballads" (*romances fronterizos*), deploying instead a heteroglossic discourse incorporating a wide variety of genres and particularly historiography in an attempt to bear witness to the instabilities of ethnic and religious identity left, in part, by the forced disappearance of the Moriscos and their legacy then taking place.[49] As the Cervantes scholar Mary Quinn notes,

The modernity of Don Quijote, in part, comes out of a new attempt to write a counter-history of the Muslim and Morisco experience and depends quite specifically not on their presence in Spain or its empire but on their absence. . . . The modern novel is thus born out of contested identity, violence, and expulsion, not out of hybridity, progress, and harmony. The absence of Muslims and Moriscos, and the attempted erasure of a Semitic past, created an aperture that Spaniards could not address within their pre-existing literary forms. (Quinn 2013, 27)

In contrast to the "Old Christian" subject presupposed by the statutes of blood purity and promulgated by the imperial state, Cervantes's characters are fractured by a history that defies any stable representation, a history indelibly marked by a now absent Muslim subject (or rather, a subject whose final elimination was then close at hand).[50] Confronting the vacuum left by the expulsion of Muslims and Moriscos, these characters are continuously thwarted by "the difficult solipsism of Christian Spain" (132) from achieving the ends they pursue. This theme, that Spain is complexly bound up with its excluded Muslim (and Jewish) heritage, also appears in one of the novel's most famous conceits, in the claim of the story's narrator that the entire account is really a translation from an Arabic text of one Cide Hamete Benengeli. As Cervantes scholars have noted, behind this rhetorical device lay serious questions about the identity of seventeenth-century Spain and about who exactly were the Spanish in the wake of eight hundred years of Muslim presence that was then, through Inquisitorial fiat, being expunged.

How might this "other Quixotic absence," the erasure of Islam and the Moriscos from early-modern Iberia, account for the appearance of Don Quixote as urtext in Agamben's reading of the waning of experience in modernity? One answer would be that the stories of loss and absence that constitute Europe and its modern culture necessarily converge and entwine. Pull on one constitutive thread of that ideological edifice and others will emerge as well. Notably such a double absence, as I have identified it, does make another appearance in *Infancy and History*. Early in the essay, in a section elaborating on Benjamin's account of the decline of modern experience, Agamben presents the reader with a variety of modern urban scenes that defy translation into the vocabularies of experience: "Neither reading the newspaper, with its abundance of news which is irretrievably remote from his life, nor sitting for minutes on end at the wheel of his car in a traffic jam. Neither the journey through the netherworld of the subway, nor the demonstration that suddenly blocks the street" (Agamben 1993, 13). Beyond these paradigmatic modern scenes, however, there is one (and only one) instance in Agamben's text where the author makes reference to a specific, identifiable location—one quite distinct from the familiar, generic sites of sensory alienation previously noted—in order to highlight the modern demise of experience. In a section in which he argues that to the extent experience takes place today, its locus is outside the individual, Agamben provides the following example: "Standing face to face with one of the great wonders of the world (*let us say the patio de los leones in the Alhambra*), the overwhelming majority of people have no wish to experience it, preferring instead that the camera should" (emphasis mine; 15).

A chance location pulled from Agamben's personal travelogue? Perhaps. Reading the text symptomatically, however, we can discern two arguments here, one voiced, the other its shadow or silent companion. The first: even the Alhambra, "one of the great wonders of the world," cannot muster the lost subject of experience from its sleep, a sleep whose conceptual and historical condition Agamben's text aims to delineate. The second: a site where Europe's Islamic legacy achieves its most compelling, aesthetically affecting form, the Alhambra is a monument to loss, to exiled historical experience, an exile, moreover, that constitutes the possibility of Christian and secular Europe (i.e., of European modernity). It is the specificity of the example (the luminous Alhambra, palace of the last Muslim kingdom on European soil) that enhances its ability to stand *as an example*, an example of loss and of historical erasure (and, for the *andalucistas*, of the melancholy of the age). These two readings, I want to suggest, work in tandem, are entwined as two threads that hold together the concept of Europe and its reason. In tracking Western experience down to its conceptual and geographic limits—the limits of its premier literary contribution, the novel; the limits of its Christian/secular genealogy; the limits of its territorial borders—the "difficult solipsism" of Europe starts to run up against its Islamic legacy just as the characters in Don Quixote find that they are never quite able to expunge from themselves the part they have cast off, have exiled. We might note as well that Agamben's text not only finds an origin in Cervantes but also that it inherits the latter's same predicament as a text structured by an absent or vanishing subject, the shadowy *moro*.

It is within this breach, an opening whose operation we witness within the procedures of Agamben's text, that Andalucismo, that border knowledge par excellence, establishes its domain. For the *andalucistas*, the pathologies of modernity—from their moments of inception to their contemporary entrenchments—take us back to al-Andalus.

THE VIEW FROM CAIRO

I arrived in Granada for the first time in 2006 not knowing much about its history but disposed in certain ways to become attuned to it. In my previous work on Islamic sermons in Egypt, I had been drawn to the aesthetic and sensory dimensions of Islamic oratory particularly as they found expression within practices of ethical listening. I had approached the Islamic tradition through the cultivated sensorium of the listener rather than the discourses and doctrines of the speaker, and this emphasis undoubtedly shaped my encounter with Andalusia and the *andalucistas*. Like other visitors coming from across the Mediterranean, I was struck by the vestiges and echoes of the Middle East I found in Granada. When I attended a concert of flamenco, I couldn't help but hear echoes of the Sufi music I had so often listened to in Cairo. Wandering through the old Muslim neighborhood of the Albayzín, I felt the kinesthetic pleasures of Sana'a or Fez. In the arabesques of the Alhambra I found many familiar faces. And although it was clear that the many tea shops around Plaza Nueva at the base of the Alhambra were designed to fulfill the Orientalist fantasies of tourists, the low benches, water pipes, and painfully strong tea did take me back to the *ahawi* (coffee houses) of Egypt where I had spent so much time. While some of the Spanish scholars I was meeting at the time saw me as yet another North American Romantic, with others—some of whom I would later come to identify as *andalucistas*—I found myself on common ground with little effort, often brought together by shared experiences in the Middle East, encounters with Middle Eastern art and music, and with the painful political realities of the region. My years in the Middle East, it seems, and my immersion in its aesthetics and politics had attuned me favorably to the world of Andalucismo, to that "third Spain."

Toward the end of that first visit to Granada, I decided I would pay a visit to the city's Muslim cemetery. My friend and onetime thesis advisor, the anthropologist Talal Asad, had mentioned that his father was buried there, and I wanted to bring him back a photo of the gravesite. Some of the Granadans I had recently met told me that they had heard the cemetery was located on a hill somewhere above the Alhambra, though none had actually been there or knew the route. A map from a guidebook I had brought with me confirmed its location, adjacent to a large Christian cemetery, high on the hills above the city.

I set out from the room I had rented in the Albayzín, climbing the steep pathway that ascends to the Alhambra complex. Passing the entrance to the monument, I turned left onto the paved road that continued upward, soon arriving at the city's vast Christian cemetery. First opened in 1805, the cemetery today covers an immense swath of the hillside, drawing tourists who come to see its exceptional examples of nineteenth-century funerary sculpture and architecture. A man who worked at the ticket office had never heard of a Muslim cemetery, nor had two guards stationed at the entrance. Making my way to the edge of the cemetery, I found a narrow dirt road that continued up the hill. A few meters ahead, a small sign on a side wall of the cemetery marked a spot where extrajudicial killings had been carried out by right-wing forces at the beginning of the civil war in 1936. Lorca, I remembered, had been killed at just such a deserted site. I continued to follow the dirt road upward for another fifteen minutes until, just as I was about to abandon the search, I came across a rusty metal gate off to the left side of the road, barely visible through the thick overgrowth. While no sign indicated the official identity of the location, the scattered white stones just visible through the wild grass and high brush covering the hillside suggested I had found what I was looking for. Climbing over the fence, I found gravesites, four to five rows, their modest stone markers broken and scattered by vandalism and neglect and almost erased from sight by the thicket of weeds. In the back corner of the cemetery I found the grave of Muhammad Asad marked by the only unbroken headstone on the site.

Muhammad Asad had been born to a Jewish family in Vienna in 1900 (his name at birth was Leopold Weiss). While still in his early twenties, he had traveled to Jerusalem, where he first came into contact with Arab Muslims and began to develop an appreciation for their religion and way of life. His observations of Palestinians, recorded in *The Road to Mecca* (Asad [1954] 1982), are recognizable in their debt to a genre of Romantic writing on the Middle East. Among his impressions, he records the following:

> I had come face to face with a life-sense that was entirely new to me. A warm, human breath seemed to flow out of these people's blood into their thoughts and gestures, with none of those painful cleavages of the spirit, those phantoms of fear, greed and inhibition that made European life so ugly and of so little promise. In the Arabs I began to find something I had always unwittingly been looking for: an emotional lightness of approach to all questions of life—a supreme common sense of feeling, if one might call it so. (99–100)

Muhammad Asad's Romantic impressions of the Middle East are reminiscent of certain *andalucista* writings. It is not at all surprising that he would have chosen Granada for his final resting place. A shared vocabulary unites the "common sense of feeling" Asad finds in Jerusalem and Ganivet's "synthetic sense" of Granada, a vocabulary we now recognize as integral to the West's construction of the "Orient" during the colonial period and beyond. In this book, however, I want to read these moments of Romantic enthusiasm as something more than machinations of power or Western flights of fancy. I want to hear in them something I hear in Du Bois: an attempt to find (better, to feel) one's way in a space of dislocation and confusion, a space of modern life marked by its constitutive expulsions and violence. For Muhammad Asad—and this holds for the *andalucistas* as well—a passion for the Orient did not exhaust itself in subjective feeling but gave impetus to a process of self-transformation and critical reason.

Importantly, Asad's Romantic embrace of life in the Middle East went hand in hand with a political sensibility infrequent among Europeans at the time and rare enough today. In the context of discussing his interactions with Jews in Palestine, of whom he still at the time saw himself as one, he writes,

> Although of Jewish origin myself, I conceived from the outset a strong objection to Zionism. Apart from my personal sympathy for the Arabs, I considered it immoral that immigrants, assisted by a foreign Great Power, should come from abroad with the avowed intention of attaining to majority in the country and thus to dispossess the people whose country it had been since time immemorial. . . . This attitude of mine was beyond the comprehension of practically all of the Jews with whom I came in contact during those months. They could not understand what I saw in the Arabs who, according to them, were no more than a mass of backward people whom they looked upon with a feeling not much different from that of the European settlers in Central Africa. (Asad [1954] 1982, 93–94)

When we dismiss such reflections as nothing more than the early twentieth-century "Jewish romance with the Orient," we deprive ourselves of the opportunity to better understand how such clear-sightedness was possible and what role the traditions of Romanticism and Orientalism played in its formation.

Some years later, Asad went on to convert to Islam, eventually becoming an important contributor to twentieth-century debates among Muslim reformers. Along the way he helped compose the first constitution of Pakistan and served as that country's ambassador to the UN before finally retiring to Spain. As a European Muslim, a converted Jew, Asad has been accused by some of being a traitor—a traitor to his race and to his civilization. The very notion of a European Muslim, I would note, can be deeply unsettling. While *andalucistas* frequently encounter a skeptical reception in Spain, I met few people during my sojourn there who did not express some level of disapproval, if not disdain, for those Spanish converts to Islam.[51] In this light, it is not surprising that I would find Asad's burial site as I did, disappearing from the winds, weeds, and neglect on a Granadan hillside somewhere along the hinge between al-Andalus and Andalusia.

Muhammad Asad's autobiography includes numerous pictures of the author, always dressed in Arabian garb, a practice not uncommon among *andalucistas* (including Lorca), and usually interpreted as a symptom of Orientalist frivolity. As with Asad, the *andalucistas* are travelers along routes of the Orientalist imagination following a line well trodden by the Romantics that runs from the cold rationality of Europe to the passional climes of the *moros* and their present-day heirs in the Middle East. Yet while it is true that one encounters "the repertoire of Orientalism" (Said 1978) across the oeuvre of Andalucismo—the sensuality of the Middle East, the fatalism of Islam—such images, I will argue, work within this tradition in a more interesting way than Said's work allows, not only as a refuge for the exoticizing mind or for a simple flight into fantasy but for a critical evaluation of European modernity through the lens provided by Iberia's medieval past. As with Muhammad Asad, *andalucistas* walk along a thin edge, trucking in the Oriental while trying to avoid succumbing to its sterile fantasies. This book necessarily navigates this same thin edge.

∴

While my focus here is on a tradition of historical reflection anchored in one corner of the European periphery, the problem space it engages extends well beyond Europe. Muslims today find themselves more and more to be people "out of place," certainly in Europe and the United States but even more desperately in China, India, Myanmar, and Israel. My initial interest in Andalusia began to emerge in the early 2000s just as the "Muslim problem" was becoming a central concern within European political debates and particularly in the aftermath of *l'affaire du foulard* in France. Andalusia, it seemed to me, provided a unique site from which to explore the deep discomfort many Europeans were feeling toward Muslim immigrants to the continent, a discomfort, moreover, that had fed popular European and American desires for military intervention in the Middle East for as long as I can remember and certainly much longer. It is hard not to see a kind of madness at play in this compulsion for endless war against the people of this region. In Andalusia, as the following chapters describe, this madness has been given a diagnosis, its etiology identified: *vivir desviviéndose*, living by denying the reality of one's existence.

The following four chapters explore the tradition of Andalucismo from four different angles. Chapter 1 examines Andalucismo from the standpoint of political activism through an exploration of the lives and words of two of the tradition's leading practitioners, the early twentieth-century Arabist and political thinker Rodolfo Gil Benumeya, and the contemporary Cordoban lawyer Antonio Manuel Rodríguez Ramos. Focusing on the multiple and often contradictory political currents that shaped the political trajectory of these two activists, the chapter aims to trace the outline of a distinct *andalucista* geographic and political imaginary and to register its impact in different moments of Spanish political life. The chapter concludes with a discussion of an ongoing debate over the religious and political status of Córdoba's celebrated Mezquita-Catedral (or Great Mosque of Córdoba), a debate that has garnered international attention and that pivots around conflicting interpretations of Iberia's medieval past.

In chapter 2 I focus on a controversy within the discipline of Spanish history precipitated by the publication of a highly unorthodox account of the Muslim conquest of Iberia in the eighth century written by Emilio González Ferrín, a professor at the University of Seville. An author deeply enmeshed in the institutional and discursive world of Andalucismo, González Ferrín provoked outrage across the discipline with his claim that the Muslim conquest had never happened, that it was an invention of ninth-century Christian ideologues. An examination of some of the contexts and contours of this debate brings into relief the political and disciplinary stakes of Andalucismo within and beyond the Spanish academy.

As I noted early in this introduction, the historical sensibilities that undergird the *andalucista* tradition are profoundly musical. While this theme will reappear across the book, in chapter 3 I turn my attention to musical practice itself, first to flamenco, as the principle genre through which *andalucistas* came to discern the presence of the medieval past, and then to what is called Arabo-Andalusi music, which I explore through the lives of some of its contemporary practitioners. Overall, the chapter can be seen as a reflection on music as a historical medium.

Chapter 4 centers on one of the primary topoi within Andalucismo's political geography, the city of Granada, home to both the Alhambra and the medieval Muslim quarter of the Albayzín, two key *lieux de mémoire* within the tradition. I approach this hybrid city through the sensibilities of three of its native sons, Ángel Ganivet, Federico García Lorca, and the contemporary scholar of Islamic art José Miguel Puerta Vílchez. Under their guidance, I seek to reveal the *andalucista* temporal geography embodied in the city's fabric and to note its rupturing force on the project of European identity. My conclusion offers a set of final reflections on the significance of this tradition today.

CHAPTER 1

The Political Cartography of Andalucismo

In Rodolfo Gil Benumeya's personal notebook from around the mid-1930s, we find a diagram concerning the political situation in Morocco at the time. A Spanish journalist from the Andalusian town of Andújar, he was living with his family in Tétouan,[1] having recently entered into a business venture with a Moroccan partner, Hagg Abdesalam Bennuna (a leader of the movement for Moroccan independence). The diagram is titled "Schematic of the diverse fields of action of the thought of 'young Moroccans' and the location of the diverse concentric zones of the Indigenous problem in relation to general problems of Islam." It is framed by an introductory comment that begins to unpack the cumbersome, if precise, title:

> The Moroccan "nationalist" movement, or rather the modernizing movement of the youth, is—in the Spanish zone—the local result of a set of international causes that therein converge. Thus, the small zone of the Spanish Protectorate is a synthesis of problems within the Mediterranean region and the Near East, and the Indigenous inhabitants of this zone, once they begin to think for themselves, instinctively take on this role of synthesis. A study of the local problems does not let them forget the general problems of the Islamic culture in which they are implicated. And their highest social or political ideals are inspired in solutions tested or realized in countries that constitute the ideal zone of the expansion of Moroccan thought.[2]

This political perspective is then further elaborated in the diagram itself, which is composed of six concentric rings, each representing a "field of action" (figure 1). The innermost ring of the schematic is occupied by the "nationalist party of the young intellectuals," a small group with whom Gil Benumeya was meeting regularly at the time and whose goal of an independent Morocco he had increasingly come to share. It is followed by the "Spanish zone, field of action based upon the education of the masses."

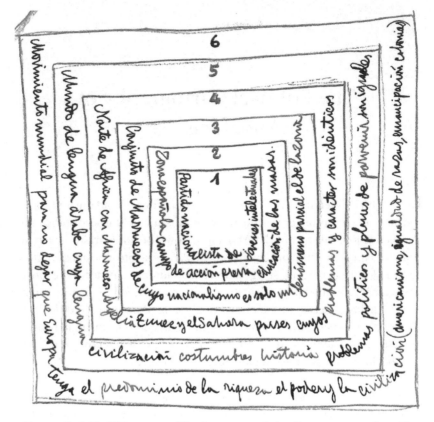

Figure 1 Rodolfo Gil Benumeya, "Cuadro esquema de los diversos campos de acción del pensamiento 'joven marroquí' y posición de las distintas zonas concéntricas del problema indígena en relación con los problemas generales del Islam," p. 3. [España] Ministerio de Educación, Cultura y Deporte, Archivo General de la Administración, Fondo Ministerio de la Presidencia del Gobierno, IDD (15)003.001, caja 81/10199.

Education was one arena where the paternalistic vision of Spanish colonial officials and the aims of the Moroccan nationalists coincided. Expanding outward, the third ring embraces the "totality of Morocco, whose nationalism is only one part of a broader regional phenomenon." This broader arena is then identified, in the fourth ring, as composed of "North Africa, with Morocco, Algeria, Tunisia, and the Sahara, countries with identical problems and features." In the next circle, Gil Benumeya refers to the civilizational space defined by language, "the world of the Arabic language, whose language, civilization, customs, history, political problems, and future plans are shared." We then come to the final ring, that defined by the global resistance to European colonialism, or as he writes, "the global movement to prevent Europe from controlling the dominant share of wealth, power, and civilization (Americanism, equality of the races, colonial emancipation)." It is this latter, global arena to which the "thought of the young Moroccan" should ideally extend, that within which the Moroccan national struggle ought to be seen and carried out.

How are we to read this personal note, written by a Spanish journalist and scholar of the Middle East, one who spent much of his life working within the institutions of Spanish colonialism? Do we encounter in Gil Benumeya another Orientalist gone native, a Lawrence seduced by the Romantic pleasures of the Moroccan medina imagining himself a strategist in the struggle for Arab freedom? Should the note be read as a vision of grandeur produced by a Spanish Romantic grappling with his country's national inferiority complex at the time accentuated by Spain's comparatively feeble colonial imprint? Certainly, support for such interpretations is not hard to find within Gil Benumeya's writing. Indeed at times the T. E. Lawrencian tones echoing from his work are deafening, as when he writes, "Buttressed by Andalusia, I have launched the new cry of the South because only from Andalusia (Levant and IndoAmerica, Mediterranean and Africa) can it be launched" (Gil Benumeya 1929, 9). Yet having acknowledged this, there is much in the career of this Andalusian that terms like *Orientalist* and *Romantic* only serve to obscure.[3]

Gil Benumeya's schema, traced into his notebook in the mid-1930s, was one variation of a political optic he would elaborate across his career, one he gave the name "Andalucismo," or "Andalucismo Árabe." Let's begin with a few of the rudiments of this vision. While Spain was usually assigned a distinctive role in Gil Benumeya's strategic thinking, it did not monopolize the center of political calculus, nor did it define the limits of political possibility.[4] Here, and in many of his other political writings, it is the Arabic-speaking world from which Gil Benumeya would assess the possibilities of political coordination and action, a world with which Spain is historically entwined and hence a natural ally and collaborator. Indeed, it is only by virtue of its historical attachment—culturally, linguistically, spiritually, racially—to the Islamic societies across the Mediterranean that Spain acquires, in Gil Benumeya's view, its singular and universal career within the global movement against European hegemony.[5]

The geopolitical space articulated by Gil Benumeya's concentric spheres of political action derives its historical possibility from the civilization produced within medieval Andalusi society, one he finds "still alive" within contemporary Morocco ("a living museum . . . of the Middle Ages"; Gil Benumeya 1942, 140), though also, latent and fragmentary, in Spain itself. Gil Benumeya will designate this space *Mediodía*.[6] Located at the intersection of Orient and Occident, *Mediodía* conjoins both a civilizational concept for which medieval al-Andalus stands as its foundational moment and a political analytic through which global struggles against the existing regime of European dominance can be articulated and coordinated and Spanish prestige in the world again reinstated. This "universe seen from Albayzín"[7]—a historical weave of aesthetic, linguistic, religious, and political affiliations and affects, of long-buried musical harmonies and cultural correspondences—held out the promise, in Gil Benumeya's view, of an antidote to the existing regime of political and geographic norms held in place by European powers to the detriment both of Spain and of the peoples of the Middle East. Spanish power and Middle Eastern resurgence were two sides of a single coin.

Mediodía belongs to the imaginary geographies of Andalucismo, a historical territory imagined, articulated, and produced within the triangular conceptual space delimited by medieval al-Andalus on one hand and contemporary North Africa and Spain on the other. What makes Gil Benumeya a particularly interesting guide to this territory is the way his own nomadic itinerary reveals this "geopsychic" space to be, not a dream landscape of the Romantic imagination, nor an instrument of Spanish colonial design, but rather a space of political, ethical, and aesthetic possibilities largely illegible within the norms of Spanish and European modernity. Indeed, if there is a protean and fantastical quality to Gil Benumeya's writing, it is because he was captivated by the dizzying world of possibilities, of reterritorializations, that Andalucismo opens up for him—possibilities of political alliance, of commerce, of linguistic and cultural belonging; in short, a reconfiguration of the global order on a new "andalucentric" basis. His essays brim with excitement over the new universe his Andalucismo Árabe offers and to which he responds with ever-changing models, plans, and strategies.

To give life to this "impractical dimension of reality,"[8] his expositions tack continuously between Andalusia's forgotten medieval past and the futures that become imaginable within the shadow it casts on the present, an exercise—as one of his close collaborators put it—necessary for "assess[ing] the factual circumstances that characterize the 'Mediterranean space' conceived as an area susceptible to being organized regionally, and the circumstances that condition the prospects of such collaboration" (Cordero Torres 1955, 9). This exercise of historical imagination is both conceptual and practical, for indeed, Gil Benumeya dedicated much of his life to constructing and nurturing the institutional and political structures that would bring the world posited by this *andalucista* vision into existence. In short, it is through the lens of his political life and activity that we can trace the contours of Andalucismo as both political imaginary and historical sensibility.

If Gil Benumeya's Andalucismo remained profoundly attuned to strategic possibilities only recognizable from within the tradition's own temporal and geographic projections, his political compass (like most other thinkers of his generation) never abandoned the problem of Spanish power. Indeed, dreams of emerging constellations of global power with Spain at the helm appear as one possible future of al-Andalus at various junctures in his work. This has led a number of scholars to interpret his work (and the oeuvre of Andalucismo more broadly) in largely instrumental terms, as a useful fiction of Spanish colonial policy.[9] I do not share this assessment. For although Gil Benumeya never entirely left the institutions of Spanish political life, including those established during the Franco regime, his vision of a Hispano-Arabic civilization chafed against the boundaries of the nation at numerous junctures, setting him, at times, in direct opposition to the policies of the state for which he frequently worked. It is this *andalucista* itinerary of his life and thought, one oriented around that space of geohistorical possibility hinted at in the diagram (figure 1) I began with, that I want to uncover over the following pages. Thus, while Gil Benumeya's writings display many aspects of the ideological currents of his day—Romanticism, nationalism, Orientalism, fascism—I trace a style of thinking that exceeds the political assumptions and historical sensibilities defined by these terms, one that repositions Spain in relation to Middle Eastern societies in unexpected ways.[10] That his vision and life encompassed irresolvable contradictions goes without saying.

As I noted in the introduction, Andalucismo is a peripheral tradition and is so in two senses: first, peripheral to the discipline of history, with its authorizing secular discourses and its institutional norms, and second, as a knowledge produced at the geographic and conceptual periphery of Europe, at the borderlands of the discursive operations that secure the coherence of this civilizational space. This chapter approaches the peripherality of this tradition through the work and life of Gil Benumeya before turning in the second half of the chapter to one of Gil Benumeya's present-day successors, Antonio Manuel Rodríguez Ramos, a journalist, lawyer, and political activist in the city of Córdoba. I examine the lives of these two Andalusians for those moments in which they veer off from European cultural and political logics, where they exert friction on the conceptual order of Spanish nationalism and its European career. I do so, however, not to find a redemptive political formula. As I have emphasized, Andalucismo is most valuable in my view in the way it unsettles political and geographic certainties rather than in what it prescribes. Instead of providing a normative po-litical compass, Andalucismo offers a remapping of possibilities (concep-tual, geographic, aesthetic, political, ethical), each entailing its own new set of liabilities, risks, dangers, and blind spots. In a moment when Euro-pean anxieties over the presence of Muslims on the continent have spiraled into a broad ethnonationalist resurgence with Islamophobia as a primary pillar, such a cartographic exercise seems particularly warranted.

SPANISH AFRICANISM

Rodolfo Gil Benumeya was born in Andújar in 1901.[11] Having been raised with an appreciation of Andalusian history and culture (his father was a scholar of Spain's Sephardic Jews), he changed his name early in life from Torres to Gil Benumeya after discovering that his mother had Morisco roots and was a descendant of Abd Allah Ibn Umayya (a member of the rul-ing Umayyad family).[12] He moved to El Escorial, just outside Madrid, for his university education, undertaking Arabic and Islamic Studies with the renowned Spanish Arabist Miguel Asín Palacios. During these years at the university, he made a number of trips to North Africa, primarily to Tunis, where he stayed with an aunt. After graduation in 1925, he was sent by the regime of Primo de Rivera to head a Spanish press corps in Morocco.

As with most Spaniards of his generation, Gil Benumeya was greatly concerned with the problem of Spanish decline and weakness, a condi-tion underscored by the loss of Spain's colonial possessions following the Spanish-American War in 1898 and the country's inability to compete—economically, politically, militarily—with England and France. Since the late nineteenth century, Spaniards had come to imagine Africa, and Mo-rocco in particular, as the site from which the recuperation of Spanish pres-tige and power might be undertaken, where the country's former status as a dominant colonial power could potentially be redeemed.[13] These imperial longings and ambitions gave impetus to Spanish Africanism, a movement among Spanish intellectuals and colonial bureaucrats who, from the late nineteenth century through the Franco period, developed a wide-ranging reflection on the significance of Africa for Spain, though with a primary focus on Morocco as the principal site of Spanish colonial interests. The or-igins of this movement can be traced to the Spanish commercial and geo-graphic societies founded during the last three decades of the nineteenth century (see Nogué 1999; Mateo Dieste 2012). Seeking to encourage Span-ish interest and activity in North Africa, these societies promoted a vision of the common bonds linking Spain to the south, bonds articulated within the reigning discourses of geography, climate, race, and history.[14] From its origins, a paternalistic attitude to "our less-fortunate brothers to the south" dominated the field.

Rodolfo Gil Grimau, the son of Gil Benumeya and a highly respected Arabist in his own right (d. 2008), has suggested that Spanish Africanism can be plotted along two—at times intersecting, at times diverging—lines of development. The first, he notes, is a colonial current "that attempts to construct for Spain a substitute for the American empire, already lost or in the process of becoming so" (Gil Grimau 1988, 277). The second, what Gil Grimau calls the "emotional" current, "sees in [Spain's] African intervention—and particularly North African—a continuation of the wars of the Christian Kingdoms against the Muslims in what is called the Reconquista, or [alternatively] one more phase of the dialectic of Hispano-Arabic civilization in which, it is now the responsibility of modern Spain, Europe, etc., to lend a hand to its less fortunate brothers" (277). Gil Grimau points to the way the medieval past harbored two entwined images for twentieth-century Spaniards: one captured in the powerful figure of the Reconquista, which by the mid-nineteenth century had become an ideological cornerstone of Spanish nationalism, the other emphasizing the fraternal bonds forged within a matrix of Hispano-Arabic civilization (and later idealized in the notion of the *convivencia* of the three religions). While these two historical images appear to stand in contradiction, both proved to be immensely useful to the Spanish state in its colonial endeavors, with the former destined primarily for internal consumption and the latter oriented to the outside.[15] While Gil Benumeya was himself highly critical of the triumphalist narrative of the Catholic victory over the Iberian Muslims, the past he sought to recuperate would remain inescapably double edged.

Throughout his career as a writer and journalist, Gil Benumeya explored the political possibilities afforded by the concept of Hispano-Arabic civilization. The Spanish Protectorate in Morocco, in his view, was a natural expression of this civilizational bond, a "moral obligation" owed to the Moroccans for reasons of history as well as race. Spanish intervention, however, had to be qualified. It was not to be an act of colonial conquest but a preliminary step toward the formation of a "federation among Spain, Portugal, and Morocco, constituting a single state on the international stage, but three autonomous and independent states for each other" (Gil Benumeya 1926, 73). For this federation to be built, however, "it was necessary [for Spain] to help Morocco, our underdeveloped brother, to organize a government capable of forming such a federation" (73). As Eric Calderwood (2018) has emphasized, this discourse on the limits of legitimate occupation was not uncommon among Spanish Africanists, many of whom believed Spain's North African colonial enterprise to be of a completely different genre than the brutal exercise of power in which the rest of Europe was involved.[16] As opposed to many of his contemporaries, Gil Benumeya's view of the Protectorate would evolve rather quickly from enthusiastic to ambivalent to highly critical. And although his writings on a "brotherhood" (*hermandad*) across the Mediterranean will come to figure prominently within the colonial propaganda of the Franco regime, he would at the same time increasingly advocate for the dissolution of the Protectorate, insisting that it was only through a federation of fully independent nations that a renewal of Spanish power would be achieved.

From his earliest essays, written when he was still in his mid-twenties, Gil Benumeya's political reflections showed a distinct *andalucista* orientation. In his text *Mediodía*, first published as a series of articles in the Africanist journal *Revista de la Raza* between 1927 and 1929, he positions Andalusia at the center of a revised global history, as the site from which "the great crises of history" have unfolded. At times, an imperial tone resounds: "Andalusia imposed itself on Roma with Seneca, on the Goths with San Isidro, on the Syrians with Averroes and Ibn Hazm, on Castile with the Sevillian school. It gave emperors to Roma and Caliphs to Islam" (Gil Benumeya 1929, 19). Yet, more than a paean to imperial glory, the book's aim (as with most of his many writings) is to excavate the Arab world lying within the Spanish. One part of the text centers on a historical account of the Muslim Kingdoms from the first Umayyad dynasty in Iberia up through 1609, when the Moriscos were expelled. This historical account is interspersed with a series of reflections on both Spanish and Middle Eastern traditions of music, architecture, dance, and festival forms, all emphasizing the overlap and genealogical connections that constituted the shared cultural-spiritual reality he saw as uniting these regions.[17] This trove of cultural and historical knowledge, distorted and effaced by the politics of purification carried out over the last three hundred years, will allow Spain to reconnect with its "genuine history." Pulling these threads together, Gil Benumeya summarizes his overall aim in the book:

> *Mediodía* has been only a prologue to an African conception of peninsular history, up to the expulsion of the Moriscos. With this expulsion, southern Spain lost its meaning and purpose, and only in 1926 [at the end of the Rif War when Spanish authority in the Protectorate was reasserted] did it resume its genuine history with the renewed fraternal contact between Moroccans and Andalusians, thanks to the new idea of "*Andalucismo Árabe*," of an integrated Andalusianism. Leaping over the pit of savagery (1610–1926), the field is free in which to link tradition to our contemporary problems. (119)

Torn apart by the early seventeenth-century expulsion of the Moriscos and maintained in isolation over subsequent centuries by a highly restrictive and exclusionary concept of national identity, Spain and Morocco were finally, in Gil Benumeya's vision, returning to their cultural and spiritual roots through the processes of exchange and collaboration set in place by the Protectorate. Andalucismo, that "fraternal ethnic religion that aims to reconstruct an Andalusian Spain that embraces the African coast" (18–19), would connect Spain to the rich traditions from which its uniqueness, intelligence, and vigor derive while at the same time remapping the terrain of political possibility in a manner highly favorable to both the Arab revival movement and to a renewal of Spanish prestige on the international stage. Spain must become "Arabic Spain" (*España Árabe*), a transformation he came to think of in terms of a vast reeducation campaign.

MUSICAL TERRITORY

As with so many of the *andalucistas* that he came to associate with from the late 1920s on—including Blas Infante, the founding father of Andalusian nationalism, and the poet Federico García Lorca—Gil Benumeya's *andalucista* sensibilities were profoundly musical, his writing saturated with the sonic figures and passional repertoires of Andalusian song. Throughout his writings he returned again and again to the musical forms of flamenco, or *cante jondo*, tracing out each line and curve of their emotional geometries as if the Mediterranean universe he was assembling demanded such a musical infrastructure. These lines and curves invariably led to the south and east, to the Arabs, Jews, and Roma whose historical experience on Iberian soil resonated in the cry of the flamenco singer and the strum of the guitar. Gil Benumeya's prose often achieved its most lyrical effects in the passages on Andalusian music:

> Andalusian song is the most powerful of enchantments; its strange witchcraft is the essential note of the millenary Semitic life, elemental and indecipherable. It is the faithful expression of brown humanity, one that shifts from long periods of lethargy and indolence to the most delirious convulsions. The Mediterranean guitar and the Bedouin dulzaina sing the eternal pain of the race, while a piece of spirit escapes from the throat and embeds itself in the ether of a cry that is both a prayer and a roar of a lion in heat. (Gil Benumeya [1928] 1996, 247)

As I explore further in chapter 3, for generations of *andalucistas*, Andalusian song has provided the door through which the territory postulated by Andalucismo can be accessed, the entryway by which this occulted historical geography will reveal itself. Gil Benumeya's writings on music often devolve into a kind of mystical poetry where his descriptive intentions are subordinated to sensory and aesthetic effects as an attempt to retune the senses of his readers to a Mediterranean world fashioned of "Semitic" elements long denied. In a section emphasizing the elements common to Andalusian musical forms and the arabesque figures that line the walls of the Alhambra, he takes the reader into a sinuous meditation on their common aesthetic gestures:

> In both of these arts, there is a continuous line that one only follows with difficulty until it is interrupted by the intersection of another, more subtle, that extends out, separates off, and narrows in order to join with others and disappear in a great bundle; a little later the same line reappears or the same note repeats as by the same law. . . . Notes and lines converge and come apart rapidly in a vertiginous cascade of colors that dissipate in space like the waves from a stone in the water. (255–56)

The world Gil Benumeya discovers within these musical and figural aesthetic forms, one in which elements coalesce and disperse, appear and disappear, parallels the Andalusian territory that is the subject of his writing, a kind of liminal space glimpsed only through fragments, traces, ruins, gestures, tastes. Gil Benumeya: "It is a music that one cannot hear well, but that one nonetheless feels; nothing concrete happens, and yet it vibrates" (256). One feels, in other words, what defies categorization within the reigning sensory epistemology, what cannot be discerned by a National Catholic ear; a "nothing," an event emptied by the Inquisitional ambition to erase all traces of Islam and Judaism from language, architecture, and music, a nonhappening that nonetheless happened and continues to "vibrate," as he says.

Bound by family resemblance to musics from the south and east, Andalusian song sounds out the hidden territory of *Mediodía*, attuning the ear to its distinct time and place. A tradition familiar to most of his readership, this music provides the affective grounding through which this imaginal geography can be felt, glimpsed, and reflected on, a first step in its realization. While Gil Benumeya offers the Arabesque as one key to this partially familiar affective territory, it is quickly followed in his text by an exploration of various North African musical traditions genealogically bound to flamenco, including *el Ala* and *el Griha*. Knowledge of the Arabic aesthetic and musical traditions, he suggests, is a necessary condition for grasping the relations on which his new historical cartography is based.

ACTIVISM

There is a mystical quality to Gil Benumeya's prose, a quality necessitated, perhaps, by the task he set himself: attuning his readers to the virtual world he hoped to actualize, accommodating a difficult dimension of the past within the Spanish present. This task, a kind of quest, is not a purely literary one for Gil Benumeya; it will inform his entire career in journalism, politics, and business. As he states in one of his early texts, *Ni oriente, ni occidente* ([1928] 1996), "The truth of the south cannot be dealt with here. It must be distilled across all of my life, in a more perfect manner than permitted by the tumultuous form of this essay" (22). The excavation of *Mediodía*, in other words, demands historical inquiry, poetic exploration, as well as political activism, what for Gil Benumeya found expression in a deepening commitment to Moroccan nationalism and to Middle Eastern anticolonial currents more generally. Almost immediately after having arrived in Morocco to work as a journalist, he began to establish relations with the leaders of the still nascent Moroccan nationalist movement, relations that in many cases became close friendships and gave rise to multiple forms of collaboration by turns commercial, intellectual, and political.[18] Thus, during these early years, he began a commercial partnership with Hagg Abdesalam Bennuna, one of the father figures of the independence movement, establishing a company that provided electricity to the city of Tétouan (López Enamorado 1998, 2). Bennuna was a cofounder of the *Ahli* School in 1925, the first educational center in Spanish Morocco organized around a nationalist curriculum and one through which many of the younger generation of nationalist leaders would pass.[19] Shortly thereafter Gil Benumeya came into contact with one of the most prominent of the young leaders of the independence movement, Abdelkhaliq Torres, when he took up a position as a professor of Hispano-Arabic art at the Free Institute of Tétouan, where Torres was acting director. Within a few years, Torres would replace Bennuna as the de facto leader of the movement. Through Torres, Gil Benumeya came to know many of the other leaders of the independence movement (among them, Ahmed Balafrej, Allal al-Fassi, El-Mekki Naciri), and for a period he became a regular participant in their weekly meetings. As Gil Grimau notes, commenting on his father's relation to these nationalist leaders, this was "a friendship that continued to the end of his life, and is still held in memory today in Morocco, where the figure of Gil Benumeya is greatly appreciated" (Gil Grimau 1996, 16).

As his network of relations with the Moroccan nationalist leaders expanded, Gil Benumeya's writings became ever more critical of Spanish colonial ambitions in North Africa. From as early as 1926, he was publishing articles in the Spanish press arguing that the time of the Protectorate had passed: "Our security requires that this anomalous regime end as soon as possible and that that there be no great colonial empires beyond our coastline, so that the Moors can govern themselves, thus making French or Spanish tutelage unnecessary. With a free Morocco, Spain will see itself on a par with the great powers and able to defeat them commercially and intellectually, by taking advantage of its proximity to Morocco and of the Islamic tradition of Andalusia" (Gil Benumeya 1926, 211). Arguing in the Africanist press that Spanish interests would best be served by an independent Morocco, he was simultaneously strategizing with the leaders of the independence movement about how to achieve this end.

Propelled by his widening contacts with nationalist leaders from the late 1920s forward, Gil Benumeya became increasingly concerned by and engaged with the wider arena of what is called the "Arabic Awakening" (al-Nahda), the broad anticolonial reform movement that began in the late nineteenth century across the Middle East and that embraced both Arab nationalist and pan-Islamist currents. In numerous articles and books he sought to educate his Spanish readership about the currents of religious and political thought that were emerging in various parts of the region in the context of the Awakening and to inform them more generally about the art, architecture, religion, and history of a region whose destiny, in his view, was inseparable from that of Spain itself.[20] Across these works, Gil Benumeya returned repeatedly to al-Andalus as the lynchpin binding the contemporary political situation in the Middle East to Spain. Thus, in an article discussing the Arabic literary renaissance that had emerged in the context of the Nahda, Gil Benumeya weaves in an account of a visit by the celebrated Egyptian poet Ahmed Shawqi to Granada and Shawqi's subsequent recognition of the historical and ongoing importance of Andalusia ("el motivo andaluz") for the Middle East (Gil Benumeya 1939, 40–41). Across his career, Gil Benumeya never abandoned this kind of pedagogical effort aimed at inculcating an andalucista perspective on the contemporary world in his Spanish audience.[21]

This effort also took the form of a series of articles, begun while Gil Benumeya was still in his twenties and extending up through the final years of his life in the mid-1970s, focused on Jewish immigration to Palestine, the founding of the state of Israel, and (somewhat later) the effects of Israeli expansionist policies on the local Muslim and Christian populations.[22] In his early writings on these issues, Gil Benumeya expressed enthusiasm for Jewish immigration to Palestine, what he saw as one face of a broader "Semitic" renaissance taking place throughout the region, a manifestation of the "eternal ideal of Semitism" (Gil Benumeya [1928] 1996, 8).[23] By the 1940s, however, this enthusiasm had waned as he became increasingly concerned with the territorial ambitions of the settlement movement and its complete disregard for the long-standing residents of the territory. Following the founding of Israel in 1948 and its adoption of an ever more aggressive and militaristic stance toward non-Jews in both Palestine and the region as a whole, Gil Benumeya's writings became increasingly critical of the country, a posture he would maintain up through the end of his life. In an essay from the early 1950s in which he sought to explain why Egypt was rightly worried about Israeli militarism, he hones in on the country's politics of relentless expansion: "The mandate of the United Nations through which Palestine was shaped in the context of English intervention was based on a commitment to establish a 'Jewish homeland' that would serve both as a center of cultural reconstruction and as a refuge for persecuted and displaced Jews who lacked a nationality. It never promised nor did it imply that in Palestine a Jewish state would be established, and even less that all of Palestine would become a Jewish state" (Gil Benumeya 1956, 82). A growing frustration is registered across these writings regarding the inability of Spanish observers to think about the Israeli-Palestinian conflict outside the lens of their perceived geopolitical interests and a simultaneous failure to recognize the country's moral and civilizational connection to the region via medieval al-Andalus. In short, Gil Benumeya's Andalucismo undergirded a sustained commitment to finding a just solution for both Jewish and Palestinian inhabitants of Palestine, the region he saw not as a distant object of strategic concern but as an integral component of *Mediodía* and hence of modern Spain as well.

In 1936, during the Spanish Civil War, Gil Benumeya was sent to Cairo as a member of Spain's cultural mission. Officially, he had been tasked with explaining to the Arab nationalists (many of whom were living at the time in exile in Cairo) why Arabs who had until then been involved in a political and military struggle against colonial armies should now support one of those armies—on the side of Franco—in a war that had little direct relevance to them (Gil Grimau 1996, 21). There is no evidence that he resisted this assignment, and it is quite likely he would have considered Franco's recruitment of Moroccan fighters to be consonant with the model of Spanish-Moroccan cooperation presupposed in his vision of civilizational fusion. During his sojourn in Cairo, he did meet and collaborate with many leading figures of pan-Arabist and pan-Islamist movements, writing and organizing in support of their cause. In addition, he served as a correspondent for the journal *Unidad Marroquí* (published in Spanish) and also taught Spanish language in the residence for Moroccan students.

The implications of Gil Benumeya's "Andalucismo Árabe" extended well beyond projects of commercial and political alliance. The Andalusianization of Spain he advocated also required a pedagogical effort within Spain itself. The construction of "Arab Spain" entailed that Spaniards begin to study Arabic as well as have a solid grasp of the principles and historical development of Islam (López Enamorado 1998, 14). "Arabic for Spanish children in Morocco, Ceuta, and Melilla (and why not also Málaga, Algeciras, Cádiz, Sevilla, Almería, Alicante, entry points to Africa?) represents contact with the language of half the Mediterranean, with classical Arabic which is no longer a dead language but has been resuscitated in Egypt and unifies the local dialects from Tunisia to India. Second origin of the Spanish language. Official language of 300 million Muslims" (Gil Benumeya 1931, 165). As the anthropologist González Alcantud notes, Gil Benumeya understood "the defense of Spanish/Arabic bilingualism as a defense against other imperialisms, and as a means to give a concrete dimension to the transnational *andalucismo* that he dreamed of" (González Alcantud 1996, 83). This educational effort, he argued, needed to be carried out in schools throughout Spain. Granada, at the time on its way to becoming a center of learning and expertise on Islam and Arabic studies, would provide a key resource for this effort. As an anchor for this project, a new university was to be founded, the University of the Alhambra, which would make the study of Hispano-Arabic civilization its primary goal and would bring together students from Spain as well as the Middle East. Some aspects of this vision were eventually given concrete form with the establishment of the Department of Semitic Studies at the University of Granada.

BALANCING CONTRADICTIONS

The central paradox of Gil Benumeya's life is that he spent his entire career working within the institutions of Spanish colonialism and foreign affairs while developing simultaneously a historical and political outlook that required Spain's displacement from its own ideological moorings. Certainly, he may have reasoned that his goal of "making Andalusia once again Andalusi," as Gil Grimau identified his father's foremost desire, might best be achieved with the backing of an authoritarian state (Gil Grimau 1996, xxxix). Indeed, it is easy to imagine that Gil Benumeya saw common ground between the Promethean discourse of fascism, with its ambition to create a "new man" and a "new culture," and his own grandiose visions of a world remade on an Andalusian foundation. His compromises with Spanish fascism aside, much of his career can be characterized as a balancing act between his commitments to Spain on one hand and to the *andalucista* territory of *Mediodía* on the other. The rhetorical ambition at the center of his vast written oeuvre was to persuade the Spanish public that these commitments could be squared with each other. His Spanish readership could be trained to understand the value and historical significance of the anticolonial impulses coursing through the Middle East and beyond and to the immense possibilities open to a Spain allied with these impulses.

The contradictions intrinsic to this stance could not always be contained. Over the years, Gil Benumeya would increasingly decry the use of his writings on a Hispano-Arabic *hermandad* by Franco's propagandists to rally popular support for the continuation of the Spanish Protectorate in Morocco.[24] Yet the regime never ceased to find utility in his *andalucista* texts. A case in point, Gil Benumeya's 1942 book *Marruecos andaluz* (Andalusian Morocco) was published by Franco's office of "popular education" and widely used within the Spanish educational system at the time as part of the ideological edifice of the regime's colonial policy, this despite the author's insistence on the text's anticolonial stance.[25] At times, repercussions from these conflicts affected Gil Benumeya's life more tangibly—as occurred, for example, when the Spanish military governor of Tangiers sought to have him imprisoned together with a number of the leaders of the Moroccan independence movement.

The frenetic pace and grandiosity of Gil Benumeya's political visions, a few of which I have outlined here, are symptoms of a most impractical attempt to find his place, and that of Spain as well, within the chronotope of *Mediodía*. Across his vast oeuvre he made recourse to a large number of pseudonyms, as if a single name could not mediate the instability of the project he was pursuing without some mutation. These included Benomar, Emir Si-Jalil el-Amagüi, Emir Sid Omar, Luís de Válor, and Muley Omar Torres Benumeya, each name navigating a different Mediterranean itinerary, a different fusion of Iberia and North Africa. A more telling demonstration of the ambiguity inherent in the *andalucista* identity Gil Benumeya was continually forging comes in a 1933 letter he wrote to one of the leaders of the Moroccan nationalist struggle in which he tried to explain some of the apparent paradoxes of his political viewpoint: "I am certainly not Moroccan, but I am a Muslim. . . . I am above all Andalusian, in other words, an Arab . . . and I work for Spain because today my country forms a part of it, with the hope of bringing about a rebirth of Arab Spain."[26] Muslim, Andalusian, Arab, Spanish—these terms unfold as if they were close synonyms, different perspectives on what Gil Benumeya took to be a singular identity. In Morocco, he was known to be a descendant of a notable Muslim family, and there is some suggestion that, on the basis of this heritage, he was considered by some to be a Muslim himself. Whether he encouraged such a view or not is unclear, though outside the passing remark made in this letter there is little evidence that he considered himself to be Muslim, at least not in any traditional sense. My sense is that Gil Benumeya, like many of the *andalucistas*, found himself to be ambiguously situated in relation to Islam, not quite a Muslim but neither the subject of Catholic Spain that historians had told him he was. Islam was integral to a civilization that he himself belonged to, one he sought to cultivate and promote. Another way to put this would be to say that *andalucistas* find themselves interpellated by Islam in ways that defy understanding within the political and conceptual world they inhabit, and this limit in turn gives impetus to their forms of inquiry, reflection, and practice. They find themselves historically constituted as subjects of Islam (and Judaism as well) even as they do not recognize themselves as adherents. Or at least not initially: one common response today to this historical interpellation is conversion to Islam, a trend more established in southern Spain than anywhere else in Europe.

FAMILY AFFAIRS

Throughout the first half of the twentieth century, Andalucismo offered the institutions of Spanish colonialism a discourse on the country's deep links to North Africa, one subsequently deployed by the mechanisms of state propaganda both in Spain and in Morocco to rally support for intervention. As one element within the broader discursive field of Spanish Africanism, the *andalucista* notion of a cross-Mediterranean *hermandad* acquired a highly paternalistic inflection, a variety of "white man's burden" that served as moral veneer for an occupation driven primarily by Spanish anxieties regarding the country's attenuated international prestige and, to a lesser extent, by commercial interests. Yet as Gil Benumeya's career suggests, despite its collaboration with Spanish colonial expansion in North Africa, Andalucismo also encompassed allegiances, solidarities, and affective attachments that sat awkwardly with the colonial enterprise and that, when articulated in political terms, could also generate an expansive recoding of colonial geography. Viewing the world produced and sustained by European dominance "from the Albayzín," imagining himself a citizen of a past and future "Arabic Spain," Gil Benumeya could see the struggles for national independence taking place in the Middle East *as his own*, as the outcome of historical processes in which he himself was implicated. *Mediodía*, in this light, was far more than an *andalucista* fantasy. It provided the compass from which Gil Benumeya's own political life found its bearings. Tellingly, his close identification with and support for the independence movement in Morocco and with Arab societies more generally did not go unappreciated. In the 1950s his name was put forward by members of the Arab League to act as a representative of that organization in Latin America (Gil Grimau 1996, xxx). The choice of Gil Benumeya for this position — not an Arab or Muslim, nor a Latin American — suggests that his notion of a Hispano-Arabic civilization — of al-Andalus as an unfinished project — was acquiring broader legibility. This honor, and the political itinerary of his life more generally, illuminate the space he called *Mediodía*, as fleeting instances of its practical realization.

The discourse on a "Hispano-Moroccan brotherhood" (beginning in the 1890s with Joaquín Costa and Ángel Ganivet and reaching its apogee during the years of the Franco regime, when it was instrumentalized within the propaganda of the Spanish Protectorate) emerged against an ideological background in which the figure of *el moro* had long been invested with intensely negative attributes as the archetypal enemy of Spain that had been vanquished by the Reconquista. Across the entire span of Spanish military campaigns in Morocco from the mid-nineteenth century until the early twentieth, and especially with the 1860 Battle of Tétouan and the Rif War (1921–1926), such Reconquista imagery was deployed extensively within Spanish media and popular culture more broadly (Velasco de Castro 2014, 209). Even when the Franco regime began to promote the *hermandad* discourse among the Moroccan elites,[27] stereotypes of the evil Moor continued to circulate in Spain much as they had before.

These entrenched stereotypes, however, did not exhaustively determine the attitudes of Spanish colonists toward the Moroccans with whom they associated. For example, although Spanish colonial policy in North Africa did include strict rules meant to keep social interactions between colonizers and colonized to the necessary minimum, in actual practice the barriers between the Spaniards and Moroccans were frequently breached. Accounts of daily life in the Protectorate in the 1930s and 40s, particularly among the popular classes, point to patterns of interaction and sociability between the two populations far more extensive than those found in the nearby French zone. Although there were urban areas designated for Spanish colonists, many Spaniards lived in what were called the "Indigenous quarters" (Mateo Dieste 2012, 243). Even Spanish military personnel, who were expected as part of their mission to rigidly abide by the norms of separation instituted within Spanish colonial policy, were known to transgress those norms.

The following note, part of a letter written by the bishop of Tangiers in 1921 in which he complains about such cross-confessional fraternization among the military, points to how the boundaries separating Spaniards and Moroccans could become considerably fluid.

Spanish soldiers continue to construct and restore buildings for the Moorish saints, and have not built even one sanctuary for Christians. Influenced by a politics of attraction (wrong, in my view), the Spanish administrators have not only left their own religious buildings to crumble, but have permitted that Spanish soldiers take part in festivals and celebration in honor of Moorish saints, to whom they offer gifts and treats, as if they were Muslims, or *as if they were indifferent to acting as Muslims, despite being Christians.* (Cited in Mateo Dieste 2012, 91–91, emphasis mine)

While the reconstruction of mosques and other religious edifices was undertaken by Spanish colonial authorities in order to help solidify the image of the occupation as being based in a relationship of fraternal harmony, the bishop's complaint about the "indifference" of the soldiers to the religious divide is striking and stands in sharp contrast to the Reconquista narratives emphasized with Spanish nationalism at the time. This is not to say that Spanish colonialism in North Africa was "gentle," as Spanish Africanists claimed in seeking to legitimate their own interventions on the continent and distinguish them from those of the rest of Europe. The Spanish in Morocco frequently resorted to the same tactics of violence used by other European nations in suppressing oppositional movements in the country. Rather, what is interesting in this context is the bishop's impression that in those instances where relations between Spanish and Moroccans appeared *too* fraternal, this behavior was attributed to the popular discourse on Hispano-Arabic solidarity ("a politics of attraction") that Gil Benumeya and others were involved in elaborating.[28]

LEGACIES OF *MEDIODÍA*

Gil Benumeya's *Mediodía* offered a space in which the present could be thought anew outside the dictates of the reigning conceptual-geographic order from the standpoint afforded by the recognition of the multiple entwinements across the sea, entwinements forged in the complex medieval society of al-Andalus and projected forward into the political and economic relations binding together the two sides of the Mediterranean. In his imaginative reworking of this Mediterranean space, Gil Benumeya was not calling on the arts of fiction but rather for an assessment of what this long ignored or rejected dimension of Spanish history might make possible and the future it might portend.

The *andalucista* tradition I have traced across Gil Benumeya's life and writings is most directly visible today in the plethora of associations that find in the Muslim period a central point of historical reference for the activities and projects they undertake. These include associations ranging from those promoting cultural exchange across the Mediterranean, the revival of Andalusi aesthetic and musical traditions, and the study of Spain's medieval past to others advocating immigrants' rights, Spanish citizenship for the descendants of the expelled Moriscos, or the revision of the nation's Catholic festivals to reflect a more religiously plural heritage. An *andalucista* imaginary also informs such state projects as the Alliance of Civilizations, a United Nations initiative first proposed in 2005 by then Spanish prime minister José Luis Zapatero as an institution dedicated to promoting interreligious and intercultural dialogue, first and foremost, between the West and the Islamic societies of the Middle East. Indeed, an analysis of this initiative in relation to Spain's diplomatic and foreign policy profile by the Spanish scholar of international relations Isaías Barreñada reads, in parts, as if it were lifted from Gil Benumeya's own prose:

> Spain's main asset as a "soft" power in cultural areas lies in its image and its cultural and linguistic heritage. In the current geostrategic context, where culture and values are becoming more important, the high symbolic value of the proposal for the Alliance of Civilizations allows Spain to link its cultural diversity, a history of successive cultural unions and miscegenation, the nature of its borders between Europe and the Arab and Islamic world, a positive image abroad and its governmental and popular bid for multilateralism and pacifism. (Barreñada 2006, 100–101)

While the Alliance has often been criticized as a naive and ineffective instrument (not unlike the UN as a whole in this regard), its limited impact cannot be taken to impugn the seriousness of the endeavor nor the historical legacies that conditioned and enabled it.

Admittedly, the expansion of the institutional web of *andalucista* initiatives in southern Spain has been significantly encouraged by the region's heavy reliance on the tourist economy, one centered on Andalusia's medieval heritage. State and corporate investment in the heritage sector and its associated institutions, including education, has directed the interests and desires of contemporary Andalusians toward a medieval history they are urged to remember nostalgically and adopt as their own. This has resulted in a vast constellation of identity-based cultural projects. However important, the fact that economic incentives have contributed to shaping contemporary interests in and attitudes toward the past does not in itself explain away the forms of thought and action that such engagements with the past may produce. The *andalucista* sensibility exemplified in the career of Gil Benumeya remains a generative dimension of Andalusian life.

CORDOBAN POLITICS

Today, those who advocate from the standpoint of an *andalucista* political imaginary tend to the liberal and left side of Spain's political spectrum far more than the right, Gil Benumeya's institutional home. Yet the earlier activist's life and work remain an important touchstone. One of the contemporary inheritors of Gil Benumeya's Andalucismo is Antonio Manuel Rodríguez Ramos, a professor of law at the University of Córdoba as well as a columnist and frequent contributor to a number of Cordoban journalistic media.

I first heard about Rodríguez Ramos during a conversation with Francisco Vigueras, a journalist and political activist in Granada. Vigueras is one of the founders of Granada Abierta (Open Granada), an initiative that seeks to challenge local forms of institutional intolerance as antithetical to Andalusia's multicultural heritage (see chap. 4). In our discussion, he singled out Rodríguez Ramos as a contemporary visionary of the Andalusian historical landscape, an heir to Castro, Lorca, Infante, and Gil Benumeya whose writings had contributed much to his own political education. Rodríguez Ramos's 2010 book, *La huella morisca: El Al Ándalus que llevamos dentro* (The Morisco Trace: The al-Andalus That We Carry Inside), earned the writer a considerable following among the many Spaniards who, like Vigueras, are drawn to *andalucista* perspectives. When I subsequently asked Elena Arigita, a professor in the Department of Semitic Studies at the University of Granada, whether she knew of Rodríguez Ramos, she acknowledged that she had read *La huella morisca* and had followed his political career as well. Like a handful of scholars I met at the university, Arigita had long been curious about and at times persuaded by some of the claims of Andalucismo, but she was also well aware that within the academy, such claims were most often dismissed as the Romantic musings of dilettantes and political ideologues. Given this context, her explorations of writers like Rodríguez Ramos necessarily took place in private circles more than professional arenas and were spoken about in subdued tones when questioned by scholars such as myself. In this case she confirmed that Rodríguez Ramos's poetic reflections on the Andalusian legacy, however unorthodox, held something of value and suggested moreover that she could arrange a meeting for me with a colleague and friend of Rodríguez Ramos the next day.

Aristóteles Moreno, whom I met over lunch the following day, indeed shared a long history of political collaboration with Rodríguez Ramos. A man in his early forties, his own trajectory echoes that of many of the other *andalucistas* with whom I spoke. A native of Córdoba, Moreno cultivated an early interest in the heritage of his city and of Andalusia more widely, an interest that eventually led him to take up Arabic studies at the University of Granada. Following his studies, he moved, initially to Baghdad and then to Cairo, where he lived for a few years (and where he met Arigita's husband, Rafael Ortega, a scholar of the Middle East, then in the process of his doctoral research). Upon returning to Córdoba and finding little demand for scholars of Arabic, he took up a job as a journalist for the popular Spanish newspaper *ABC*, where he works today. Over the years, he has collaborated with Rodríguez Ramos on a number of political projects, one of which—the Manifesto de Córdoba—I discuss below. After our initial conversation, he agreed to set up a meeting with Rodríguez Ramos a week later in a café in Córdoba.

Antonio Manuel Rodríguez Ramos was born in Almodóvar del Río, a town not far from Córdoba, best known for its medieval Muslim castle. In his youth, he joined the Juventudes Andalucistas (Andalucista Youth), a wing of the Andalusian nationalist party, the Partido Andalucista, and served as a regional secretary for the group. Over the subsequent years he has participated in and has frequently been a founding member of a wide range of associations, most with a progressivist political agenda and a clear *andalucista* tint: Andaluces Levantaos (Andalucians Rise Up), Parlamento por Andalucía, Foro Andaluz, Paralelo 36 Andalucía, Andalusians por unas Elecciones Propias (Andalusians for our Own Elections), the Fundación Blas Infante, to name a few.[29] At the time of writing, he was the secretary general of the Ateneo de Andalusia, a cultural association that supports events that celebrate and strengthen Andalusia's pluralist heritage and provides a forum for dialogue on regional issues. Rodríguez Ramos also ran as a candidate for the left-wing political party Podemos in 2016, an association that was short-lived once it became clear to him that the party "had no intention of treating Andalucía as a political subject on the level of Cataluña, Galicia, and Euskadi," as he explained to me during one of our meetings. Rodríguez Ramos's political career, with its succession of shifting affiliations and initiatives, betrays a restlessness, as if the political imaginary of his Andalucismo, awkwardly constrained within today's institutional norms, compelled the proliferation of ever-new embodiments, just as Gil Benumeya's political imaginary resulted in a seemingly endless succession of new cartographies and grand schema. Their politics, we might say, embraces an ethics of disorientation, a recognition of the need to find one's way across an unsurveyable political geography, a task for which the tools of a Romantic imagination prove to be essential. Political thinking for both Gil Benumeya and Rodríguez Ramos must draw on the powers of art and music.

The political optic of Rodríguez Ramos's Andalucismo takes as its primary focus the subordination of the Andalusian community to the dictates of the Spanish state and the consequent loss of freedom, social equality, and economic viability the community has suffered. From its origins in the first decade of the twentieth century through today, these have been the key structural problems that have, in his view, animated Andalusian nationalism. As he told me over coffee at our first meeting in February 2016, "These problems were there in 1910, when Blas Infante founded the movement and it articulated its vision, in 1977 when the community rose up in mass demonstrations to demand the same status of autonomy as then being conferred on Catalonia, Euskadi, and Galicia, and today, as Andalusia suffers from the highest rates of unemployment, the greatest social inequality, and the worst education system within all of Spain." In Rodríguez Ramos's opinion, the country's integration into the EU has further eroded the possibilities for social and economic justice in the community. "Spain's entrance in the European Union," he recounted, "has brought about a dismantling of the country's [productive] strength, and especially in Andalusia, in order to convert it into a service-providing country. We lost the opportunity to become a world power in agriculture or energy."

For Rodríguez Ramos, the modern history of Andalusian impoverishment and marginality is inseparable from a much earlier historical event: the subjection of the religiously heterogeneous society of medieval al-Andalus to persecution and repression at the hands of the Catholic conquerors. While the forms of persecution unleashed have shifted over the centuries, they emerge and repeat within an abiding structure forged by an alliance of the Castilian state with the Church, a form that took the shape of National Catholicism during the Franco regime and that continues today in an ongoing concordat between Church and state. Andalucismo in this sense is an expression of a culture of resistance that emerged across the sixteenth century in the Morisco struggle for survival against the increasingly repressive apparatus of the Catholic regime. This struggle, Rodríguez Ramos argues in *The Morisco Trace*, did not end with the expulsion of the Moriscos in the early seventeenth century because (and contrary to what the vast majority of historians of the period maintain) they were not expelled, or rather only some of them were. The majority, Rodríguez Ramos asserts, successfully evaded expulsion, vanishing into the fabric of rural Andalusian society, the Inquisition having exhausted the financial and moral resources necessary to track them down (Rodríguez Ramos 2010, 65). Through dissimulation and concealment, and eventually through a willful forgetting of who they were, they survived undetected. To do so, they negatively inhabited their own cultural and religious traditions, adopting the customs of their conquerors that best concealed their Muslim habits from dress to bathing, the consumption of pork, and the drinking of wine (79–80). These adoptions and modifications of their own practices, however, did not erase the prior cultural forms of Muslim and Jewish society. Traces of this inheritance, argues Rodríguez Ramos, continued to pervade the new cultural forms. What was lost, expunged as a condition of survival, rather, was the memory of where such traces came from, their embeddedness in an Islamic civilization and the plurireligious culture it had fostered. The cultural forms of the Moriscos survived precisely by being denied, rendered invisible by a practice of collective blindness adopted as a strategy of survival.

As Rodríguez Ramos put it to me in conversation, "the first characteristic of an Andalusian's identity is that his memory is the product of having lost his memory." This culture is what Rodríguez Ramos refers to as "the third Spain": "Between the uniform and repressive Spain that emerged with the definitive territorial conquest of al-Andalus, and the diverse and repressed Spain that died with the expulsion of the Spanish Moriscos, there is a third Spain, traumatized and clandestine. The real Spain, if there is one" (Rodríguez Ramos 2010, 29).[30] This "third Spain," prevailing in the south of the peninsula, was in this view not a tiny minority, a small residue left in the wake of the destruction of the Muslim kingdoms. Not only did the Moriscos, now concealed within their own skin, constitute a significant segment of the population at the time of the expulsion, but their practices and customs continued to exert a dominant cultural influence.

As with many other *andalucistas*, flamenco will prove key in Rodríguez Ramos's understanding of the culture that emerges from the wound of Inquisitorial persecution.

> The first generations of persecuted overcome the trauma by forgetting, even forgetting why they had to forget. Possibly this collective amnesia is accompanied by a kind of bipolar neurosis (schizoid or hysterical) that over time gives birth to the culture of flamenco. The children of their children inherit unconsciously the memory of the wound, encrypted in the instinctive and visceral creations that emerge during its cauterization. Thus we can understand the paroxysms of the dancers. Between sober pain and inebriated joy. (58–59)

For Rodríguez Ramos (and adhering closely to a vision we encountered in Gil Benumeya), flamenco designates "much more than an artistic expression" (60). The term embraces the culture of struggle and resistance produced by the Moriscos and their descendants up to the present, a period he refers to as "the flamenco era": "Andalusia became the natural catalyst for that Morisco essence, nomadic and converted, metabolized during the flamenco era into a highly original culture with a humanist and universalist ideal that reached its political epiphany on the fourth of December, 1977" (61). Here, the struggle by contemporary Andalusians against the repressive and parasitical central state—a struggle that culminated in the mass popular uprising of 1977 in which Andalusians demanded and received the same conditions of independence then being granted to the other autonomous regions of Spain—is continuous with the battle for survival by the Moriscos against the predations of the Catholic monarchs during the early-modern period. Andalucismo, in this light, is not simply a politics of identity but a demand for social justice (*reivindicación social*). As Rodríguez Ramos told me, "when Andalusians come out in the street to demand more Andalusia, they are asking for greater social equality, for work, and for an exit from the subordinate and parasitical relations that the community has with the state."

The Morisco Trace offers a passionate narration of the birth of Spain, the "third Spain," from the suffering and resistance of the Moriscos and the imprints left by this process in the linguistic and cultural forms of present-day Andalusians as the unconscious background of their political agency. As with Gil Benumeya's generation, North Africa lies along the path of Spanish political reform as the only mirror in which Spain can learn to see itself: "To certify the Morisco origins of our culture," writes Rodríguez Ramos, "it will be very useful to compare it to that which we find still intact in the places of exile beyond the peninsula. There where the devastating effects of the process of cultural uniformity sweeping the planet have not completely erased these traces" (Rodríguez Ramos 2010, 34). Echoing a common *andalucista* refrain, Rodríguez Ramos speaks here of a loss of self, of a void left within it, one for which even an inaccurate image of that missing part— found across the sea, in this case—is needed to dress the wound left by that amputation. And as with most other *andalucistas*, Rodríguez Ramos's trajectory has repeatedly taken him to North Africa, including numerous trips to Morocco to participate in events concerning the legacies of al-Andalus and the history of the Moriscos.

For Gil Benumeya, a *Mediodía* anchored in the historical legacy of al-Andalus was the key conceptual and political site from which the global anticolonial struggle against European domination could be waged.

Rodríguez Ramos's Andalusia is, similarly, a Mediterranean space whose cultural position—within Spain and outside it, both European and Middle Eastern—gives to it a universal political significance. Today, however, it is not colonialism against which Andalusian difference aligns itself but rather neoliberalism and its corrosive, homogenizing force. As Rodríguez Ramos told me at one point, "the fourth of December of our fathers is our 15M" (15M is the moniker of the Spanish antiausterity movement that began on of May 15, 2011). Andalucismo is, moreover, by the historical conditions of its emergence at the heart of the struggle against racism, discrimination, and intolerance, attitudes deeply lodged within Spanish political thought via the repressive operation that obliterates the Muslim and Jewish past. This denial of the Islamic and Jewish features of Spain not only saturates Spanish public discourse but has distorted the entire tradition of European historiography, a tradition in which "there are a plethora of terms to describe Muslims living under Christian rule (*Mudejar*), Christians under Muslim rule (*Mozarab*), Muslims converted to Christianity (*Morisco*), but no term to designate a Muslim born on Iberian soil despite the fact that by the fifteenth century the majority of them had been. Islam, in other words, has no place in Spain except as a foreign element" (Rodríguez Ramos 2010, 49–50).

LA MEZQUITA-CATEDRAL

In recent years Córdoba, Rodríguez Ramos's adopted home, has become an international flashpoint for contemporary conflicts over the significance of that foundational expulsion. The focal point of these conflicts is the medieval edifice at the city's center, commonly known as the Great Mosque of Córdoba or the Mezquita-Catedral (the Mosque-Cathedral), a UNESCO world heritage site and one of the most spectacular and frequently visited architectural wonders from the period of Islamic rule in Spain. Rodríguez Ramos has been a central protagonist in the unfolding struggle over the ownership and administration of this edifice for close to fifteen years. An analysis of this struggle highlights the contemporary political context of Andalucismo.[31]

First constructed between the eighth and tenth centuries, the Mezquita-Catedral combines a mosque and a Catholic chapel, the chapel having been built within the inner sanctuary of the mosque during the sixteenth century. Since the construction of the chapel five centuries ago up through the present, only Roman Catholic ritual practice has been permitted within the edifice. Beginning in the early 2000s, however, a growing movement among Muslims in Spain and internationally has petitioned the Church to allow for Muslim prayer as well. On a few occasions, over the last two decades, Muslim visitors have defied the ban, enacting the words and gestures of Muslim prayer within the space of the Mezquita-Catedral, an act that has resulted in their immediate ejection and, at least on one occasion, arrest.

In the context of this small but growing movement to open the edifice to Muslim worship, the Catholic Church in Spain took two steps. First, the Church began to undertake a program aimed at redefining the building as a purely Christian space. To this end they gradually eliminated most references to the Islamic history of the site from print and electronic literature aimed at visitors. It now became simply the "Cathedral of Córdoba." The elimination of Islam from the historical framing of the edifice offered to visitors found scholarly backing in the extensive works of the Church's official historian for the site, Manuel Nieto Cumplido. Often described in the Spanish press as "the world's leading expert on the Mezquita-Catedral," Nieto Cumplido has propounded an interpretation of the edifice that restricts the role of its Muslim architects to having assembled what for the most part are elements derived from Christian contexts. His description of the origin of the many lamps that illuminate the interior of the sanctuary is characteristic: "I have made various trips to Algeria, Egypt, and Tunisia in order to understand what the original lamps were like. Each time, they were of Christian origin, not a Muslim creation. Everything original about the monument is not derived from Islam."[32] Following a broader trend within the historiography of al-Andalus, Nieto Cumplido desubstantializes the Mezquita-Catedral's Islamic elements, leaving Islam as the vehicle through which the non-Islamic Mediterranean, here envisioned as primarily Byzantine Christian, is channeled.[33]

The Church also began archaeological projects aimed at showing that the remnants of a Visigothic church (the Basilica of Saint Vincent) lie beneath the floor of the edifice and that the mosque, therefore, is a foreign and temporary interruption within an ancient and continuous Christian space.[34] Adopting a polemical tone, a revised tourist brochure published by the Church gestures to the archaeological remains of the Basilica in order to refute the popular perception of al-Andalus as a period of enlightened rule: "It is an historical fact that the Basilica of Saint Vincent was expropriated and destroyed in order to build on top of it the subsequent mosque in the Islamic period, throwing into question the tolerance allegedly cultivated in medieval Córdoba."

When I first visited the Mezquita-Catedral in 2008, the effort to detach the sanctuary from its Islamic elements was already evident in the narration offered by my tour guide. As he led our group through the entranceway and into the vast expanse of red and white stone pillars, the guide paused, concerned that we approach the great edifice with the right ethnic and historical lens: "There is a common misunderstanding that this edifice was built by Arabs. This is wrong. Those who constructed this place were Moors [*moros*], you know, Moors from Mauritania. They were blacks. Blacks! The Arabs had nothing to do it." No direct denial of the Islamic faith of the builders was made nor needed, as the racial marker already served to supposedly block any association with Islam.

As a second step, the Church which had administered the building since it was first seized from the defeated Muslims in 1258, filed a petition with the public registry of property in March 2006 to have the building legally registered under the name Santa Iglesia Catedral de Córdoba as the private property of the Church. The petition is written in the following terms:

> The city having been reconquered by Ferdinand III, the monarch set forth that in the festival of the Apostles Peter and Paul, in the year 1236, that the cathedral be dedicated to María, mother of God, and consecrated that same day by the bishop, Osma Don Juan Dominguez. . . . The ceremony of tracing, with a staff, letters written in Greek and Latin alphabets on a strip of ash in the form of a diagonal cross on the floor of the building gave canonical and liturgical expression to the church's act of taking possession of the church. (Reina 2014)

A medieval act, if ever there were one. In the face of an attempt by Muslims to gain permission to pray within the Mezquita-Catedral, the Church responded with a reminder, inscribing within the official property register the fact and date of the earlier defeat and expulsion of the Muslims of Córdoba—the so-called Reconquista—while simultaneously securing the equivalence of an ecclesial act and a modern juridical one, an act of consecration with a deed of legal transfer.[35] Thus, although the Spanish Constitution of 1978 states that "no religion shall have a state character," in practice, ongoing political alliances with the Church have ensured a certain ambivalence in the distinction between ecclesial and state authority, and as a consequence, between the time of the Church and that of the nation.

This fusion of Church and state is effected in a striking manner in the petition's invocation of the Reconquista. The concept of the Reconquista, indexed by the Church as the basis of its claim to ownership of the sanctuary, first appeared within Spanish political life during the late nineteenth century as one key element within an emerging nationalist discourse.[36] By the mid-twentieth century it had become a central reference point in popular discourses of Spanish identity, indexing an event now described as the birth of the nation. The concept served to articulate a number of key aspects of Spanish national identity, particularly the idea of Spain as a unity extending back to the period of the Goths, with the Muslim period framed as a bracketed interval of foreign occupation (see, e.g., García Fitz 2009). The eight hundred years of Muslim presence on the peninsula was in this way circumscribed and extirpated from the historical surface of the nation. Moreover, a fundamental unity, forged of a common enterprise to expel a common enemy—Muslims and Jews—was extended over the many fractures dividing the territory and bound this national unity to a militant Catholicism. National history thereby acquired a transcendent meaning embodied in the eternal mission of the Church (García Fitz 2009).

Although this myth was embraced by historians and political thinkers on both sides of the civil war, it was given pride of place within the ideological apparatuses of National Catholicism, including the educational system (where, I would add, parts of it remain largely intact; for an example, see Navarro, cited in Flesler 2008b). Indeed, within fascist propaganda, Franco's "war of liberation" against the "atheist Communists" was frequently compared to the earlier struggle against the so-called foreign Moorish occupiers who, as with the Communists, threatened the unity of the nation and its sacred heart, the Catholic Church. As a book for children explained at the time of Franco's ascendance to power, "Just as now the Carlist [pro-Catholic and monarch] militia fights against the Communists, so then the good Spanish people warred against the Moors, who had taken over almost all of the ancestral home of the Spanish."[37]

Assigned the status of origin myth within the story of the Spanish nation, the Reconquista posited the indissoluble unity of the Catholic Church and the Spanish state, merging ecclesial time and secular time. It also gave mythical status to a struggle against Islam as the foundational act of the nation and as such, the existential ground of the authority of the state. This mythical structure takes its clearest ritual expression in the yearly celebration of the Moros y Cristianos festivals in many parts of southern Spain as well as in the Day of Conquest (*Día de la Toma*) festival celebrated each year in Granada (see chap. 4).

A recent comment by Nieto Cumplido, responding to a question about the request to allow for Muslim prayer in the sanctuary, gives a sense of the rather strange temporality of the Church's battle with Islam:

> Muslims think that everything they walk upon belongs to them. . . . And besides, there exist maps of North Africa in which Córdoba is integrated into the Muslim World. For that reason, when political claims are made—not religious claims, but political ones—our politician leaders should recognize, with respect to Muslim immigration into Spain,

that they should welcome them, but should also be aware that problems soon will come.[38]

Nieto Cumplido's anxiety is telling. The fact that Muslims "walked upon" Iberian soil, that they left footprints on the land, bequeaths to Spain an interminable problem, what Nieto Cumplido identifies in terms of a Muslim ambition to reclaim what they will always consider theirs. The *andalucistas*, for their part, treat this anxiety as a symptom of an identity forged by the compulsion to continuously expunge an integral part of oneself. This theme, already well evident in Cervantes's Quixote in the early seventeenth century (see the introduction), has been explored by many Spanish historians and literary scholars of an *andalucista* stripe, including Américo Castro, whose diagnosis of this condition—"to live by denying the reality of one's existence" (*vivir desviviéndose*)—we encountered earlier.

DISSOLVING MUSLIM DIFFERENCE

Spain's nationalist historiography has attempted to deal with the problem of eight centuries of Muslim rule in Iberia through a variety of means. Thus, Asín Palacios, the country's most prominent mid-twentieth-century Arabist, argued that Islam as practiced in the Iberian context was in actuality Christian or rather a current of Christianity in which a number of doctrinal errors had sedimented over the years (see Parra Monserrat 2012a, 115–17). An alternative argument, first articulated by the fascist thinker Ignacio Olagüe and today embraced by a variety of left-wing scholars as well as by many in the convert community, posits that Islam was not a foreign intruder on Iberian soil but an autochthonous development, a temporary solution adopted by an endangered Unitarian community in the eighth century (see chap. 2). Both left- and right-wing solutions, in other words, respond to a nationalist impulse to eliminate the obstacle that Islam represents for Spain and its European identity, guarding against the foreign footprint Islam leaves on Spanish soil.

These twentieth-century discourses on the nondifference that Islam makes for Spain and Europe, however, build on a theological foundation articulated during the sixteenth and early seventeenth centuries at a time when the region's Christian authorities were still wrestling with the problem of how to assimilate Spain's recent Muslim converts to Christianity (Moriscos) before this program was finally discarded in favor of forced exile in the early 1700s. Suspicions about the Moriscos' hidden attachment to the practices of their former religion ensured they would always be treated as heretics by the Old Christians and hence become the site of a permanent social rift. Their ongoing attachment to their previous styles of dress, bathing, music, and celebration were widely viewed as evidence of this heretical belief. Moreover, anxieties born of the evangelizing project in the New World about Indigenous syncretism also contributed to these worries. While concerns about Morisco heresy increasingly drew the attention of ecclesial authorities during the latter decades of the sixteenth century, scholars at the time were skeptical about the ability of the interrogators of the Inquisition to ferret out Morisco unbelief. For example, in one influential text from the early seventeenth century, *Tratado acerca de los moriscos de España*, Pedro de Valencia, a philologist and royal chronicler in the court of Philip III, argued that not only were some forms of Morisco heresy inaccessible to Inquisitional authority but that recourse to the institutions of the Inquisition would only deepen the divide between New and Old Christians, thus rendering assimilation all the more difficult.

As the historian of early-modern Spain Seth Kimmel has argued, the solution to this problem propounded by Valencia and others at the time was to secularize heresy; that is, the goals of orthodoxy could best be served if the Church "sometimes pretended that crimes against the Church were offenses against the Crown" and allowed irregular religious practices to be adjudicated through a "secular tribunal" (*tribunal seglar*) rather than an ecclesiastical court. As Kimmel notes, for Valencia "the noble end of effective New Christian assimilation justified the deceptive means necessary to accomplish such jurisdictional surgery. . . . It mattered not whether the Moriscos and their representatives were duplicitous; Morisco dissimulation and assimilation each depended upon a shifting sense of collective Spanish political identity rather than Morisco insincerity or sincerity. Because duplicity and earnestness were products of social and political conditions, those interested in New Christian orthodoxy should focus on changing these conditions" (Kimmel 2013, 300). Valencia's proposal, one that found numerous scholarly echoes, theorized and provided a theological basis for a new arena of *cultural* diversity—as opposed to *religious* heresy—an arena oriented, paradoxically, around the disciplinary formation of religious subjects.

While my purposes here do not require any further exploration of the complex historical shifts that underlay this process of refashioning the boundaries of Christianity in Iberia, what I want to highlight in calling attention to this early moment in the development of a secular discourse is the way Morisco difference was shorn of its religious significance, all in the name of achieving pastoral goals. The residues of attachment to Islam could thereby be policed and regulated through fines and penalties meted out by civic authorities. In this, I suggest, we can see an early moment in the development of a discourse, evident in the comments of Nieto Cumplido mentioned above, on the immunity of a Christian Europe to the Muslim footprints left on its soil.

RECONQUISTA NOW

The Reconquista framework of Spanish historiography did not disappear with the end of the Franco regime in 1975 but has found continued life in the writings of both Catholic and lay intellectuals in Spain as well as— particularly since the terrorist attack of 2004—among best-selling authors and journalists. Ex–prime minister José María Aznar's frequent invocations of this framework give evidence of its ongoing vitality. In 2003 Aznar agreed, in the face of immense popular opposition, to send a contingent of Spanish troops to join in the US-led invasion of Iraq. In preparation for the mission, the Spanish military produced a new badge for the soldiers emblazoned with the emblem of Santiago Matamoros, St. James the Moor Killer. With its sword-point tip and brilliant red color, the cross has long served as a symbol within Spain for the defeat and elimination of the Iberian Muslims by Christian armies. Spanish troops, now armed with this symbol, were sent off to Iraq to patrol the city of al-Najaf—one of the holiest cities in Shi'a Islam.

The choice of the Moor-Killer emblem was not incongruous with Aznar's strident anti-Muslim rhetoric or with his historical optic. In a talk on "global threats" he gave in Washington in 2006, Aznar drew the connection between the fight against Muslim radicals and the Reconquista: "It's them or us. The West did not attack Islam, it was they who attacked us. . . . We are constantly under attack and we must defend ourselves. I support Ferdinand and Isabella."[39] At the same event, while defending Pope Benedict's controversial claim that Islam was an inherently violent religion, Aznar suggested that Muslims should apologize for having invaded Spain in the eighth century. For many Spaniards today, the political and historical compass exemplified in Aznar's comments and the policies of his right-wing successors in the Spanish government are the result of the ongoing presence of tensions and divisions left unresolved from the country's civil war. The conflicts crystallized in the course of the war continue to striate Spanish political life, including the Catholic identity of the nation and the role of the Church in the public sphere.

The Spanish essayist Javier Gomá Lanzón has argued that Spain's entrance into the modern era was marked by the lack of any event that could separate it from its current attachment (here construed as anachronistic) to a particular past:

The so-called "Reconquista" during the Middle Ages and during the modern epoch, the combination of the discovery of America and the anachronistic ideal of a political-religious empire—a form of untimely continuation of the medieval Reconquista—produced an extremely problematic entrance of Spain into the contemporary era, a country without a liberal revolution, nor a bourgeois revolution, nor an industrial revolution, nor a workers' revolution, or at least interrupted, irregular, or failed.[40]

For Gomá Lanzón, the so-called transition that marked the end of Franco's long rule initiated an attempt to found—"in one blow"—a new political demos, enacted with great energy and enthusiasm but without the prior institutional transformations needed to make its realization possible.

The diagnosis of Spanish untimeliness, however, can also be viewed from a rather different standpoint: not as the product of a lack, the absence of the historical developments that are understood to constitute and define Europe, but rather as the result of the consistent attempt to erase or supersede a medieval world through the positing of a total historical rupture (captured by the temporal logics of the Reconquista). This is the view held by Rodríguez Ramos. As discussed above, Rodríguez Ramos presents a historical account in which the attempts to erase Islam from the Iberian Peninsula—to expunge Muslim populations as well as the imprint they had left on language, architecture, customs, art, and dress—failed. The failure of this genocidal effort and its repression from consciousness produced a trauma within the Spanish psyche, one that continues to nourish "the racist and xenophobic unreason of today" (Rodríguez Ramos 2010, 83). In his view, the Catholic Church's efforts to conceal the Islamic dimensions of the Mezquita-Catedral, to efface one of the most aesthetically powerful traces of a Spain resistant to Inquisitorial impulses, reflects just this unreason.

In 2006, in response to these moves taken by the Church, Rodríguez Ramos formed a group together with a number of Cordoban liberals and leftists (many with *andalucista* biographies) going by the name Plataforma Mezquita-Catedral: Patrimonio de Todos (Mosque-Cathedral Platform: Patrimony of All). The group quickly began a campaign to mobilize local and international opposition to the measures taken by the Church and to challenge the legality of the Church's claim to ownership.[41] Acting as official spokesman for the group, Rodríguez Ramos has written and spoken tirelessly for their cause. The measures taken by the Church, as he sees it, are "an amputation of collective memory," an attempt to expunge Córdoba's pluralist heritage (Rodríguez Ramos 2013). "The Mezquita," as he told me, "is the most important Islamic architectural trace (*huella*) found in the West, and the historical obsession of National Catholicism to erase and adulterate this period of our past is obvious to all" (interview with the author). Faced with growing local and national pressure to reverse its course—pressure generated, in large part, by the efforts of the Plataforma—the Church recently agreed to reattach the title "Mezquita" back onto "Catedral" in its official publicity for the edifice, though the question of ownership remains (at the time of publication) unresolved.

Rodríguez Ramos describes *The Morisco Trace* as a work not of history or reason or politics but of passion, and this description could easily be extended—to differing degrees—to the entire corpus of Andalucismo. And how could it be otherwise? Through what modern reason could an Arab (or Morisco) wound be found at home in, be discovered to inhabit, a European soul (other than perhaps in Romantic poetry or nostalgic longing, genres not quite fit to address the pressing issues of our time)? The entire edifice of European history and knowledge seems to be built to foreclose that possibility just as the closure of the border today aims to limit the possibility that an Arab or African can inhabit a European city (except as a "guest worker," an immigrant, an Arab). To think otherwise requires a radical break with our normative frames of reference.

Rodríguez Ramos for many years now has spearheaded a campaign to petition the Spanish government to extend the right of citizenship to the descendants of the Moriscos now residing in North Africa.[42] This effort to right what some have come to see as a historical wrong follows a long history of similar efforts by other generations of *andalucistas*. An early gesture in this direction took place in 1899 among a group of Granadan poets and artists known as the Cofradía del Avellano, a group whose most famous contributor was Ángel Ganivet. Just a few months after Ganivet's suicide in late 1898, the remaining members of the group published a letter to the "Moors of Morocco" reminding them that Granada was still their home and inviting them to visit should they ever wish to (see González Alcantud 2014, 56).

This gesture, one that has been repeated many times in different forms by *andalucistas* over the last hundred years, has often been dismissed as little more than Romantic whimsy fueled by the Maurophilic fashion of the day. In contrast, when the Spanish government in 2015 passed a law offering Spanish citizenship to descendants of the Sephardic Jews expelled from Iberia in the fifteenth century, this gesture was not trivialized. The text of the law, rather, emphasized the continuity of historical memory for Spain's medieval Jewish population: "In truth, the Jewish presence in Iberian lands was firm and ancient, palpable even today in vestiges of word and stone"

(Law 12/2015 of June 24, 2015). The law granting the right of Jews to acquire Spanish citizenship, a law that "repairs the injustice committed 500 years ago," according to the Spanish Minister of Justice Rafael Catalá,[43] is grounded in the presence of Spanish words still tinged with their Hebrew roots and in the crumbling medieval synagogues that draw thousands of tourists to the ancient *juderías* of Córdoba and Girona. Those words and stones speak of both greatness and destruction and hold contemporary Spaniards accountable for the story they tell. The voice of the Muslim past, in contrast, speaks today to many only as the phantom whispers of a ghost.

CHAPTER 2

The Difficult *Convivencia*
of Spanish History

The Spanish historiography of medieval Iberia, a field entrusted to maintain order over the inconvenient and unwieldy eight hundred years of Muslim rule on the peninsula, is (not surprisingly) marked by tensions and
ideological fractures. These tensions both inhabit the narrative history of
the nation-state and exceed it: just as Spain today bears the duty to police the flow of immigrants entering Europe from its southern border, so
must its historians police the continent's southern history, maintaining
the conceptual integrity of the project against renegade accounts. One locus of disciplinary anxiety and conflict within this scholarly arena is found
in the notion of *convivencia* (living-togetherness, or coexistence),[1] a term
that has acquired a burgeoning career outside of academia with journalists,
politicians, and popular writers as shorthand for the celebrated harmony
among Jews, Christians, and Muslims associated with al-Andalus. While
the first appearances of the term date back to the late eighteenth century,
its contemporary usage is generally associated with the work of Américo
Castro, for whom it served as conceptual anchor for a vision of coexistence
and symbiosis among Jews, Muslims, and Christians in medieval Iberia, a
form of dynamic synthesis from which later Spanish cultural and literary
forms emerged.[2] Castro's emphasis on the interdependencies and creative
entwinements forged at the intersection of these religiously based collectives was taken up and subsequently simplified as the term entered popular
usage, where it eventually came to stand for the possibility of harmonious
relations among adherents of diverse religions.[3]

While most historians writing today tend to avoid using what has become such a politically charged term or only do so after stripping it of what
are seen to be its overidealized assumptions, *convivencia* as a concept has
continued to elicit vehement, pointed denunciations by scholars of Spain's
medieval period. Its most prominent critics range from Castro's contemporary and primary critic, the historian Claudio Sánchez-Albornoz, who
insists that medieval Muslim-Christian relations were never anything other

than "superficial and hostile" (Sánchez-Albornoz 1975, 196), to contemporary professor of Arabic Serafín Fanjul, who characterizes al-Andalus as "a regime more like South African apartheid, *mutatis mutandis*, than the idyllic Arcadia invented by Castro" (Fanjul 2004, 29). These more strident takes notwithstanding, most scholars of medieval and early-modern Spain keep their distance from Castro's interpretation of Iberian coexistence and even more from its exuberant reception within popular culture. Indeed, I rarely met a Spanish historian of the medieval period who did not feel it their responsibility upon first meeting to warn me off from the false seductions of *convivencia*. Such moments were reminiscent of certain experiences I had in Egypt, where, as a non-Muslim, I would at times be addressed as one who had been led astray, someone yet to convert and therefore requiring correction and concern.

Ryan Szpiech, a professor of medieval Iberian literature, has written perceptively in regard to the anxieties provoked by the notion of *convivencia* within the Spanish academy. Szpiech's analysis highlights the unique trajectory followed by Arabic studies in the country.[4] As opposed to scholars of Arabic and the Middle East elsewhere in Europe, the Spanish Arabists took their own medieval past as the primary object of concern, thus binding their inquiries to the problems and tasks of national identity.[5] As a result the field came to be closely entwined with cultural and religious studies, fields of scholarship greatly responsive to the historiographical demands of Spanish nationalism. Subsequently, as Francoism dissolved in the mid-1970s, a new generation of scholars viewed the methods and forms of inquiry of their predecessors as overly identified with the reformist idealism and conservative Catholic nationalism that culminated in the repression and violence of fascism. As Szpiech comments,

> It is not surprising that Spanish Arabist philology—still within living memory of Francoism and its own conflicted identity as a part of western Orientalism—is now very much on guard against interpretive or poetic histories that use philology as a technique for Bildung, whether national or individual; and that consequently it hews very close to the righteous rigors of philology as a fundamentalist science of post-Romantic Wissenschaft. (Szpiech 2013, 150)

For contemporary Spanish scholars of medieval Iberia, then, a commitment to positivist philology has been both a condition of academic legitimacy and a prophylactic against the dangers of ideology cast in historical disguise. And herein lies the significant problem with Castro's *convivencia*. A literary scholar trained in the Romantic traditions of interpretive history, Castro rejected the idea of a scientific history, of a fixed past objectively knowable through rigorous empirical methods.[6] The past, in his view, could only be grasped through poesis, could only be "made present in us like a link between a possibility and its realization" (Castro 1956, 22, cited in Szpiech 2009, 145). In accord with this Romantic view of history, the notion of *convivencia* that Castro elaborated does not describe a set of empirical circumstances but rather is a figural term, one that aims to illuminate poetically patterns of mutuality and interdependence found in the hybrid forms and practices of the heterogeneous collectives that inhabited medieval and early-modern Iberia.

For most contemporary scholars of this period, such a foray into Romantic interpretation cannot be viewed without trepidation: not only does it fail the test of empirical accuracy as defined within the protocols of secular historiography, it also participates in the dangerous practice of articulating an essentialized Spanish collective identity, a practice with strong National Catholic associations, including in its contemporary post-Franco political reformulations. The paradox here is that the notion of *convivencia* elaborated by Castro while in exile in the United States was precisely a critique of the petrified and homogenous versions of national culture that dominated mainstream Spanish society and political life during the Franco era.

Consequently, the name Américo Castro still provokes unease in many quarters of Spanish academia. On my numerous visits to the Department of Arabic and Islamic Studies at the Consejo Superior de Investigaciones Científicas (CSIC)—a department whose authority and institutional power within this field is unrivalled in Spain—my invocation of Castro was frequently met with suspicion. Many scholars feared I had caught the Romantic disease that North Americans coming to Spain have been prey to ever since Washington Irving was captivated by the mythical world of the Alhambra in the 1820s, a disease for which Castro provided a (dangerous) veneer of academic respectability. When I first brought up Castro's work to CSIC's prominent early-modern historian Mercedes García-Arenal, she exclaimed, "no, not Castro again!," clearly tired of having foreign researchers invoke a scholar whose work is considered to hold little value for the field of Iberian Studies today. Not unlike the perspective I encountered among other Arabists and historians at CSIC, García-Arenal acknowledged the brilliance and originality of Castro's work but felt its historiographical claims were vitiated by the identarian lens that dominated Spanish historical studies at the time of his writing, centered as it was around an investigation of an essential Spanish identity. As she cautioned me in a note sent shortly after our first meeting back in August of 2009: "The problem with

Castro, as well as with Sánchez Albornoz and the others, is that they look for the immanent definition of Spanish identity, essential and eternal. They seek to find the past that we have inherited. Don't fall into the same danger, which you already fall into a little, perhaps because you present 'Spanish-ness' [*lo español*]—whatever that means—to an American public that will like something a little Romantic, picturesque, almost incomprehensible." García-Arenal's reservations build on a great deal of historical experience. For much of its modern history, Spain found itself assigned the role of Europe's exotic Other within European scholarly and popular discourses, with the country's Muslim and Jewish past often identified as a primary source of its exuberant primitivism. Scholarly accounts that explore historical continuities across the medieval-modern border—such as found in Castro—are potentially redolent of this stigmatized identity and the marginality that it both marked and enacted.

Like many historians in Spain today, García-Arenal believes that the ideological pressures that previously subverted the possibility of an objective historiography in the country have since retreated, particularly as Spain's inclusion in the family of countries making up Europe has become an institutional reality. Indeed, many of the Spanish Arabists I spoke with emphasized the historical profession's new self-confidence, evident both in the international recognition it has increasingly garnered and in the discipline's own prominence within broader Spanish intellectual circles. In the present context of heightened anxiety over the increasing number of immigrants from North Africa in the country, historians in this field play an important public role in interpreting and defining the significance of al-Andalus and its historical legacy within contemporary political debates about the place of Islam in Spain.

They do so, however, still haunted by the ghosts of the civil war. In 2014 in the context of the political dominance of the conservative People's Party, a celebration of the foundation of the Consejo Superior was held, one in which the institution's fascist mandate as a center of "Catholic science" was honored. Interviewed about the commemoration by the Catholic journal *Religión en Libertad*, a biologist from CSIC exalted its Franco-era Catholic mission: "CSIC must be considered the greatest achievement made by lay members of the Catholic Church for the universal development of science in the twentieth century."[7] For many other scholars now working at CSIC (including the Arabists and historians I spoke with), to celebrate the seventy-fifth anniversary of an institution founded as part of the fascist purging of Spanish academia—one that involved the forced exile or execution of many scholars—is not only to continue to extend legitimacy to the brutalities of the Franco regime but also to signal the continuing purchase of National Catholic legacies within the country. As the CSIC Arabist Maribel Fierro, exasperated by the direction in which she saw CSIC to be moving, explained to me, "science in Spain moves likes a pendulum according to whoever is in power—it's terrifying."

There is no doubt that the rhetorics of Andalucismo and those of National Catholicism converge in moments around a shared Romantic vocabulary. Take the 1939 inaugural discourse by CSIC's founder and first president, José Ibáñez Martín: "We want a Catholic science. So let us erase at this time all of the scientific heresies that have *dried up and parched the channels of our national genius* and plunged us into lethargy and decadence" (emphasis mine).[8] For many of the contemporary scholars working within this institution, this diagnosis of a "national genius" desiccated by the country's abandonment of its true transhistorical essence (Catholicism) is not markedly different than the *andalucista* idea of a country alienated from, or outright rejecting, its own Islamic and Jewish historical experience. In contrast, for Gil Benumeya, Castro, and their followers today, the problem is not essentialism—the attempt to identify abiding features of Spanish experience—but the denial and erasure of a key dimension of that experience rooted in medieval and early-modern Iberian culture.

In this chapter, I survey the problem that al-Andalus represents for Spanish historiography and, to some extent, for the wider European historiographical tradition of which it forms a constitutive part. This problem can be described in broad strokes as that of finding a place for Islam and Judaism within a historical space that had been politically and epistemologically constructed on the premise of their elimination. This task corresponds to what could be called the theological-political function of the discipline, and it is carried out today through a discourse that incorporates these "foreign elements" into peninsular history while confining the sphere of their relevance to the distant past—safely exterior to Europe and its modern career.[9]

Andalucismo, from its peripheral location, disturbs the calm waters of this enterprise, making visible a range of anxieties beneath its surface. As I explore below, these anxieties, inherent to the task of domesticating Iberia's complicated and uncomfortable past, are inflected by a variety of contemporary political concerns, including unresolved tensions left over from the civil war, worries about Spain's status within the community of European nations, and fears provoked by the growing presence of Muslim immigrants in the country, many from that onetime *hermandad* across the sea, Morocco. Illuminated by these present-day apprehensions within Spanish political life, Andalucismo, as I show, provokes within the historical discipline a felt need to performatively reenact that foundational erasure of Islam from the continent. The chapter, in this sense, attests to a long-standing disturbance within Spanish and European historical thought and practice.

In order to underscore the stakes of Andalucismo for historical studies, I take up the work of Emilio González Ferrín, a historian of Islam and *andalucista* of sorts whose ideas have come under intense criticism among mainstream Spanish historians. In 2006 González Ferrín published *Historia general de Al Ándalus*, a work that put forward a radical—if not entirely unprecedented—interpretation of the early history of Islam in Iberia. Based on a rereading of the limited historical evidence currently available, González Ferrín rejects the traditional account that attributes the arrival of Islam to a contingent of Muslim warriors who crossed the Strait of Gibraltar in 711, defeating the Visigothic armies they encountered on the other side and, in a few short years, sweeping northward to claim most of the Iberian Peninsula. Islam did not arrive in the form of a military conquest in 711, he argues, because it could not insomuch as Islam did not yet exist, at least not as a distinct civilizational identity around which an army might be mobilized. As González Ferrín puts it, "Islam, in its early stages, at least until the year 800 or so, didn't do anything, but was 'done.'"[10] According to this view, Islam coalesced as one monotheistic religious form in a context of competing and overlapping Unitarian and Trinitarian religious options that composed the highly conflictual world of eighth- and ninth-century Iberia. The idea of an organized invasion, González Ferrín argues, was the invention of later, tenth-century Christian ideologues who found that such a fictional account served their political interests well.

González Ferrín's work can be considered a contribution to the scholarship of Andalucismo, and indeed, it has become a key point of reference for *andalucista* writers and activists (Rodríguez Ramos's *La huella morisca* turns to it repeatedly for historical scaffolding) as well as for members of the convert community. In much of the rest of this chapter, I explore some of his ideas and the impassioned responses they have provoked among Spanish historians and Arabists. The controversy sparked by *Historia general*, I suggest, can usefully be read as a diagnostic of the problem of finding a place for Islam within Spain insomuch as the country is embraced and defined today by its European civilizational identity.

INVASIONS

Before I turn to González Ferrín's scholarship and the controversy it has generated, I want to take a step back to consider some of the political pressures bearing on the contemporary historiography of al-Andalus. To do so,

I want to draw on the critiques of Andalucismo made by two historians, both affiliated with CSIC. From the perspective of most contemporary Spanish scholars of al-Andalus, two primary flaws infect and disqualify the historical inquiries of writers following in the *andalucista* tradition associated with Américo Castro: the error of positing social and cultural continuities across vast historical periods, and the methodological recourse to "identity" as the category through which to analyze historical processes. A very clear statement of this critique can be found in a piece by Fernando Rodríguez Mediano, a well-respected historian of both Spain and Morocco and a colleague of, and frequent collaborator with, García-Arenal. Rodríguez Mediano's thoughtful survey focuses on how the Spanish historiography of al-Andalus has so often been harnessed to the project of defining a Spanish national identity, and at considerable cost to historical accuracy. Taking examples from two widely separated moments in the historiographical literature of al-Andalus, one sixteenth- and one twentieth-century text, Rodríguez Mediano demonstrates how the compulsion to seek ancient roots or origins for contemporary identity formations has led repeatedly to the production of historical fictions, "illusions of stable and permanent identities" (Rodríguez Mediano 2011, 78) radically inadequate to the actual complexity of the objects they purportedly describe. The task of the historian, he argues, must be to show that such claims to stable identity mask the actual flux of human societies, immersed, as he describes, "in processes that extend out in different and at times contradictory directions, each with its own rhythm, if not outright discontinuity" (78). Rodríguez Mediano's conclusion is unequivocal and worth quoting fully:

> It is worth asking whether every invocation of identity, of a founding matrix, of roots, is not yet another manifestation of a sacred history, of its efforts to impose itself—its history and memory—on the history of men. Without doubt, those who continue to speak about cultural identity, using al-Andalus to ascribe it historical legitimacy, do nothing but project onto the past their will to define in an exclusive manner contemporary political communities. In this text, I have tried to provide some examples that belie attempts to define Spanish or European identity on the basis of some singular and determinate set of roots and show how these attempts have no correspondence in reality except that of the context in which they are enunciated. (93)

Rodríguez Mediano's diagnosis of the ideological demands that have long plagued Spanish historiography is both acute and salutary. Not only is his skepticism toward the function of terms like *origins* and *civilizational identity* within historical writing justified, his argument bears witness to the relative freedom of the current generation of Arabists and historians from the demand to either champion or denounce the achievements of Muslim Spain.[11]

It strikes me, however, that this call for caution moves too quickly and categorically in its disqualification of a broad range of arguments, peremptorily dismissing a set of claims that cannot be so easily done away with. Can we really assert that all invocations of cultural identity that refer to al-Andalus are "nothing but" the expression of a reductive politics of identity? Must such claims always have "no correspondence in reality"? Surely the present is not created anew in every moment, ex nihilo, but necessarily involves coming to terms with enduring features of the past (including those rooted in prior attempts to discount that past). Rodríguez Mediano seeks to create a theoretical space for such presentism by recruiting an ontology of flux that, within the rhetorical context of his argument, serves to undermine any claims to continuity and stability as necessarily the motivated fictions of a political strategy. Hence his setting up of an opposition, cast in the subjunctive formulation of the interrogative, between "the history of men" (the actual events) and the histories of identity (the always false representation given by the names societies apply to themselves)—the latter denounced as the fantasies of religious passion. Yet can we not argue, in turn, that the history of human beings cannot be told without reference to the terms those men and women have applied to themselves, have argued over, disagreed about, or understood as an inheritance on which to model their own lives and respond to the changes they have faced?[12]

In short, exploiting a modern positivist sensibility, one well entrenched in the historical discipline, Rodríguez Mediano renders suspicious any attempt to trace lines of continuity and stability, with the present exhaustively determining its own ground of action and thought. And yet, while Rodríguez Mediano's article casts doubt on the motivation and historical adequacy of claims linking medieval al-Andalus to the present, his own argument, I should note, itself relies on notions of stable spatial and temporal horizons. Specifically, he locates the historiographical operation that posits ancient roots in order to secure claims to civilizational identity as integral to an early-modern reordering of the field of knowledge continuous with the present: "In effect, in Europe, beginning in the sixteenth century, a reconstruction of the field of knowledge took place, one that gave rise to new disciplines concerned with the significance of the past and the interpretation of distinct languages and cultures" (Rodríguez Mediano 2011, 79). The site of this epistemological reordering is identified as "Europe," an odd reference given the article's critique of notions of "European identity." The notion of Europe, it seems, acquires temporal depth and stability in his argument to the extent that al-Andalus loses it. For the historical practice on which Rodríguez Mediano pegs the unity and identity of Europe across five centuries—that is, the claim of contemporary society to having ancient roots—is the same as that which vouchsafes the fictional (or religious) quality of claims concerning the legacies of al-Andalus. The site from which a modern suspicion of historical claims can be deployed is the very same as that which can singularly escape that suspicion: Europe.

The methodological strains evident in Rodríguez Mediano's argument bear witness, I want to suggest, to ongoing anxieties about the place of Islam within Spain's historical fabric, specifically, about the consequences of its Muslim past for the country's European pedigree and about the social, political, and economic advantages that pedigree serves to anchor. Insomuch as the scholarly discourse on al-Andalus is inevitably entwined with the question of Spain's place within Europe, scholars of this period necessarily navigate a fraught historical minefield. In our conversations, Rodríguez Mediano expressed his own view of these matters in frank terms. Notably, he felt that the postcolonial turn within historical studies—a turn taken by a growing number of scholars of medieval Europe[13]—threatened to give impetus to a cultural relativism destructive of the values of the European Enlightenment. This danger was evident today, he argued, in the way certain minority groups in Europe had increasingly come to embrace a discourse of cultural identity in order to justify practices of patriarchal control and repression. Referring to himself as "a modernist, against the anti-modernists," he emphasized his distrust of this "elevation of culture to politics" and his concern that Europe not unmake itself—that is to say, abandon its many historical accomplishments—so as to accommodate all the cultures of the world.

While this defense of the Enlightenment, viewed as the intellectual foundation of secular-liberal society, reflects a political worry that has become common today across Europe in the context of a growing Muslim minority, its articulation within the halls of CSIC (an institution founded by the Franco regime and still subject to its looming shadow) bears witness to the way al-Andalus has come to be refracted through the lens of the civil war and through the sense of institutional fragility left in the war's aftermath. My point here is not to suggest that Rodríguez Mediano's personal political reflections provide some interpretive key to his historical methodology. His historical inquiries adhere to the discipline's highest standards, and it would be an injustice to reduce them to this or any other political standpoint. His reflections, however, help illuminate what are felt by many Spanish historians to be the stakes in the field, the conflicting pressures that bear on it in its dealings with Islam, past and present.

Agreeing with Rodríguez Mediano's critical assessment of an ideologically driven historiography focused on legitimating identity claims, Eduardo Manzano Moreno (a scholar also affiliated with CSIC) further elucidates the political apprehensions bearing on the historical discipline's approach to al-Andalus. Manzano Moreno's argument stresses the twin pitfalls that the so-called game of historical mirrors (2009, 72) poses for Spanish historians of the medieval period. The first ties Spanish identity to the heroic Catholic crusade, the Reconquista, while the ("now ascendant") second is centered on an idealized image of Muslim Iberia as the foundation for the modern liberal nation. Manzano Moreno asks his readers to imagine the "nightmare" of a Spanish classroom, "not too far off," where Christian and Muslim students are set against each other as partisans of two contradictory versions of history, one "identified with the legacy and historical references of 'Christian Spain,'" the other with "the historical splendor that has nourished the myth of al-Andalus" (68). The (rather improbable) outcome he anticipates, one with clear medieval resonances, is a society (once again!) divided into opposing Muslim and Christian camps: "The result will be a disassociated historical memory alternating between El Cid and al-Manzor, relegated to either mosques or cathedrals, and eventually frustrating any idea of common citizenship" (68–69).

One feels, upon reading Manzano Moreno's argument, that the daunting task of the medieval historian is to navigate the narrow channel between the Scylla of National Catholicism and the Charybdis of what Gil Benumeya called (approvingly, in his case) *España Árabe*. To stay this course requires an emotional disidentification with the past, a task that the discipline of history is uniquely qualified to undertake insomuch as its methodological imperatives ensure the discontinuity of the present from what preceded it, the dissolution of any affective resonance across times.[14] In history, as Manzano Moreno envisions it properly taught in his imaginary classroom,

> there is no place for a past onto which the ideals of either patriots or believers are projected, nor for a braided discourse on the deeds of our supposed ancestors, for the simple reason that these ancestors are not really ours — nor did they live or die thinking of us. In reality, in this history class, the only thing that should be taught are the processes of change occurring across time, changes that allow us to understand the great abyss that the centuries have wrought. (Manzano Moreno 2009, 72)

Thanks to this great abyss separating us from the past (no longer ours), it can now be approached "dispassionately" and thus become the sort of "pure and simple knowledge" that life in a modern, heterogeneous society demands (73).

While it is the enthusiasm for al-Andalus that most concerns Manzano Moreno as a threat to the integrity of the cultural fabric, his worry extends to Spain's regional nationalisms more generally, where the drive to excavate historical roots correlates directly with the fragmentation of national unity. His arguments, in this sense, reflect a Madrid-centric, Castillianist perspective. The unity of the nation requires the erasure of differences that make a difference. Those differences must become properly historical in the sense of being discontinuous with the present and irrelevant to its ongoing production and reformation. And as with many other historians I spoke with, the experience of the Franco years hangs heavily over the question at hand:

> For those of us who have suffered and know well the mechanisms of historical indoctrination, certain manifestations and arguments made in regard to the Andalusi legacy are disconcerting. . . . All of that is enough to put us on guard with respect to the consequences that gratuitous exaltations of the past may provoke, even if that past is as lyrically moving and poetically evocative as is the Andalusi. (Manzano Moreno 2009, 72)

Against the siren song of al-Andalus, with its lyrical and poetic seductions, the European historian must hold firm. Here again, we see how the legacies of al-Andalus are viewed through the complex prism of the civil war, with all of its unresolved conflicts and political legacies. Moreover, the fact that aspects of Andalucismo were embraced by the Franco regime (and that a number of prominent *andalucistas,* such as Gil Benumeya, themselves held official positions within the regime) serves to further solidify a skeptical judgment.

During the transition to democracy in the mid-1970s, Europe came to be viewed by many Spanish intellectuals not only as key to bringing about the needed political and economic transformations but also as "a form of insurance policy against any return to authoritarian rule" (Dorothy Kelly, cited in Flesler 2008b, 18). Integration into Europe would restrain the reactionary tendencies of National Catholicism (still powerful, if dethroned) and ensure Spain's progress along its modernizing path. In this context, and in light of these political concerns, the question of Spain's European pedigree, its unambiguous membership within the civilizational narrative of Europe, emerged as an urgent problem. Spain's Catholic identity, moreover, has come to acquire contradictory valences. On the one hand, Catholicism, tainted by its associations with fascism and still a force to be reckoned with in Spanish political life, is viewed by many intellectuals and ordinary Spaniards as an obstacle to the progressive movement of social change, an obstacle to be overcome through further secular reform. On the other hand, as arguments about European identity in recent years have increasingly come to pivot around the notion of a shared Christian heritage and of shared Christian (and Judeo-Christian) values, Catholicism has emerged as a marker of Spain's membership within Europe. Paradoxically, what was once held up as a sign of Spain's tenuous status as a fully European nation has now become the coin of the realm. Al-Andalus, for its part, has become, yet again, a liability, a stain. As one scholar handily puts it, "It should not be any surprise . . . that in Spain we try to abominate our Islamic roots . . . for international prestige purposes. How are we going to get in the 'VIP countries' club with such an un-European past?" (Navarro 1997, 20).

A COUNTERHISTORY OF ISLAM IN EUROPE

No event has more dramatically revealed the fault lines running through the historiography of al-Andalus in recent years than the publication of Emilio González Ferrín's *Historia general de Al Ándalus* in 2006. The book has received near universal condemnation among Spanish academics in the field, while its author has been charged with every variety of moral and political sin. More than one reviewer has suggested that González Ferrín's claim that Islam arrived in Spain less through military conquest than through a process of gradual assimilation is comparable to an act of Holocaust denial.[15] Trained as a philologist, González Ferrín is a specialist in Arabic and Islamic thought at the University of Seville. While he is not Andalusian by birth, it forms both his adopted home as well as an intellectual and personal vocation. He traces his own intellectual genealogy to Castro and his students, though also back to such Spanish thinkers as Unamuno, Ganivet, and Ortega y Gassett (González Ferrín 2014a, 2014b). Defining his own writings as contributions to the field of "historiology," González Ferrín follows Castro in rejecting a scientific interpretation of the historical enterprise, emphasizing its necessary reliance on the imaginative activity of the historian and the conventions of literary form (González Ferrín [2006] 2016, 16–19).

González Ferrín's extensive writings and interviews provide an important contemporary reference for sustaining and extending a tradition of historical inquiry that runs from Ángel Ganivet to Rodolfo Gil Benumeya to Américo Castro to Juan Goytisolo, and his work is frequently cited in *anda-*

lucista writings (including *La huella morisca*) and foregrounded on the convert website WebIslam. He is also a frequent participant in *andalucista* fora, having served as director of the "al-Andalus Chair" at the Fundación Tres Culturas (Three Cultures Foundation) and as a member of the think tank "Regarding al-Andalus," hosted by the Spanish foundation Casa Árabe. He has shared a stage with his friend Rodríguez Ramos on multiple occasions. González Ferrín's scholarship, in short, has struck a powerful chord within the institutional networks of Andalucismo.

When I first met with González Ferrín at a restaurant in Seville, I asked him about his relation to the *andalucista* tradition. Though he resisted applying the term to himself, in light of having been born in Madrid (though it should be noted, of parents from Melilla, one of two remaining Spanish territories in North Africa), he acknowledged his attraction to the tradition: "I have always been drawn to the project of the *andalucistas*, as a group of people trying to understand their land and history. Plus, the idea of Mediterraneanizing Europe is a healthy one" (February 10, 2014). Indeed, while Iberia is the proximate object of his studies, his analytical purview embraces Europe itself: "Al-Andalus is not a bygone epoch, and nothing more; it is a component. Of what? Well, in my view, of Europe; of a Europe that we recognize as the matrix of the West and that precisely in al-Andalus made a jump from the medieval to the early Renaissance" (González Ferrín 2016, 35). As with other scholars I had met who were attracted to *andalucista* perspectives, the biographical trajectory that appeared from González Ferrín's descriptions of his life was one that moved continuously outside the boundaries of Europe, frequently to the Middle East. His intellectual map stretched from Pakistan to Iran, Egypt to Morocco, with many stops in between, and it included a two-year sojourn in Cairo. A similar geography of thought characterizes his writing, where the words of Ibn Tufayl, Ibn Khaldun, and Muhammad Abduh frequently share the page with Ángel Ganivet, Walter Benjamin, and Max Weber. In this and other ways, González Ferrín marks his proximity to the project of Andalucismo.

The thesis González Ferrín lays out in his *Historia general* builds on two key lines of investigation within the historical literature on Islam. The first of these centers around a critique of the period concept "late antiquity" as it informs European historical perspectives and particularly the way this concept serves to radically disassociate Islam from the broader Mediterranean world in which it emerged. As he comments, "In general terms, I believe that Islam is erroneously considered as a sudden and counterhistorical alteration insomuch as it is seen to have severed an organic unfolding of history, bringing to a close late antiquity and setting the stage for a medieval dichotomy—Christianity against Islam—one still unresolved through today" (González Ferrín 2015, 32).[16] Islam, he argues, did not emerge in the seventh century in isolation from the broader context of Mediterranean thought and practice; rather, much like Christianity at the time, it was thoroughly entwined with the surrounding religious, social, and philosophical currents of the Byzantine and Persian empires and of Greek and Roman thought, through processes of argument, borrowing, imitation, and critique.[17] An adequate concept of late antiquity would recognize Islam as a development integral to an arena of social, economic, and intellectual exchange and interchange that embraced both Eastern and Western poles of the Mediterranean and continued until sometime around the year 1000.

The second line of inquiry informing González Ferrín's scholarly argument is based in a body of research focused on what is called "early Islam." Drawing from a disparate set of historical inquiries, González Ferrín argues that before the ninth century, Islam had yet to coalesce into a distinct civilizational entity, a stable political-religious formation. Instead, the prophecy of Muhammad was understood as one more Unitarian vision (or heresy), unique but not radically outside the arena in which other competing Jewish and Christian currents circulated within an overarching Christian Mediterranean context. Islam, from this perspective, was not born, fully formed, from the soil of the Arabian desert, as it has so often been described by Western scholars, but emerged gradually from a cauldron of only loosely distinguishable Unitarian currents composed of an "amalgam of Jews, neo-Muslims, non-dogmatic Christian movements such as Nestorianism, Arianism, Donatism, Pricilianism" (González Ferrín (2006) 2016, 102), drawn together by their common opposition to the dominant Trinitarian orthodoxy. As opposed to Western scholarly views that, González Ferrín argues, have tended to always associate the spread of Islam with military conquest, he situates Islam as one element within a broader trans-Mediterranean world bound together by trade, politics, and by the dynamics of religious contestation and dissent.

According to González Ferrín, the conventional image of the arrival of Islam to the Iberian Peninsula in the eighth century—as one billiard ball, the invading Arab Muslims, crashing into another, the Visigothic kingdoms—is highly distorted. Hispania (the Roman name for the Iberian Peninsula and still in use by the Visigoths in the eighth century) was a cauldron of religious and political conflict at this time, organized around the opposition between a Trinitarian orthodoxy imposed by the Visigothic kings and a variety of Unitarian currents formed of Jews, Christians, and what González Ferrín calls proto-Muslims, those drawn to the Qur'anic revelation but nonetheless existing before the regional crystallization of Islam as a distinct religious identity. The Visigoths had followed the Unitarian theology of Arianism up until the closing decades of the sixth century when Recaredo, the Visigothic king, announced his acceptance of the Nicene Creed and imposed Trinitarianism as the law of the land. From that point onward, opposition to the Visigothic state came to be articulated in terms of abiding Unitarian attachments, a context in which Islam would emerge as one variation. González Ferrín foregrounds chemical metaphors—for example, decantation, liquid culture, distillation—to describe the process by which Islam gradually emerges as a distinct civilizational option out of the soup of religious controversy and contestation that characterized Iberia between the eighth and tenth centuries. The shift in perspective is radical:

> Islam is the effect and not the cause of a long convulsive period. That an initial diversity will give rise later to a civilizing unity, and above all that Islam did nothing in its initial phase, for the reason that at that time it was precisely Islam that was being constructed. And before the beginning of the ninth century—around the year 820—it is impossible to speak of a civilizing entity or of concrete religious frontiers called Islam or Islamic. (González Ferrín [2006] 2016, 19)

While González Ferrín's thesis has been subject to a barrage of criticism from historians of medieval Iberia and most emphatically from the historians and Arabists of CSIC, it has encountered a vastly different reception from *andalucistas* as well as from Andalusia's community of converts to Islam.[18] Among these groups, his work has been championed as a major contribution, correcting the highly biased historical account shaped both by the Reconquista ideology at the heart of Spanish nationalism and the anti-Muslim impulse within contemporary discourses of European identity. Insomuch as his work provides historical support for the claim that Islam is not a foreign intruder on Iberia's Christian soil but, in some sense, a native fruit born of Iberia's own religious and intellectual ferment during the eighth and ninth centuries and still extending its legacy today, it resonates with a deeply seated *andalucista* sentiment, one that embraces al-Andalus as continuous with the Spain of today.

As with his muse Américo Castro, González Ferrín is a theorist of the "third Spain," that historical figure (also invoked by Rodríguez Ramos) forged of the suppressed but unrelinquished memory of the Moriscos and of Arab Iberia more generally. Against an Inquisitorial Spain that "wanted to forget" and also contrasting with that other Spain "forced to leave or die," a "third attempted to remember in secret and outside suspicion" (sin ser vista y sospechada) (González Ferrín [2006] 2016, 565).[19]

A point of continuing resistance to the imperatives of the Catholic Church
and the centralizing will of Castillianism, this third Spain, guardian of the
alma morisca (Morisco soul), found a refuge, according to Ferrín, in the
theology of the sixteenth-century Dutch humanist Erasmus of Rotterdam,
whose critique of confessionalism and formalism within the Church found
an enthusiastic readership among the Spanish laity despite having been
banned by ecclesiastical authorities by the mid-1500s. Erasmus's insistence
on doctrinal flexibility, on the need to resist the drive toward rigid confes-
sional boundaries defined by dogma, and particularly his concept of the
mystical body of Christ, wherein a wide diversity of Christian practical and
devotional forms found ultimate unity and concord—these aspects of Erasmus's thought together articulated a theological space that could embrace
and sustain some aspects of the embattled pluralist culture and society then
disappearing under a regime of silence, secrecy, and forgetting.[20] González
Ferrín writes, "Erasmus was proclaiming an ethical revolution. A Christian
experience based in an interior spirituality, far from the extravagant formalism carried to excess by Spanish Catholicism, exaggerated—no doubt—by
the need to put on display (i.e., to feign) the fervor of a neophyte in a Spain
where the Morisco soul still remained" (González Ferrín 2008). Erasmus's
notion of the mystical body of Christ provided a shelter from the anxieties
of conformism that accompanied the Counter-Reformation. As opposed
to the National Catholic genealogy of Spain, one that traces a line from
Ferdinand and Isabel through to Franco and embracing contemporary
right-wing movements, González Ferrín's alternative lineage of national
belonging runs from Averroes to Erasmus, from Cervantes to Ganivet and
Unamuno, to culminate in Castro and his *andalucista* heirs.

Among the cultural forms that constitute this third Spain, González
Ferrín mentions Mudejar art and architecture—a medieval aesthetic form
that brought together elements and techniques from a diversity of both
Christian and Muslim traditions. Under Hapsburg rule in the sixteenth and
seventeenth centuries, Mudejar aesthetic forms (including clothing and
ceramics as well as architecture) were largely shorn of their Islamic signifi-
cations, becoming instead expressions of a distinct Iberian style. Viewed
from this cultural and aesthetic lens, the third Spain emerges as a site of
complexity or heterogeneity not lost but forgotten, dormant in the material objects of everyday use and appreciation.[21]

In Miguel de Cervantes's *Don Quixote*, a work built on the play of dissimulation and disguise among its Christian, Muslim, and Morisco characters, González Ferrín finds the highest literary expression of this third
Spain. Invoking Juan Goytisolo's definition of the work as "a weapon
against forgetting," González Ferrín highlights the way the Quixote bears

witness to the persecution and effacement of the Morisco world and to the corruption and hypocrisy of orthodoxy at the time. The metafictional dialectic organizing the narrative between the story's Arabic author, Cide Hamete Benengeli, its unnamed Morisco translator, and its editor (as Cervantes identified himself), highlights the confused play of appearance and reality that characterized early seventeenth-century Iberia.[22]

For González Ferrín, the third Spain is the hidden container of vital cultural energies and progressive political impulses, the force behind not only Spain's Golden Age but also the liberal political currents that rose up during the nineteenth century and the radical democratic movements of today:

> The Third Spain of the old Morisco soul accorded with modern and revolutionary ideas of Europe. Both the Morisco soul and the Reform movement were subject to persecution and later to historiographical confusion. That possible "mystical body"—egalitarian society—a more inclusive alternative to reactionary Catholicism, was capable of holding together post-Jews, converts, Mudejars, crypto-Moriscos, illuminati and Erasmists of all stripes, all threatened by the so-called "tyranny of habit"—in Erasmist terminology. (González Ferrín 2008)

This alternate cultural-aesthetic space, González Ferrín argues, offers the "possibility of secularization" (González Ferrín [2006] 2016, 572)—itself generated by the attempt, undertaken within an Erasmist framework, to create a space for New Christians (the forcibly converted Moriscos) and their cultural practices within what by the seventeenth century had become a paranoid and dogmatic Catholic society.[23] There are echoes here of Antonio Manuel Rodríguez Ramos's notion that Andalusia's cultural heritage, forged of the experience of medieval and early-modern society, provides a barrier to the tyrannies of National Catholicism and its centralizing dictates. In both cases, we find a historical narrative that connects the early-modern struggle of the Moriscos to secure the conditions of their survival to a contemporary political vision that opposes the exclusionary logics of Spanish and European identity.

IGNACIO OLAGÜE VIDELA

As I noted above, González Ferrín's work has touched a deep and inflamed nerve among Spanish scholars of medieval Iberia. Positioned as a pariah of historical studies, González Ferrín is accused not simply of lacking methodological rigor but of purveying dangerous falsehoods. The charges leveled against him, however, have focused less on his own writing than on the work of another writer: Ignacio Olagüe Videla. A Spanish paleontologist and amateur historian, Olagüe published *Les Arabes n'ont jamais envahi l'Espagne* (The Arabs never invaded Spain) in French in 1969, a work that anticipated a number of González Ferrín's central claims and that is acknowledged by the latter at numerous junctures in his own writing.

Olagüe's work has had a fascinating reception within Spain. Translated into Spanish in 1974, his book went on to become, by the 1990s, a key point of reference among *andalucistas* and particularly among converts to Islam, where the text has encountered its most enthusiastic audience.[24] On the many occasions when I met with converts to Islam in Granada and Córdoba, rarely did Olagüe's name not arise in the course of conversation. Many described their initial encounter with his book as having precipitated the shift in perspective that had led them eventually to embrace Islam. Among this community, Olagüe is revered for having dared to push aside the ideological curtain—sustained by the fictions of nationalist historiography—bolstering Spain's eternal Christian identity. Instead, and anticipating González Ferrín, Olagüe argues that al-Andalus was not the artifact of a violent foreign intrusion but an autochthonous, fully Spanish phenomenon; that is, that there was no occupation of southern Iberia by Muslims from North Africa and the Middle East in the eighth century but rather a mass conversion by the local community. The burgeoning enthusiasm among contemporary *andalucistas* and converts for Olagüe's book led to its republication in 2004.

In contrast to the uniformly positive reception among *andalucistas* in the south, contemporary historians and other scholars have denounced Olagüe's work as a dangerous fiction, with González Ferrín as its contemporary and similarly dangerous heir. In Olagüe, however, critics of González Ferrín have found more than simply an intellectual forerunner. Beyond this, Olagüe's biography has provided them with a particularly damning piece of evidence in support of the charge of intellectual bankruptcy: Olagüe was an ardent nationalist and close associate of the fascist thinker Ramiro Ledesma Ramos.

In an insightful essay on Olagüe's life and work, the CSIC Arabist Maribel Fierro highlights the writer's relation to Ledesma Ramos and the broader political and intellectual climate of midcentury fascism that shaped his thought. Olagüe's work, she notes, emerged from an intellectual context strongly oriented around the question of an essential Spanish identity (*ser de España*) and the attempt to produce a coherent historical vision that could encompass and mobilize a nationalism capable of meeting the tasks of the future (Fierro 2009, 344). In the words of Ernesto Giménez Caballero, a Falangist (specifically, Francoist) writer and friend of Olagüe whose writings Fierro cites, the task of fascist thought was "to produce a version of the history of Spain that would allow for the construction of a nationalism capable of looking backward while not losing sight of the future, a kind of permanence, of perpetuity in which heroes should proceed from the discovery of this 'genius,' of this authenticity that lies in the heart of this community" (cited in Fierro 2009, 344).[25] While for Giménez Caballero and other Falangists associated with the Franco regime Catholicism constituted the principal anchor of this essential and timeless national identity, for the fascist current associated with Ledesma Ramos, "the influence of the Catholic tradition in the whole of Spanish society had constituted a serious obstacle to the crystallization of a solid and authentic nationalist ideology, one profane and independent of the Church and the monarchy, and that, in consequence, would be capable of sustaining under its aegis the entirety of the population" (Fierro 2009, 345).

Within this particular nationalist current, the necessity of sidelining the Church went hand in hand with a demand to eliminate foreign influences, a requirement for which the eight centuries of Muslim rule in Iberia, commonly understood as a period of foreign occupation, represented a particular difficulty. Fierro reads Olagüe's *Les Arabes n'ont jamais envahi l'Espagne* as an attempt to respond to this demand. Islam was not a foreign intruder on Iberian soil but an autochthonous development, a temporary solution adopted by an endangered Unitarian community (Fierro 2009, 347), an argument that reappears, albeit with some important modifications, in González Ferrín's work, as Fierro notes.

By reading Olagüe through the context of midcentury Spanish fascism, Fierro arrives at a damning judgment, one echoed by many of González Ferrín's critics as well: the fantastical history produced by Olagüe/González Ferrín is one more expression of a nationalist desire for a foreigner-free Spain. This singular desire has right- and left-wing variants in Spain. For the right, such an account satisfies the fantasy of a purely Spanish heritage, a convergence of history, territory, culture, and to some extent even religion, as Islam is dematerialized against the Christian background that preceded and succeeded it. For the left, a political current that would include many of today's *andalucistas*, the Olagüe/ González Ferrín version of history similarly serves the impulse to expunge the foreign by erasing the distance and difference between the two sides of the Mediterranean or rather fusing them into a single cultural or religious homogeneity. Gil Benumeya's concept space of *Mediodía* stands as an obvious precursor here, and it is thus not surprising that some critics have identified him as an earlier contributor to a shared project.[26] Fierro's text invites us to recognize, beneath these apparently divergent political alignments, a common and dangerous political reflex.

It is important to note, nonetheless, that this critique of ideology—

focused on Olagüe/González Ferrín but also addressing Andalucismo as a whole—shares one important feature with those it is directed against. Namely, both the texts of Andalucismo and those of historians such as Fierro who warn of historical distortion frame their claims as a response to a historically recurring danger within Spanish political life: the drive for purity, whether historical, racial, cultural, or religious. Where they diverge, however, is in regard to what they identify as the historical nexus of this impulse. On one hand, for the *andalucistas*, this originary nexus stretches back to the statutes of blood purity developed by the Spanish Inquisition that resulted in the campaign to expel every Jewish and Muslim trace from Iberian soil only then to deny and forget every remainder of their presence. Drawing sustenance and purpose from the site where that campaign ran aground against the shores of memory—the south, Andalusia, *Mediodía*— Andalucismo represents a countermovement aimed at resisting that ever-mutating yet relentless campaign. On the other hand, for the community of historians of which Fierro is a part (practitioners of a discipline entrusted with the duty to ensure that the medieval does not infringe on the modern, Fasolt [2005] reminds us), this drive for a purified history—for what Juan Goytisolo has called a "clean-shaven Spanish history"—is above all an artifact left in the wake of the civil war, a residue from the political movements of nineteenth- and twentieth-century nationalism rather than a centuries-long inheritance. As I stated at the outset of this chapter in referring to Szpiech's analysis of the "*convivencia* wars," Spanish Arabism remains haunted by early associations with and accommodations made under National Catholicism.[27]

While Fierro dedicates much of her essay to exploring Olagüe's debt to the nationalist currents of his day, she also locates his work within a longer history of scholarship, one that has its initial opening in the work of the eighteenth-century Jesuit scholar Juan Andrés y Morell. Andrés, as Fierro notes, was an early exponent of what is referred to as the "Arabist theory": the claim that the origins of modernity—the traditions of modern science, philosophy, medicine, and literature—are not located in northern Europe but rather on its southern periphery in the cultural and religious fusion produced in medieval Iberia. Responding to Spain's relegation to the backwaters of universal history within a dominant French intellectual culture (a view articulated with particular force by Montesquieu), Andrés countered with a thesis that placed the origin of European literature outside of Europe and in the Arabic poetic traditions of the Middle East. Brought to Europe's southern shores starting in the eighth century, these traditions, in Andrés's account, provided the seed that, once planted in Spanish soil, grew to become the basis of Europe's own literary efflorescence of the fifteenth and sixteenth centuries.[28] The creative spark that gave birth to modern European literature (as well as philosophy and medicine) did not emanate from Provence, as Montesquieu had claimed, but from Baghdad: "So, throughout the vast Arab domains, in all the three parts of the world [the ones known at the time: Asia, Africa, and Europe] where their empire had been extended, we see Saracen letters enter triumphantly, and dominate, like their armies, the globe. Since the ninth century of our era, the light of Arabic literature began to shine, and for six or seven centuries it kept glittering bright" (Andrés, cited in Dainotto 2006, 21–22).[29]

Yet despite Andrés's postulation of a Middle Eastern origin for European modernity, his revised geographic imaginary was not meant in any way to topple Europe from its historical pedestal, only to downgrade France's role. While giving recognition to an Arabic contribution to the constitution of Europe, he simultaneously desubstantialized it, stripping it of any content that could not be traced back to an exercise of European creativity. As Roberto Dainotto notes, "nowhere does [Andrés'] *Origin* show much sympathy towards the Arab, 'itinerant and nomadic nation,' pyromaniac of Alexandria's library, and bamboozled by Mohammed '*famoso impostore.*' . . . Whatever the Arab had given Europe was purified and codified into a modern European idiom without any trace of the Arab origin" (Dainotto 2006, 23). The historical gesture Andrés inaugurates, a simultaneous inclusion and exclusion of Islam and the Middle East in the processes that constituted Europe, has long been a staple of the European historical tool kit. Accordingly, Islam will make its appearance in the narratives of European history but in a manner that minimizes its relevance to the contemporary subject of that history, just as school children in liberal Spain can now be taught that al-Andalus was a wonderful moment in the development of their country and entirely irrelevant to who they are.

Fierro positions Andrés as a precursor to Olagüe (and by implication, González Ferrín), a reading that assimilates the Arabist theory, of which Andrés is an important and early exponent, to the reactionary nationalism of midcentury Spanish fascism. Although this is certainly one of the directions that Andrés' perspective leads, it is not the only one. For Dainotto, Andrés' Eurocentrism prevented him from recognizing how his postulation of an Arab origin for modern European literature could not but leave unsettled the cultural geography he purports to draw from, one based on the polarity of East and West. Dainotto reads Andrés as a diagnostic of a problem that remains with us today: "rather than representing any solution, Andrés remains the allegory of the problems and difficulties that we may still face when attempting to provincialize Europe from its interior borders" (Dainotto 2006, 25). In my view, the passionate controversy provoked by González Ferrín's work is itself a symptom of the problems and difficulties Dainotto refers to here. The tradition of Andalucismo, in this light, may be seen as the site where the contradictions inherent in this attempt to rewrite the boundaries between Europe and the Middle East appear in their starkest form.

Fierro's cautionary warning, I suggest, itself bears witness to the anxieties that continue to surround this project. Notably, what links Andrés to Olagüe and González Ferrín in her reading is not a shared rejection of the idea of an Islamic invasion. Andrés, contrary to these other writers, affirms the conventional view of a Muslim conquest. Rather, the common element conjoining (and incriminating) these authors, as Fierro describes them, is their insistence that Europe owes a "debt" to the cultural efflorescence that took place on medieval Europe's southern border. This "preoccupation" with a European "debt" is mentioned three times in Fierro's text in relation to the works of Olagüe, González Ferrín, and Andrés, respectively, each time registering her strong opposition to such a claim. Why, we might ask, does this particular aspect of their thinking provoke such a response? Why must this claim in particular be so strongly denounced? The implication here is that the ideological commitment that most exemplifies this dangerous current of thought is expressed in this judgment that Europe is "indebted" to the societies that existed under Muslim rule during the Middle Ages. Yet wouldn't we say (and wouldn't much of Fierro's own exemplary historical work precisely affirm) that the achievements in science, medicine, philosophy, and literature that we identify with the European Renaissance were built on—were "indebted" to—the works of Muslim, Jewish, and Christian scholars situated in medieval Iberia? While remaining on guard against the use of Iberia's Arabic and Islamic legacy for recognizably dangerous nationalist ends, her text also has the effect of removing that legacy from the story of Europe, its constitutive entanglements with the Middle East expunged in the process.

Notably, the concept of a "historical debt" reflects a sensibility specific to capitalist societies, those where *debt* is connected to particular anxieties and fears. Insomuch as the concept presupposes a distinction between two separate agents, the debtor and the debtee, when applied to the analysis of historical facts, it tends to interpret processes of adaptation and incorporation as the action of subjects who remain autonomous and self-identical across such transformations—hence, the prominent place of this notion within nationalist historiographies. Contrast this notion of a debt that one society owes to another with the idea that one society *builds on* elements derived from anther. Such a society can no longer be radically distinguished from the other from which at one point it absorbed a certain feature. The idea of "building on," therefore, may be experienced as more threatening than that of debt from a nationalist standpoint, which may explain why scholars anxious about the clarity of the border separating Spain from the Middle East avoid it.

NEGATIONISM

The most sustained (though also most shrill) denunciation of Olagüe/ González Ferrín is found in Alejandro García Sanjuán's *La conquista islámica de la Península Ibérica y la tergiversación del pasado* (2013) (The Islamic conquest of the Iberian Peninsula and the misrepresentation of the past). No other writer has given such passionate expression to the anger and disdain provoked by González Ferrín's *Historia general* among Spanish Arabists and medieval historians. For García Sanjuán, González Ferrín's work belongs to what he calls the "discourse of negationism," a set of arguments first elaborated by Infante and Gil Benumeya, he avers, but only articulated fully by Olagüe and his heir, González Ferrín. In comparing González Ferrín's work to the discourse of Holocaust denial, the term *negationism*'s primary referent, García Sanjuán invites us to view the text as a morally reprehensible act of historical distortion, a view reinforced across the text by his repeated reference to "historiographical fraud" (García Sanjuán 2013, 70).[30] In his insistence that González Ferrín's work be read not simply as an erroneous interpretation of historical evidence but as moral violation, an act of scholarly evil, García Sanjuán goes so far as to impute corrupt motivations to *Historia general*'s author: "What we have before us is a clear opportunistic improvisation meant to satisfy disgraceful [*inconfesable*] personal ambitions" (121).

Negationism, García Sanjuán notes, finds its most fertile soil in the south, specifically in Andalusia, among both converts to Islam and Andalusian nationalists. The idealization of al-Andalus promoted by Andalucismo requires the erasure of the violence of the Muslim conquest that produced it. García Sanjuán writes,

> The oeuvre of Blas Infante himself indicates that the denial [*negación*] of the conquest constitutes an inevitable premise of a historical memory that calls for the establishment of emotional and national ties to al-Andalus. It is worth affirming, in fact, that negationism represents an inescapable requirement of *andalucismo*, given the relevance attributed to the Andalusi period within that discourse. The identity Al-Andalus/

Andalusia, a foundation of the *andalucista* mythology, demands that the origin of the Andalusi be delinked from any trace that might associate it with violence or imposition. (García Sanjuán 2013, 92–93)

The first third of García Sanjuán's text is dedicated to disclosing a menacing conspiracy based on the ideas of Olagüe and González Ferrín, a conspiracy disseminated via a network of *andalucista* foundations, websites, and publishing houses, and given legitimacy by prominent literary figures (Antonio Gala, Juan Goytisolo), journalists (Francisco Vigueras Roldán), and academics (the Arabist Juan Marto, the modern historian Ricardo García Cárcel). Even the anthropologist José Antonio González Alcantud, a scholar who has dedicated much of his career to a critical (though not entirely unsympathetic) assessment of the discourse of Andalucismo, is accused of having been "seduced by the 'siren song' of negationism" for having suggested that Olagüe's ideas have tended to be disqualified on political grounds rather than discussed objectively (127).

Despite the excess of contempt and vitriol directed at González Ferrín throughout the work, García Sanjuán eventually arrives, in the latter two-thirds of the text, at a close consideration of González Ferrín's reading of the historical record, a reading that, he argues, fails to do justice to the available historical evidence. Presenting a series of reasoned arguments justifying his interpretation of the scarce historical record and countering those presented in *Historia general*, these sections of the book provide a valuable resource for those interested in the early centuries of Islamic rule in Iberia.[31] A relentless effort, however, to characterize González Ferrín's scholarship as an unconscionable distortion of truth, a kind of madness ("delírios," 120), ultimately leads him to produce a highly distorted account of the work he is criticizing.

In a review of García Sanjuán's book, the medieval historian Kenneth Baxter Wolf highlights how García Sanjuán's determination to demolish González Ferrín's credibility leads him to misrepresent or too readily dismiss the serious aspects of the latter's work. While Wolf rejects many of González Ferrín's claims, he argues that those claims nonetheless are far from absurd and reflect an interpretation that has considerable overlap with the viewpoints of other widely respected medievalists: "I am simply pointing out," Wolf writes, "that there is a logic to González Ferrín's negationism that is grounded in more than some andalucista 'myth.' As problematic a thesis as it is, one could (and for the sake of fairness one probably should) argue that negationism is reminiscent of theories about the 'rise of Islam' advanced by historians whose reputations are beyond reproach" (Wolf 2014, 10).[32]

For Wolf, García Sanjuán's campaign to discredit every aspect of the negationist thesis leads him not only to undervalue the parts of the thesis that cohere with current historical research but to seemingly embrace much of the conventional account propounded by National Catholicism, a view that García Sanjuán explicitly rejects as a nationalist "myth."[33] As Wolf notes, the very speed of the Arab conquest has always been a problem for the traditional account, and has led many scholars to posit a slower process for which military power was only one, possibly minor, aspect:

> It is awfully hard to imagine a small Arab force making the kind of headway that it did if the local inhabitants had senses that their lives—or even their ways of life—were at risk. This simple observation strongly suggests to me that the Islamic conquests, east and west, were conquests with a very small 'c'; no doubt there was a change of regime, but it was effected by a pragmatic and strategic balance between the threat of force and the offering of attractive terms. Unfortunately, rather than give the negationists some credit for getting this one right (more or less), García Sanjuán sets out to prove that the conquest of 711 was indeed a violent one. (Wolf 2014, 11)

A tenet of Reconquista nationalism is thus reaffirmed—that the Arab presence in Spain arrived as a violent foreign force—within a historical work that defines its target as the myths of nationalism.

The fact that scholars who are acutely attuned to the dangers of Spanish nationalism end up reaffirming some of the more problematic tenets of nationalist historiography (Islam as a violent intruder into Iberia, erasure of the Arab contribution to building what eventually becomes Europe) points to the political and ideological pressures under which historians of the period labor. One of the starkest testimonies to these pressures can be found in a response to Wolf's review of García Sanjuán's book on the website of the journal where the review appeared. Only a handful of responses were left on the site, though they include sharp rebuttals from Fierro, Manzano Moreno, and García Sanjuán himself. However, it is the first in the series of comments, by the Spanish author and journalist Francisco de Borja Loma, that lays bare some of the central anxieties giving shape to this debate. Borja Loma's rather feverish response focuses on an issue that has been a long-standing target of Spanish intellectuals: the highly distorted and disparaging views of Spain and its history proffered by foreign scholars from at least the sixteenth century. He writes "American historians and Hispanists are bereft of the minimum intellectual value when it comes to writing about Spain. They are liars and idlers who let themselves be swept away by the Black Legend, given that it is easier to hold onto one's biases than search out and discover the truth."[34] The Black Legend (*Leyenda Negra*) alluded to here refers to a style of anti-Spanish historical writing produced by rival European countries and characterized by a highly disparaging view of the country, emphasizing its decadence, repressiveness, and brutality. Such literature epitomizes what had been Spain's long-standing denigration by its European neighbors, its forced exile from the story of European progress and civilization that was put to rest, so I was told, with the end of Francoism in the mid-1970s.

Many of Spain's early-modern critics explicitly attributed Spanish decadence to the corrupting influence of Iberia's Muslims and Jews on the Spanish character.[35] Indeed, Borja Loma addresses this charge directly not by denying that Muslims and Jews had a corrupting influence but by rejecting outright that they had any influence at all. This refutation is all the more striking given that Wolf's review never once addresses the issue of a Muslim or Jewish legacy. Borja Loma states, "The influence of Near Eastern and North African social structures in the development of Andalusian history? Come on! This influence, according to the Anglo Hispanists, extends across all of Spain, not only Andalusia. And all of Spain is the result of this influence since the eighth century. Or so they have continued to tell us insistently since the nineteenth century. And without greater precision. I don't believe it at all. Let them sell this idiocy to those who have already bought it: the American students, for example, educated, like their professors, in the Black Legend."[36] What Borja Loma's criticisms lack in elegance they gain in directness. The claim that medieval Iberia's multireligious society left an abiding imprint on what later became Spain—as argued by Castro, from exile (not coincidentally) in the United States—is here condemned as a plot sustained by lazy foreigners, part of the machinations by which Spain is subordinated by foreign powers.

To excise the traces of the Near East and North Africa from Spanish soil, as Borja Loma does, is to erase the difference that enables this subordination and that threatens Spain's inclusion within Europe. Although Borja Loma's comment appears eccentric, I frequently encountered more polite versions of it in my conversations with Spanish academics, who insisted that Castro had become irrelevant for scholars of Spanish history or that the question of an Andalusi legacy was one of concern only to American academics still spellbound by a Romantic view of Spain. The question, they would continue, had lost its relevance to the Spanish themselves particularly in light of the new self-assuredness engendered by the country's integration into the European Union. These observations, common among contemporary Spanish historians, evacuate the Arab/Islamic contribution to Spain by rendering it a nonquestion, obsolete—a standpoint, moreover, made inadmissible by the methodological imperatives of a positivist historiography.[37]

IMMIGRANT HISTORIES

While González Ferrín's downplaying of the military dimension of the arrival of Islam in Iberia is certainly unconventional, many parts of his narrative on the porosity and slow consolidation of Islam during the eighth and ninth centuries have gained increasing acceptance in recent decades. Mercedes García-Arenal herself makes positive reference to this shifting perspective in a review of a book by Manzano Moreno, where she notes, "During the early years of Islam, Muslims—who did not refer to themselves as Muslims, but as *Mu'minin*, faithful, had yet to establish absolute boundaries between themselves and believers of other Abrahamic religions" (García-Arenal 2007). In this light, the virulent response provoked by González Ferrín's narrative (and Olagüe's before him) bears witness to the way he more radically troubles the historical waters, blurring the boundaries separating Spanish from Muslim, Spain from Islam, European from Middle Eastern.

In Spain's transition to democracy and the linked process of the county's integration into Europe, Spanish historians encountered a shifting ground of expectations and pressures. Released from the imperatives of National Catholicism to craft a past amenable to the ideological needs of the Franco regime, the profession encountered new exigencies tied to the felt need to support Europeanization in the face of an entrenched conservatism. The new freedom to explore their own past, in other words, also came with a renewed demand to forget (or remember anew?) episodes from this history so as to produce an image of the enlightened, liberal society that Spain was now to become. This project of producing a modern and European identity for the country, as Eduardo Subirats has noted, entailed new practices of "censorship and occultation of memory":

> In the first place, the cultural and political project of National Catholicism had to be displaced. It had to be reformulated as if it were an anomalous and isolated phenomenon within Spanish history, without historical antecedents in the past or consequences for the future. . . . [This was conjoined with] the official silence on the expulsion of the Moriscos in the seventeenth century, the displacements and forced resettlement of

populations, the inquisitorial persecutions, and the prohibition on the use of the Arabic language that accompanied them. (Subirats 2003, 11–12)

The suasive force of this project is evident, for example, in continuing recourse among historians to the claim that the Moriscos were expelled from the Iberian Peninsula on the ground that their hidden attachment to Islam represented an unacceptable disruption within the social fabric.[38] It would be wrong, however, to read such acts of historical erasure as solely an artifact of the contingencies of Spanish politics. The repetition of such gestures of expulsion (from territory, culture, thought, and memory) across Spanish history indicate an abiding structure (as Castro diagnosed), a theological-political foundation of Reconquista Spain, but also of European reason itself, as Anidjar (2008) reminds us.

The contemporary attachment to the 711 invasion narrative, of course, must also be viewed in relation to what some in Spain will call the second invasion of *los moros*: the more recent arrival of Muslim, and particularly Moroccan, immigrants into Iberia, many of them coming across the straits following the trajectory taken by their eighth-century forerunners. In Spain today, these immigrants are commonly referred to as *moros*, and their immigration to Iberian shores is routinely identified in popular media as a new "Islamic invasion" of Spain. To speak of the return of the repressed in this context is entirely appropriate. The historical masks these immigrants are made to wear north of the border are multiple, each folding over the other: Muslim invaders who held Christian Iberia captive for centuries, fearsome *Regulares*, the Moroccans recruited into Franco's army and deployed as shock troops during the civil war, the "Oriental" face of Spain itself, stripped of its European disguise by misfortune and circumstance.[39]

As Daniela Flesler notes, this threatening liability of Spanish history is now, simultaneously, perceived as an opportunity for the country to become more fully European: "Spain's current status on the receiving end of migration has a psychological significance—besides a historical and political one—that means more than the issue does to other European countries. Having to deal with the so-called immigration problem becomes an index of Spain's belonging to First-World Europe" (Flesler 2008b, 30). Spain's 1985 adoption of the *Ley de Extranjería* (Foreigner's Law), a more restrictive law than found elsewhere in Europe, suggests a national enthusiasm for the country's new role as guardian of Europe's southern borders (Flesler 2008b, 30–31). In short, the popular interpretation of the Reconquista as Spain's heroic rescue of Europe from its destruction at the hand of the infidel Moor—a national myth at once cautioned against and, as I have argued, reified by a dominant, positivist historical position—has acquired new resonance today as the country's military and juridical forces are deployed against the *pateras* arriving from across the straits.

MUSICAL HISTORY

Without music, there can be no Andalucismo. In a recently published autobiography, González Ferrín (2018) frames his narrative with two musical encounters, one in the first chapter, one in the last. Both of the anecdotes he presents foreground moments of intuitive feeling, the experience of hearing musical connections between Spain and the Arab world, even when the language to describe them was not forthcoming. In the first account, he writes of a summer spent, while still a student, exploring Morocco by car, accompanied throughout by the radio broadcasts of popular Moroccan musical groups, many of Sufi inspiration. Although he had never listened to this genre of music before, some part of it, he writes, was familiar to him. The music carried echoes of another genre he had discovered in Seville some years before, in the early 1980s, what was then called "Andalusi rock" (*rock andaluz*) and that brought together elements of flamenco with progressive rock. (Antonio Manuel Rodríguez Ramos led an Andalusi rock band earlier in his life.) Reflecting back on this experience of a commonality bridging the two genres, González Ferrín muses that this commonality was "perhaps less musical than social: it was natural that I would feel and understand that Andalusi rock and those Moroccan groups expressed the same, demonstrated the same aesthetic, the same singular and hostile relation against an officialdom . . . a sentiment of bitter resentment against a certain pressure, perhaps centralizing, from the countries of which they came" (González Ferrín 2018, 26). His brief account here, as I read it, is an introductory invitation to his readers to think—via the musical—beyond the usual boundaries of recognition, identity, and influence and to consider the epistemic value of such felt relations within historical inquiry.

In the second anecdote, González Ferrín recounts an occasion when he was listening to the composer Scarlatti on a classical music station. During a break in the music, the host of the program took calls from listeners. One of the callers asked whether Scarlatti, in light of his extensive sojourn in Spain, had been influenced by Hispano-Arabic music. Listening to the host's rather disdainful rejection of such a suggestion, González Ferrín decided to investigate the matter himself, listening first to a sonata by the composer and then to a fandango, a musical form widely thought to have Andalusian origins, concluding in the end that, indeed, Scarlatti's music bore the imprint of what the host had disparagingly called "flirtations of oriental music" (González Ferrín [2006] 2016, 330–31). Bookends to a text recording the personal and intellectual trajectory that gave shape to the author's unique perspective on the past, these scenes of aural sensibility attune the reader to the importance of the senses for approaching the complex relational histories that compose Andalusia.

In *European Modernity and the Arab Mediterranean* (2010), Karla Mallette explores how nineteenth- and early twentieth-century scholars working from Europe's southern periphery confronted the limits of philological method in their attempts to make sense of the "Semitic-Romantic hybridity," the crisscrossings of Arabic, Latin, and Hebrew that characterized the scant historical texts at their disposal. Philology, a discipline of ancient origin, reformulated in the nineteenth century in accord with the categories and imperatives of modern nationalism, provided a powerful tool in parsing these texts but ultimately could not overcome its own conceptual confines when faced with a world composed according to principles radically distinct from those undergirding the system of nation-states. Mallette writes, "When multiple parentage generates a hybrid text, when disparate elements are amalgamated and engender something rich and strange, can analytical paradigms plumb their mysteries?" (Mallette 2010, 164). In her wonderfully generative reading of this scholarship, Mallette highlights how, at key moments of analytical impasse, these southern European scholars would supplement the rigors of philology with intuitive leaps, flights of poetic liberty, and in so doing open the way for immense interpretive advances in their field of inquiry.

Among the scholars discussed by Mallette is Emilio García Gómez, one of the leading Arabists of his generation and a professor of Arabic at the University of Granada during the 1930s. García Gómez is best known for having solved the mystery of the *kharja*, a medieval Andalusi poetic form written in Arabic script but—as he discovered—actually a form of antique Spanish. The recognition of the *kharja* as one of the foundational moments in the development of a European literary tradition provided a key opening to a reconsideration of Europe's relation to the Middle East. García Gómez's work located an Arabic poetic form as one element within the development of a national language. While this discovery was of immense importance for scholars of Spanish history, his writings on the *kharja* inspire few readers today: by casting this poetic form as "a voice of Spain" (Mallette 2010, 195), he ended up flattening some of the complexity that had made the *kharja* such a rich and generative site of interest. In contrast, it is his poetic testimonial to the Alhambra, a book titled *Silla del moro* (Seat of the Moor), that continues to speak to contemporary audiences. In this work, García Gómez weaves together voices from across Granada's history, from Muslim poets to Romantic enthusiasts, all the while giving expression to the turmoil and anxiety left in the wake of the Spanish Civil War. The result was a unique achievement, a work that, as Mallette describes, "sacrifices neither historical pleasure nor the sumptuous sensual pleasures to be derived from close reading," a book both "passionately historicist and passionately intuitive; the two urges, rather than denying the legitimacy the one to the other, rather support and affirm each other" (195), thus reflecting and enacting the amalgams and ensembles of the city itself. And across this book, echoing like restless ghosts from the past and wandering troubadours from the present, filling every street that winds beneath the Muslim palace, while weaving the pages of the book together in a symphonic whole — the music of Arab lute players, flamenco singers, boleros, fandangos, and *ghazals*.

As we have seen throughout this book, Andalucismo turns to sound and music in order to open up dimensions of the past that defy categorization within normative analytical frameworks. These spaces present what Cora Diamond (2003) calls "difficulties of reality" and are illuminated by the very limits of language as spaces that only sounds may plumb. González Ferrín thinks of these moments when historical analysis falls back on life, on a writer's felt sense of connection or recognition, in terms of their generativity in opening up new avenues of inquiry and discovery, avenues whose value is necessarily conditioned by the circumstances and concerns that define the writer's life. Such moments of affect and intuition within the historian's tool kit, however, are not strictly subjective or individual but rather can be recognized as sensibilities integral to the tradition of Andalucismo — as, thus, patterned and authorized within the matrix of institutions and practices that sustain that tradition. As "modes of encountering and inhabiting the present's relation to the past and the future" (Abeysekara 2019, 2), these sensibilities shape the temporal geography we have encountered in Gil Benumeya's *Mediodía*, in Rodríguez Ramos's "Flamenco era," and in González Ferrín's "third Spain."

An epigraph by Francisco Márquez Villanueva, a student of Américo Castro, marks the opening of González Ferrín's recent book *Cuando fuimos árabes* (When we were Arabs). It speaks to the exploratory aspect of Andalucismo, a tradition that unsettles old perspectives as much as it opens the door to new ones, and I will call on it to close this chapter: "The key to Américo Castro's reading of our history consists in braiding an oriental thread into Spanish culture, an approach that responded to many of our questions and also elicited others" (Francisco Márquez Villanueva, in González Ferrín 2018, 5).

CHAPTER 3

Sounding Out the Past

Listening to the inarticulate cry of the Andalusian *cante jondo*, a sound of human anguish in which he discerns both regional and universal elements, Federico García Lorca registers the voice of the exiled and persecuted: a *gitano* (Roma) voice, to be sure, but also that of the Moriscos defeated, repressed, and finally expelled from their Iberian home. The experience to which the *cante* gave voice has, he finds, Arabic and Persian undertones to it, expressive gestures Lorca seeks to bring to light through his exploration of the works of Muslim poets. Lorca's intervention regarding the genealogy of the Andalusian musical tradition stands in contrast to that of the Catalan musicologist and composer Felipe Pedrell. In comments made a few years before those of Lorca, Pedrell asserts that the essential features of *cante jondo*, what he calls "primitive Andalusian song" (*cante primitivo andaluz*), were derived from the sacred music of the Byzantine liturgy. The Arabs, in his view, had simply served as a *channel* for their transmission, contributing nothing to the substance of the musical genre. As he declares, referring to the Muslim impact on Spanish music, "their influence did not touch anything essential. They were the ones to be influenced" (Pedrell 1900, 74–76). His stance is consonant with the long-standing practice, encountered frequently over the preceding chapters, of expunging the Arab and Islamic elements from Spanish and European cultural forms—a project that acquired renewed vigor in Pedrell's day during the last years of the nineteenth century as Spain became embroiled in a protracted conflict in Morocco (Labajo 1997).

The composer Manuel de Falla, a disciple of Pedrell's who, together with Lorca, co-organized the renowned Concurso del Cante Jondo (Conference of Deep Song) in Granada in June of 1922, held a third view on the origins of this musical tradition. In his lecture on the topic, delivered on the occasion of the Concurso, Falla begins by affirming Pedrell's observation on the origins of *cante* within the Byzantine liturgy but then takes issue with his mentor's conclusion that the Arabs added nothing to the Spanish form (Falla 1950, 122–39). As part of his training as a composer, Falla studied Arabic musical genres through a number of collections available at the time and had noted the influence of the music within Andalusian song.[1] Countering the claims of Pedrell, he insists that various genres of music on both sides of the Mediterranean reveal a common Andalusi origin: "There is no doubt that the music still known in Morocco, Algeria, and Tunisia by the name 'Andalusian music of the Moors of Granada' not only includes a personal character that distinguishes it from other musics of Arabic origin, but in its rhythmic dance forms we easily recognize the origin of many of our Andalusian dances: *sevillanas, zapateados, seguidillas,* etc." (Falla 1950, 125).[2]

Parallel to Lorca's poetic explorations, Falla incorporates rhythmic and melodic elements from Andalusian folk traditions (as well as from Arabic music more directly) into his musical vocabulary, most strikingly in the compositions *El amor brujo, El sombrero de tres picos,* and *Fantasía Bética.* His exploration of Andalusian themes would evoke an ambivalent response from Spanish critics, some applauding the "quintessentially Spanish" character of his work, others deriding it for presenting a caricature of Spain and Spanishness, one based in the same romanticized stereotypes that dominated popular images of the country abroad. Indeed, one critic commenting on his composition for the ballet *El sombrero de tres picos* suggested the piece was on a par with "a chapter out of the Black Legend," a term, as mentioned above, used to indicate a style of European historiography that presented a highly disparaging view of Spain as a country mired in decadence and brutality. While celebrated by many, Falla's Andalucismo would remain vulnerable to the charge of provincialism and exoticism, less a contribution to musical modernism than a picture postcard from the folkloric, exotic climes of southern Spain (Hess 2001).

Falla's musical trajectory during the mid and latter stages of his career was largely shaped by an impetus to overcome this pronouncement on the folkloric quality of his music. By the late 1920s he had largely eliminated Andalucismo from his musical palette, his point of musical reference having shifted north to the seventeenth- and eighteenth-century Spanish composers strongly associated with Castille. Characterized by what his contemporary critics described as a more austere, abstract, and mystical musical vocabulary devoid of the sensualism ascribed to his Andalusian works, Falla's compositions were now hailed as having transcended the localism of his Andalucismo period to attain a universal significance—a shift registered in his critics' recourse to the term *neoclassical* to designate the new works (Hess 2001, 232–61). Commenting on Falla's *Harpsichord Concerto,* Carol Hess highlights the extent to which critics saw the universality of the piece as grounded in its profound indebtedness to Spanish Catholicism: "Falla had done much more than merely abandon Andalucismo in favor of a modernist idiom. Rather, he had allied that very idiom with prevailing constructions of Spanish Catholicism, the discourse of which, in turn, was entirely compatible with the values of European neoclassicism" (245). Importantly, some of the emerging constructions of Spanish Catholic identity signaled in Hess's comment were moving at the time in a distinctly fascist direction. In this context, it is rather striking that the key term used by contemporary Spanish commentators to describe the new musical values of Falla's concerto was *depuración*—purification. Echoing a long-dominant narrative within Spanish historiography, Falla's Andalusian period comes to be cast as a transitory stage on the pathway toward both a purified Spanish Catholicism and European universalism. His Romantic flirtation with the charms of the Orient here gives way to the serious business of a modern European nation and its Christian identity. Expelling the Andalusi tinge from his music was a necessary first step in this direction.

I start with these brief observations on the career of Manuel de Falla in order to introduce the central theme of this chapter—musical Andalucismo—and to highlight some of the ideological contours of the terrain over which the musical legacies of al-Andalus extend. As I have noted at multiple junctures, music has served as a privileged arena through which the presence of Spain's Arab and Islamic composition has been conceptually explored and aesthetically elaborated. From the first stirrings of the *andalucista* movement, one finds flamenco there in the foreground (at times under the moniker of *cante jondo*),[3] an authentic voice of the people (though which people?) whose horizons extend temporally back to al-Andalus and geographically to the south and the distant east, the chronotope of *Mediodía*. It is striking that almost every important contributor to the tradition of Andalucismo from the late nineteenth century forward has found in flamenco a key to thinking about the unity and continuity of contemporary Spain with its medieval Muslim and Jewish past—or rather, less a key to *thinking about* than *passionately encountering* that past. And not only flamenco: music of one kind or another pervades the discourse on Andalusia tout court.[4] Already in Washington Irving, for example, we hear "all Andalusia was thus music mad" (Irving 1869, 364), and he saturates his Romantic stories of the Alhambra with the sound of lutes and singing voices. The Arabist Emilio García Gómez, for his part, likens his short monograph on the city of Granada, *Silla del moro*, to a composition for piano (García Gómez 1948, 10). The ghost of al-Andalus finds a body in sound.

Yet to speak of ghosts is not quite right. The sonic figures and constructions of Andalucismo do not summon something otherwise absent by fashioning its (ghostly) image in sound and music. Something else is at play, in my view, in Andalucismo's compulsion to draw on the sonic. During a conversation I had in Seville with the flamenco expert Cristina Cruces Roldán, she introduced a term that I find useful for thinking about sound as a historical medium. "What flamenco and the Andalusi tradition share," she noted, "is a common *sonorous foundation* [*un fondo sonoro*], one that makes it easy for flamenco musicians to relate to, experiment with, and understand Andalusi music" (interview with author, February 2011). She described a conversation she had with Gerardo Núñez, a celebrated flamenco guitarist and a leader in explorations across these traditions: "Gerardo put it to me this way: 'Their [the Moroccans'] Andalusi music is something universal that we [Spanish flamenco musicians] can move about in quite easily because of the shared *fondo sonoro*. With Andalusi musicians, when I play something, they know how to build on it, extend it, they recognize how to move within it. When I first played jazz, I could build on it because I had the technical skills, but I had no intuitive grasp of it. It was like a foreign language, though one I could learn. Andalusi music, however, is more like a language I once knew but forgot, or one I can speak without knowing.' This is how Gerardo puts It."[5]

I want to think with the notion of a *fondo sonoro*, as described by Cruces Roldán, not just as a musical figure but also a temporal one. The improvisational space the *fondo* affords to the skilled musician (or listener)—the connections it makes possible—is simultaneously musical and historical—an articulation of sound and of time forged not with the resources of narrative but by rhythm, timbre, scale, and tone. As I have suggested in prior chapters, Andalucismo involves a cultivated feel for the way the Iberian past and present hold together much as a musician has a feel for the way different musical styles intersect to form a common ground, one laden with emergent musical possibility. In this encounter of horizons, the sensitive musician attempts to reveal patterns latent in this *fondo*, a territory of aesthetic and affective connection. This territory, the sonic image of a Mediterranean world—a variety of Gil Benumeya's *Mediodía* or González Ferrín's "third Spain"—will provide the *andalucistas* with the affective materials to shape a vision of history outside the normative political geography of Spain and its European career.

Flamenco affords Andalucismo the aesthetic tools for the honing of a unique epistemic attitude, one attuned to the subtle yet pervasive presence of an inherited medieval world and its thematization as an important condition of contemporary social and political life. Within the sensory-emotional opening afforded by flamenco's sonic palette, *andalucistas* find the possibility to feel and think across the *fondo sonoro* linking al-Andalus

with Andalusia and the Middle East with Europe, a space of historical reflection unsustainable within the dominant epistemological frames that
constitute modern Spain as an integral part of a broader European civilization. As I have discussed, within dominant traditions of narrating the
Spanish nation, the date 1492—and the Reconquista narrative that structures its significance—stands as a historiographical barrier to this impetus, positing as it does a nonrelation to Islam and the Middle East as at
the core of the historical and conceptual procedures that define the nation.
From within this conceptual space, continuities with Iberia's Muslim and
Jewish past can only ever be assigned to the modality of Romantic fiction,
Orientalist fantasy, or nostalgic (i.e., inauthentic) longing, none of which
constitute a responsible ethical and political orientation to the present.[6] In
this discursive context, flamenco both marks the limits of the "sayable" and
creates the ground for a passional relation to the past that allows it to be
thought and lived otherwise—on the basis of new possibilities emerging
within the resonance chamber located between al-Andalus, Andalusia, and
the Middle East. Instead of viewing the musical passion of Andalucismo as
a flight from historical reality into the false idealizations of ideology, I read
it here as a historical sensibility cultivated and practiced on the periphery
of Europe.

Over the following pages I explore these dimensions of the musical af-
terlife of al-Andalus, beginning with flamenco, a tradition exemplifying
some of the tensions and contradictions within Spain's relation to its medieval past. The second section of the chapter shifts to an ethnographic
mode, wherein I focus on a set of contemporary musical practices centered
around a project of recuperating and performing medieval traditions of
Arabo-Andalusi music. Within musical scholarship, such projects of historical recuperation tend to be approached through two interpretive frames,
one emphasizing the discourse of heritage as part of the ideological edifice
of modern cultural nationalism, the second highlighting the emergence of
the "world music" industry and its role in creating the tastes, desires, and
commercial infrastructure necessary for such musical projects. While the
analysis I develop here necessarily addresses the importance of the heritage and world music industries in creating the context for the circulation
and performance of Arabo-Andalusi music, I also point to the limits of an
approach that remains within the analytical purview that these two frameworks afford. The recuperative musical project I explore here articulates,
I argue, a transgressive historical space. The ethical and aesthetic sensibilities it mobilizes work away at the barrier that exiles al-Andalus from contemporary Andalusia, setting in motion forms of attachment and belonging
that rub up against the norms of Spanish and European identity.[7]

ECHOES TO THE SOUTH

In 1924 Blas Infante, the "father of Andalusian nationalism," set out on a journey to the city of Agmat, Morocco. As he later described,

> I was determined to renew the wanderings that our fathers made at one time to the tomb of one of the men who most characterized the spirit of our land, [the eleventh-century poet] Abu-l-Qâsim ibn 'Abbâd, al-Mu'tamid, the true king of Sevilla, Córdoba, Málaga and Algarbe. . . . Six centuries and Andalucía has not sent its condolences (*saudad*) in the living body of one of its children to the tomb of the Poet King, who died in the distant desert invoking his homeland with his pain-filled verses. (Infante 2008, 117)

Infante had come to share with his fellow *andalucista* and interlocutor Gil Benumeya the view that a key symbolic and historical reference for Andalusia's social and political renewal was to be found in al-Andalus, the historical site of the region's distinctive culture and pinnacle of its creative expression. In his own metaphysical terms, al-Andalus was "the foundation of our distinct will to exist" (Iniesta Coullaut-Valera 2001). Moreover, in the persecution and expulsion of the Moriscos Infante saw a historical injury committed against the people of Andalusia that remained exposed and untreated across the centuries, one from which contemporary grievances drew their force and historical weight. This orientation to Andalusia's medieval history had led him, some years earlier, to research and write a theatrical piece on the life of al-Mu'tamid. Infante's 1924 journey to Agmat was undertaken for the purpose of honoring and resuscitating the memory of this celebrated Andalusian, and on it he met with some of the descendants of the Muslims and Moriscos who were exiled from Iberia between the fifteenth and seventeenth centuries.[8]

Infante followed up his visit to al-Mu'tamid's tomb in Agmat with a stop in Rabat, where he attended a gathering of descendants of Rabati Andalusians, together forming the audience for a performance of Andalusi music.[9] Listening to the performance of Andalusi *nubas*—a classical musical form found primarily in North Africa but of Andalusian origins—Infante was struck by the music's profound resonance with southern Spain's own flamenco traditions and by the shared tragic sense at the expressive core of both musical genres. Commenting on the experience, he wrote,

> The Nuba continues to intone the lyrical sadness (*saudade*) of Andalucía in exile. . . . This kind of chant is choral. In its native home, in peninsular

Andalucía, the same musical form only finds expression by individual singers. Andalusi music, forbidden by society, came to take refuge in the individual; no longer choral it became secret, inaccessible, though at the same time, it became intensified. (Infante 1989)

Moved by the musical intimacies binding the exiled Andalusians of Morocco with the Spanish inhabitants of their onetime home, Infante dedicated his next few years to a historical and ethnographic study of the origins and expressive repertoire of flamenco, an abridged version of which was finally published posthumously in 1980 with the title *Orígenes de lo flamenco y el secreto del cante jondo* (The origins of flamenco and the secret of deep song).[10]

In the last chapter of *Orígenes de lo flamenco*, Infante draws together the many threads of his study in order to support his conclusion about the social and ethnic matrix from which flamenco first emerged. Flamenco, he argues, is the child of an encounter between two persecuted peoples, Moriscos and *gitanos* (Roma).[11] As the Moriscos faced ever greater repression from the sixteenth to the early seventeenth centuries, including the expropriation of their lands, they came, Infante avers, to seek refuge among the *gitanos*, a group whose itinerant lifestyle, social marginality, and openness toward other persecuted groups provided a temporary safe haven for the increasingly imperiled Moriscos.[12] The music they brought with them, and to which their *gitano* hosts added their own imprint, acquired the name of the Moriscos' own precarious condition: that of exiled or expelled peasants, in Infante's rendering, *"fellah mengu"* (from the Arabic, *falāh*, peasant, + *najā*, to escape) (Infante 1980, 165–66). As an Arabic expression, and thus a marker of a group that by the early seventeenth century had no legal protection within Iberia, *fellah mengu* (from which, Infante asserts, the Spanish term *flamenco* was derived) was used only in tightly circumscribed arenas until the mid-nineteenth century. Born of this alliance of the downtrodden, flamenco would become the expression of the downcast Andalusian soul (and of Spain's most impoverished, marginalized province). As Infante concludes, "Thus began the elaboration of flamenco by the Andalusians, exiled or expelled to the mountains of Africa and Spain. These men conserved the music of their homeland, and this music enabled them to analyze their pain and affirm their spirit: the slow rhythm, the comatose exhaustion" (166).

Most scholarship on the origins of the term *flamenco* has judged Infante's etymology to be dubious at best and has emphasized the paucity of historical evidence available to resolve this question in a determinate fashion. What I want to highlight, however, is how Infante's intuitive leap, in the absence of sufficient historical evidence, gave impetus to an exploration of the legacies of Morisco society that had previously received little attention. In flamenco, Infante can hear the sad voice of Andalusia, a voice that intoned, simultaneously, the distant suffering of Iberian Muslims forced into hiding and exile in the seventeenth century and the dark travails of the contemporary Andalusian soul. Flamenco became a voice, a sound— most often, a cry—of a historical subject whose experience encompassed both Muslim past and Spanish present. In doing so, Infante seeks to transform the felt relationship between contemporary Andalusians and their distant (Muslim) kin in order to highlight the meaningful nexus by which this shared past articulated with the present. More than establish a connection, he gestures toward the *practice* (one taken up and developed by subsequent generations of *andalucistas*) of listening and reflecting on the musical territory expressed by this aesthetic form as central to an Andalusian ethos and perspective.

As mentioned above, Blas Infante's thesis on the origins of flamenco has met with a range of largely negative responses from within the contemporary field of flamencology. As in other areas of Spanish historiographical inquiry, debates about flamenco's beginnings have long been bound to a broader question concerning the value and historical significance to be attributed to Spain's Arabic and Islamic heritage.[13] While a few scholars of this musical tradition (such as Cristina Cruces Roldán) have written extensively on the common musical foundations of flamenco and Arabo-Andalusi music (Cruces Roldán 2003), skeptical views of such a connection predominate. Thus, for the prominent flamencologist Gerhard Steingress, the search for flamenco's ancient origins is itself a legacy of nineteenth-century Romanticism and therefore inadequate as a historical method. Whatever fragments of medieval musical traditions may be excavated from within the contemporary genre, the form itself acquired its coherence as a discrete and recognizable set of musical practices only in the latter part of the nineteenth century. As Steingress summarizes, "we consider classical flamenco (*Mairenista*) as an aesthetic-ideological manifestation of modernity, rooted in essentialism and rationalism as foundations in the construction of objectivist identity, anchored in either a national and/or class conscience" (Steingress 2005, 122). While the genre's Muslim and *gitano* elements are not denied in this argument, their significance for contemporary Spain—the difference they make in how the genre articulates with the aesthetic, social, political, and commercial contexts in which it circulates—is here understood to be exhaustively determined by processes of identity formation, folklorization, and heritage production. To speak of flamenco before the 1860s is, then, to leave history for more ideological climes (Steingress 1993, 2002; Sant Cassia 2000). Flamenco holds a privileged place among *andalucista* thinkers, these critics assert, because as the most abstract and emotional of the arts, music offers the most fertile soil for the illusions of the Romantic imagination on which Andalucismo is founded.[14]

SOUND RESISTANCE

Scholars of flamenco necessarily encounter difficulties intrinsic to studying musical forms that do not accord with the nationalist assumptions undergirding the field of musicology, though they also must navigate ongoing anxieties concerning the Arabic and Jewish genealogy of European cultural forms. Even among scholars expressly concerned with the musical relationship between Spain and the Middle East, the affirmation that Middle Eastern elements adhere in Spanish musical forms often takes a highly circuitous formulation. In a conversation with Cruces Roldán, whose work has extensively documented the many diverse points of connection binding Andalusi music with flamenco, she began, much to my surprise, by emphasizing difference rather than commonality: "There are few direct connections between flamenco and Andalusi music. The scales, the rhythms, the instruments: one finds more divergence than convergence. Just as we have little in common with Moroccan culture." In the introduction to her book on the commonalities linking these two musical genres, Cruces Roldán hesitates to take any position on the relation or nonrelation of the two, stating rather that "the pages that follow serve, not to seal an argument for or against one viewpoint or the other, but as an attempt to suggest criteria of judgment in connection to both" (Cruces Roldán 2003, 14). It is only in her conclusion to this work, indeed, in its last sentence, itself hedged and hesitant, that she finally arrives at a positive statement:

> If there indeed exists a broad set of correspondences in the structural and expressive forms of the oriental musical tradition, we cannot establish a singular nexus, but rather can conclude with a decisive affirmation: the necessary presence of the model of the Andalusi music system in the historical processes and the cultural exchanges through which the seeds of flamenco, happily, were sown. (127)

If Cruces Roldán is a tentative inheritor of Infante's musical Andalucismo, Antonio Manuel Rodríguez Ramos, in contrast, has embraced Infante's vision to its full extent. During our multiple meetings, flamenco was never far from the center of conversation. Rodríguez Ramos had long been interested in the influence of Islamic mystical traditions on the de-velopment of Andalusian folk musics and was always keen to discuss this topic with me given my previous work on the tradition of ethical listening in Islam. His thought on this topic eventually coalesced into a book pub-lished just over a year after our last meeting (Rodríguez Ramos 2018). In this work, Rodríguez Ramos undertakes an exhaustive (and often specula-tive) etymology of the key terminology of flamenco so to reveal the buried Arabic and Hebraic experience rooted in the musical form and to reclaim this experience as a living, though obscured, wellspring of contemporary Andalusian culture.

At one of our meetings, Rodríguez Ramos offered an interpretation of why flamenco had become so important to the *andalucista* tradition. Its musical style, he suggested, served as a repository for Andalusia's univer-salist culture, one particularly suited to resisting the forms of religious and secular power developed in early-modern Spain. Informed by the contem-porary ascension of Cartesian rationalism, the fusion of Church and state that emerged in the sixteenth century (and that eventually would evolve into Franco's National Catholicism) was based on a division of powers that assigned the state authority over the domain of thought and reason and left the Church with a monopoly over the realms of human feeling, or over the soul, their locus. The Church's efforts to assimilate Andalusian cultural forms within its own disciplinary purview, however, encountered a barrier in flamenco insomuch as the form was embedded in deeply rooted oral tra-ditions of learning and transmission and was sung in an Andalusi dialect rather than in Spanish. As Rodríguez Ramos put it, "All attempts to dispos-sess a society of its stones, its documents, its religions, its people, encoun-ter a barrier, something that cannot be so easily dispossessed: that is the heart and the throat. Sounds are not so easy to take away, nor is the heart" (conversation with the author, February 2016).

I hear Rodríguez Ramos here to be suggesting that what he terms a "flamenco society"—produced in the Morisco resistance to Catholic repression—was, to an important degree, articulated sonically, through the musical practices that such resistance gave shape to and the affects that these practices orchestrated and expressed. Indelibly marked by the ex-periences and aesthetics of Muslims, Jews, and Roma peoples, flamenco contained a fundamental otherness that the Church might tolerate as an element of "popular culture" but that it could never fully appropriate or re-define. While the source of this otherness might have been long forgotten, a condition for survival in the face of Inquisitorial suspicion and threat, it would continue to anchor an affective life resistant to the projects of cen-tralized power emanating from Madrid. The time of the voice, I hear him to say, is not the time of history (of empty homogenous time). The cry of the flamenco singer, as Rodríguez Ramos hears it, is a repository of sensory memory, of fragments of past experience that encompass both sides of the Mediterranean and that when heard properly articulate the temporality of that postulated territory of al-Andalus/Andalusia. I read the poetics of Andalucismo, its tireless celebration of flamenco's musical aesthetic, as an effort to attune the ear to this erstwhile continent of memory.

As the Italian thinker Giorgio Agamben has recently noted, for the ancient Greeks, music bore an intimate relation to politics. By giving expression to that which cannot be said in language, to the limits of the sayable, music demarcates the foundation on which any word, language, or discourse will necessarily depend. Glossing the views of Plato and Aristotle, Agamben writes,

> In every age, humans are always more or less intentionally educated to politics and prepared for it through music, even before this happens through traditions and precepts that are transmitted by means of language. . . . Just as, for a soldier, the trumpet blast or the drumbeat is as effective as the order of a superior (or even more than it), so in every field and before every discourse, the feelings and moods that precede action and thought are musically determined and oriented. In this sense, the state of music defines the political condition of a given society better than and prior to any other index. (2018, 101–2)

In Agamben's view, music—at least potentially—reminds us, and celebrates the fact, that a fundamental aspect of our lives cannot be said in language, that language is not our voice, or not all of it. We might say music can effect a break between who we are and what we say, a break, I want to suggest, that is also a new foundation (call it a sonorous foundation) for what we can subsequently articulate linguistically. Within the tradition of Andalucismo, flamenco constitutes just such a sonorous foundation, one that breaks the historicist hold on the potential meanings of medieval Iberia so as to interrupt the prohibitions that ensure the "purified" identity of Spain (purely Catholic, purely European). In doing so, it becomes the site for a reconfiguring of the affective and epistemic dispositions from which the virtual territories of Andalucismo can be charted. The historical poetics of flamenco—as elaborated by such proponents of the tradition as Infante, Gil Benumeya, and Rodríguez Ramos—seek to excavate the sounds of an Arabic society from within the Andalusian musical form so as to lay a sensory foundation for the practices of historical and political reflection and critique they engage in. Forged at the juncture of al-Andalus, Andalusia,

and North Africa, this *fondo sonoro* offers the tradition the space of improvisation within which its claims can be articulated.

Another Andalusian who contributed extensively to the development
of this sonorous thought was Lorca, the Granadan poet whose short life
was extinguished by pro-Franco forces in 1936. Lorca's most well-known
encounter with Andalusian song took place at the 1922 Concurso del Cante
Jondo, as described at the beginning of this chapter. In his presentation
at the conference (and thus as a preface to the musical performances that
would follow thereafter), he underscores the "gestures and lineaments"
of Islamic poetry that lie within the Andalusian musical tradition, reciting verses from three Muslim poets while giving particular emphasis to the
"sublime Ghazzals of love of Hafiz," the fourteenth-century Persian poet
(Lorca 1994, 223). Juxtaposing verses of *cante jondo* and those of Hafiz,
Lorca traces the proximities of image, emotion, and theme across the two
poetic repertoires, giving special attention to the shared vocabularies of
love, anguish, and the presentiment of death—as if the dark, blood-soaked
sentiments he hears in this musical form could only be glimpsed in the mirror provided by the verses of the Arab and Persian poets. "When Hafiz addresses the theme of weeping," he notes, "he does so with the same expressions as our popular poets, with the same spectral construction and on the
basis of the same sentiments" (224).

A sensitive observer of his time and place, Lorca crafted a poetic voice
through an historical anthropology of his home city, Granada—an inquiry
that led him repeatedly outside the literary and conceptual confines of Europe. The Islamic world he was drawn to was not that of the luxuriant ha-
rem, the noble Moor, or even the utopia of inclusion and belonging figured
by the notion of *convivencia*. Rather, to decipher the palimpsest of Granada
required knowledge of the Islamic traditions that had long before left their
indelible marks on the cityscape. Granada spoke to Lorca in a voice composed of multiple strands from across the Mediterranean, a voice he sought
to capture not through imitation but via a creative elaboration that would
do justice to the past, present, and future of the lifeworld he valued. This
voice achieved its purest form not in human speech but in the inarticulate,
almost animal cry of anguish he discerned at the heart of Andalusian *cante
jondo*—what Lorca designated as *la Pena Negra*, the Black Dread.

While readers of Lorca have celebrated his poetic elaboration of the
theme of Andalusian sadness and pain, *la Pena Negra*, his association of
that experiential condition with the Iberian Muslims and their demise is
widely viewed as a flight from history into Orientalist fantasy.[15] Something
is lost in this view, however. As I see it, Lorca's attunement to the Arabic
voice within the flamenco singer's cry takes the form not of a myth but of a

poetic practice that constitutes one of the most productive literary encounters across the Mediterranean of the twentieth century, one that discloses a historical and aesthetic space not easily explored within the normative discourses of civilizational identity that surrounded him.

What is clear is that for many Andalusians, music (and flamenco in particular) becomes a thread that binds them, on the one hand, to the medieval Muslim past, and on the other, across the straits to Morocco, North Africa, and farther on to the east. Moreover, this musical geography of Andalucismo is not limited to the Mediterranean. A particularly interesting account of discovering a shared aesthetic vocabulary linking flamenco to traditions of South Asian Islam is the case of Aziz Balouch.[16] In the early 1930s Balouch traveled from his home in the province of Sindh to Spain for reasons of study. When friends subsequently introduced him to some flamenco records, he was struck by its similarities to Sufi music he knew from Sindh. He recounts, "On hearing this music for the first time, I had an extraordinary spiritual experience, a sense of upliftment impossible to describe in words. At that moment, I could have sworn I had once been a *cantaor*" (Balouch 1968, 5). Balouch went on to write an analysis of the connections between the geographically distant musical styles, attributing the commonalities to medieval trade routes linking al-Andalus with Damascus and Damascus to South Asia. He later went on to study the Spanish art with some of the virtuosos of the day and became an accomplished flamenco artist himself (Calado Olivo 2013).

For most scholars of Andalusian folk musics, Balouch's thesis is not considered a serious contribution to the historical study of flamenco. The relations it posits between the Sufi music of Sindh and twentieth-century flamenco are too distant, too faint, to serve as the basis for a historical claim. From the standpoint of flamencology, a discourse whose central concerns and epistemological assumptions were shaped by nineteenth-century historicism, such distant relations are a curiosity but hardly constitute a valid historical object. Balouch's ear, however, hears these distant relations as more than a curiosity—hears them as something more akin to two estranged family members resembling each other in some aspects but entirely dissimilar in others. Passionately compelled by what he hears, he writes a book documenting these family resemblances (Wittgenstein 1973), but also hones and develops his skill as a performer of flamenco, becoming a virtuoso in his own right. In contrast to teaching manuals for students of flamenco found in Spain, the approach he develops and offers as a guide to other students of the genre shows a marked debt to South Asian ascetic principles: among them, abstention from alcohol, special dietary restrictions with a preference for vegetarianism, and limited sexual activity.

The complex and often indecipherable network of relations across the music of these times and places articulates a sonic territory—a *fondo sonoro*—one that musicians from the mid-twentieth century forward would increasingly set out to explore. These journeys have resulted in a wide spectrum of musical collaborations, bringing together Spanish flamenco artists, specialists in medieval European music, Moroccan performers of Andalusi music, as well as musicians specializing in other Arabic genres. Exploiting the possibilities of musical connection, affordances of sound and style grounded in affinities both historical and acoustic, these collaborative ventures have produced a rich variety of musical mélanges, blendings of diverse yet related traditions that, in the view of some observers, exemplify the heterogeneous and inherently open object that flamenco has always been (Cruces Roldán 2008)—and that al-Andalus has sometimes stood to symbolize.

Admittedly, these musical fusions have been propelled in part by incentives emanating from the world music industry, which has over the last thirty years fashioned an audience for such north-south sounds.[17] Indeed, the celebration of cultural hybridity that this industry stages and promotes easily aligns itself with the discourse of *convivencia* that at times has accompanied and framed collaborations by Spaniards and North Africans. Such musical collaborations, however, have been shaped by more than the marketplace. Notably, they unfold along lines that reflect possibilities, affinities, and harmonies immanent to the music itself as well as potentialities internal to the wider conditions of skill and expertise, of sensibility and aesthetic judgment, of association and communication that the elaboration and performance of this music requires and effects. As I explore below, the sociability of this music, the web of relationship it sets in motion, describes a cartography of association and belonging, of ways of fitting heterogeneous things together in a single organized space. This space, one witnessed and explored by Blas Infante, takes the form of a musical geography stretching from Spain into the Middle East—and back, as a distant echo, to al-Andalus.

PERFORMING AL-ANDALUS

The Tetería Tetuán (Tétouan teahouse) is located just a few blocks from Plaza Nueva, the touristic heart of Granada, with the medieval Muslim quarter of the Albayzín rising on one side and the Alhambra looming from the cliffs above on the other. The first day I visited the locale's Moroccan owners, Ridwan and Ahmed, had hired a photographer to come by and take some promotional pictures of the musical group they had formed, an ensemble specializing in what they called *maghrebi-andalusi* music. The shop itself, as with all of the many other tourist-vying teahouses along the street, was laid out in full Oriental regalia: the turbaned-man-in-the-casbah paintings; the low, velvet-draped benches and cushioned chairs; the incense and water pipes; the ouds and inlayed platters set on the walls. Members of the group arrived and changed into the special dress they had brought for the photo: for the men, a white *jalabiyya*, tarbush, and pointy Moroccan shoes; for the women, colorful *jalabiyyas* and sandals. The group was composed of four Spaniards (two women and two men, all but one converts to Islam) and three Moroccan men. As they prepared for the photograph, they chatted and joked with each other in Moroccan Arabic and Spanish, sometimes resorting to classical Arabic as an occasional lingua franca of the ensemble.

The linguistic heteroglossia of the group corresponds to the hybrid musical form they play, evident in the appellation used to describe the genre: *maghrebi-andalusi*. The hyphen, however, needs a little explanation. There is a genre of music performed in Morocco today called Andalusi, variations of which are found in other North African and Middle Eastern countries, most prominently Algeria and Syria.[18] This genre is a direct descendant of musical traditions of medieval Iberia and is recognized as such in Morocco, although it has also undergone many revisions and accretions over the intervening centuries. In Spain, however, the term Andalusi is usually used to designate the musical forms specific to medieval Muslim Iberia, forms that were lost at the end of the Muslim presence in the region (forcibly suppressed by the burgeoning Christian powers). Thus the term *maghrebi-andalusi* (used by some musicians today as a national variant of *Arabo-Andalusi*) suggests a music that recuperates and interprets the medieval Iberian tradition via its contemporary North African forms. The hyphen, in other words, corresponds to geographic and historical differences but also to the aspiration to transcend them.

Javier plays the clarinet. He had converted to Islam some years ago, shortly after having begun his university studies.[19] Before conversion, as he told me, he had been a committed Catholic and was even a member of the Catholic-nationalist association Opus Dei. He narrates his decision to convert this way: "I was always very religious and therefore curious to learn about other religions. During my first year at the university, I took a class in Islamic studies. Islam's unified and comprehensive theology resonated with my own rationalist inclinations. After having studied it for a semester, I made the decision to covert" (conversation with the author, Granada, June 2011). Javier decided to pursue a major in Arabic studies at the University of Granada, a decision that, among other things, led him to spend a year at a language school in Yemen. He also began on his own to learn as much as he could about Andalusian musical traditions, reading literature on the topic in both Spanish and Arabic; finding ways to meet and play with some of Granada's leading Andalusi musicians (many from Morocco); traveling to Fez, Tangier, and Tétouan to listen to Maghrebi musicians, often at *zawiyyas*, the Sufi sites of ritual practice and learning where Andalusi music is performed. After a few years of study, he developed and taught a course at the university on Andalusi music. Beyond his current group, he has pioneered a number of initiatives to promote awareness of the music, including organizing a series of public workshops as well as setting up a website that provides translation of key concepts and aesthetic vocabulary alongside historical information on such themes as its medieval textual sources and contemporary Middle Eastern variants.

In contrast to many Andalusian converts or nationalist activists, Javier is often very skeptical of claims about similarities between medieval Andalusian cultural forms and present-day musical and aesthetic practices:

> Converts are always telling you that this or that musical form is Andalusi and how much they love it, but most of the time what they are listening to is Egyptian pop or some generic oriental stuff sold to tourists as authentic but that actually has none of the tonal patterns or rhythmic structures of Andalusi music. People always like to say that flamenco shares much with Andalusi music, but the scales, the instrumentation, the performance styles, it's all different.

Javier's attitude on this point reflects his distaste for what he views as the naive enthusiasm for things Andalusian promoted by regional nationalists and converts—though, as I mentioned above, few scholars of flamenco would dispute the claim that flamenco has certain connections to Arabo-Andalusi musical traditions (see Farmer 1925; Reynolds 2009; Washabaugh 1995). The recuperation and performance of this medieval tradition for a contemporary Spanish public requires the discerning ear of the musicologist, in Javier's view, lest the task of reviving a valued local musical form be compromised by the Romantic fictions that commonly deceive the untrained listener.

Across the decade of the 2000s, opportunities to perform Arabo-Andalusi music declined in southern Spain due both to cutbacks in state funding for cultural events following the economic downturn of 2008 and to the cultural policies of the conservative party ruling at the time, the Partido Popular, which tended to favor what they view to be properly Spanish musical styles (a designation that includes flamenco), over those with a Middle Eastern provenance. In this context of limited opportunity,

Javier and some of his musical collaborators have accepted employment performing in the medieval fairs that are frequently held in towns throughout Andalusia. Recruited by the organizers to play medieval troubadour music, they stroll through the crowd dressed in attire characteristically worn today by Andalusi musicians in Morocco while performing songs forged from a blend of flamenco, Andalusi, and Arabic styles. Such musical mélanges, Javier complains, are in increasing demand by concert promoters and sponsors, a trend that he fears will lead to an erosion of Andalusi musical knowledge as its complicated time signatures and quarter tone intervals are simplified and assimilated to flamenco musical norms.

Despite his concerns for the historical authenticity of the music he plays, Javier often finds himself obliged to make obeisance to the contemporary tastes and musical proclivities of Spanish audiences. This involves the balancing and combining of aesthetic criteria from diverse traditions. Spanish audiences, for example, do not have the patience to sit through a performance lasting many hours, as Andalusi music traditionally entails and as it is still performed in Morocco. Rather than impose this strenuous effort on his listeners, Javier and his ensemble seek to gently retune the sensibilities of their listeners by interspersing the long segments that audiences find tiring with shorter pieces that incorporate elements from flamenco, the familiarity of the motifs providing a rest for the ears of audiences unaccustomed to the lengthy performances.

His description of a recent project offers another significant example of the creative synthesis he has taken on:

> In the most "commercial" repertory of Arabic music, there is a song that is played everywhere because it has a melody pleasing to Western audiences: "Lamma bada yatathanna." It is an oriental composition from an Egyptian or Syrian composer of the late nineteenth or early twentieth century, I have to check, and not part of the Andalusian heritage. The rhythm, for example, is 10/8, called *sama'i*, of Turkish origin. But the poetry over which the melody was written is a *muwashshah* considered to be Andalusian, though I don't know from which anthology it was taken. (conversation with the author, 2011)

A little background on the poetry used in Andalusi music will be useful here. The poetic form at the heart of the Andalusi repertoire is called the *muwashshah*. Originating in Andalusia around the ninth or tenth century, this strophic form was written in classical Arabic and is structured around two alternating rhyme patterns. However, the last few lines of the *muwashshah*, known as the *kharja*, or "departure," are written in a different lexical register, sometimes in colloquial Arabic or Hebrew, though also in Aljamiado (i.e., Hispano-Romance, or a mixture of Romance, Hebrew, and Arabic written with Arabic script). The *kharjas* had remained a mystery until the middle decades of the twentieth century when the British scholar S. M. Stern and the Spanish Arabist García Gómez were able to decipher the antique Spanish lying beneath the Arabic calligraphy (see Mallette 2010). As Karla Mallette observes, this discovery "culminated in the integration of an Arab past into a narrative of national origin and the identification of an Arab voice as the earliest expression of a modern European identity" (168).[20]

Javier goes on to describe how in responding to his friends' requests for a Spanish version of an Andalusi song, he was himself led to the Aljamiado *kharjas*:

> Anyway, when our group was making a recording, our friends and families insisted that we also sing something in Spanish, so in a few of the songs we translated, more or less, some of the strophes and sang them in Spanish. But with the *Lamma bada*, a song that had already been sung in Spanish, I thought I would try to find a *kharja* with the same meter in the published collections of *kharjas* by different authors. I didn't have to look long, as one of the most cited *kharjas* in the scholarly literature fit the theme of the song perfectly. Because this *kharja* fit so well with the meter and meaning of the Arabic poetry of the *Lamma*, we inserted it into the song and recorded it that way. (conversation with the author, 2011)

The *kharja* that Javier incorporated into the *Lamma bada* is usually attributed to Muqaddam ibn Muafá al-Qabrí, the ninth- and tenth-century poet often thought to have composed the first *muwashshah*. Since Stern and García Gómez's initial discovery of the Hispano-Romance words behind the Arabic letters, the poem has been transliterated and translated in many different ways. The version used by Javier's ensemble reads:

> bay-se mio coraçon de mib
> ya rabbi si se'n tornarad
> tan mal mi doler al-garib
> enfermo yed quand sanarad

> (My heart leaves me
> Oh Lord, will he come back?
> My suffering is so great, oh my friend!
> It is sick, when it will be cured)

I want to pause for a moment to consider Javier's process of composition, the forms of knowledge it draws on, the geopolitical conditions that enable it, and the linguistic and musical competencies it requires. Guided by a personal ethic around the historical authenticity of things Andalusian, Javier is quick to point out the non-Andalusian origin of some of the *Lamma*'s components and particularly the extent to which its popularity and circulation owe to its fit with the aesthetic sensibilities of Western listeners shaped in part by the burgeoning world music industry. However, despite the song's compromised status, Javier puts it to use, an act impelled, as he tells it, by affective ties to "friends and family." His solution, however, is not to produce a modern translation of an ancient textual fragment but rather to uncover an artifact capable of inhabiting—and bridging—multiple languages at once (the verse in Aljamiado, again a hybrid of colloquial Arabic and medieval Spanish), an aesthetic gesture that reworks a contemporary musical form to provide space for an ancient one.

This act of composition, it might be claimed, is modeled on the *kharja* itself. In Andalusi poetry, the *muwashshah*—spoken in classical Arabic—corresponds to the voice of the lover, while the *kharja*—spoken in the colloquial, often a hybrid of Arabic, Hebrew, and Romance—expresses the response of the beloved. Like the *kharja*, Javier's response to the ties of relationship is to shift voice: from Arabic, a foreign language to his audience, to a hybrid form (Aljamiado) within which his listeners can orient themselves, if awkwardly. Note as well that the aesthetics of the *kharja* corresponded to a particular sociological condition, as a gesture from the Arabic-speaking poet to the plurilingual context of his performance—a gesture repeated in Javier's recrafting of the *Lamma*. Importantly, this gesture does not invent a history where none existed. The *kharja* is already what can be called a compromised form, less the exemplar of a poetic tradition than a hybrid, the work of a bricoleur, crafted of necessity from the poetic resources generated by the medieval encounter of hierarchically related languages. The incorporation of the *kharja* into the musical structure of the *Lamma* today and its ability to resonate with the tastes and language skills of contemporary listeners is founded on the poetic form's own heteroglossia, one that enables it to move across both languages and historical contexts.

To speak of heteroglossia is also to speak of power. The genre expresses a relationship between two voices, a unitary and homogenous voice of the (male) lover and a fractured and heterogeneous voice of the (female) beloved. The tensions and oppositions that shape the amorous attachment are those intrinsic to the hierarchical society from which this poetry emerged. Is the heterogeneous voice of the beloved destined to be never quite at home, or does it open up possibilities of belonging, of living together out-side the master order of territory-language-religion? This question is not just hypothetical but ever present in the life of this musical ensemble.

Two months after the photography session, one of the female singers decided to leave the group. Her reason for leaving, as she later told me, was that she was frustrated by the fact that all the solo vocal parts were sung by the male singer, with the two women only singing during the choral sections. Notably, this gendered distribution of voices stands in contrast to current practice in Morocco, and more specifically, Tétouan, where it has become common for women to take on prominent vocal roles in An-dalusian musical performances. It would seem that Granada's embrace of its own Mediterranean past does not always extend to the Mediterranean present. *Mediodía*, in other words, is no utopia of inclusion.[21]

Certainly Javier's engagement with the Andalusi musical tradition in many ways bears the imprint of its modern European context: Andalusia's heritage industry ensures an interested public, as does the creation and marketing of a hybrid Andalusian sound by the world music industry. The close if unequal economic relations between Spain and Morocco ensure access to Moroccan musicians and musical expertise, making it affordable for Javier to study under the guidance of Moroccan experts in the genre. Moreover, his ensemble's practice space is a *tetería* in the Albayzín owned by his Moroccan bandmates and kept afloat economically by the Orien-talist fantasies of travelers and tourists who come to Granada looking for the treasures of the East (while staying safely within Europe). Yet while Javier's musical practice is enabled by these economic and political factors, it is not, I am arguing, exhaustively determined by them. The aesthetic sen-sibilities he cultivates and teaches, the geography of knowledge he artic-ulates in practice—weaving together both sides of the Mediterranean in order to recover a lost musical form—his acquisition of comprehension and fluency in medieval Arabic poetic forms, the patterns of friendship, association, and belonging enacted along the course of this endeavor: in all of these ways, Javier's musical wanderings trace the cartography of a Europe deeply entwined with Arabo-Islamic aesthetics and constitutively bound to the other side of the Mediterranean. While the economic sustain-ability of Andalusi music today depends on the fascination and romance of al-Andalus as promoted by the heritage industry and through the cultural politics of the Andalusian state, the songs bear witness to a different polit-ical and cultural geography than that promoted by mainstream tourism or state managers of cultural identity. Such a practice of learning, sociability, and performance reshapes the way dimensions of the past articulate with the present and future, offering for some a palpable vision of a different

Spain or Europe than that being presently consolidated around an anti-immigrant political platform.

MUSICAL HERMANDAD

Ahmed, co-owner of the *tetería* and the group's violinist (though a master of the oud and banjo as well), came to Granada thirty years ago in order to study Spanish literature at the University of Granada. The university has long been a destination for young Moroccans, an artifact of the role assigned to the institution early in the twentieth century in the context of Spanish colonialism as a site where Moroccan students could be trained in the competencies and concerns appropriate to a modernizing colonial population. As with so many Arab visitors to and residents of Granada, he expresses his sense of ease and familiarity with the city through the oft-heard refrain, "it feels like home here, like Fez." He arrived already an accomplished musician, having studied at a conservatory in Morocco, though also having learned much through his participation in Sufi performances. By his own account, it was not until he came to Granada—"Andalusi music's home," as he says—that he became seriously interested in the genre. Among the North African musicians I came to know in Granada, this story was commonplace: trained in other musical genres, some with careers in pop or rock and roll, after some time in Granada they had been drawn to Andalusi music, a genre of opportunity for Arab immigrants, to be sure, but also, as I repeatedly heard, a natural expression of their own historical attachment to southern Spain, a testament to their claim of belonging. In the context of pervasive tensions over the place of Muslims in Europe, Andalusi music, an Iberian aesthetic form, offered both a livelihood and an image of belonging where few such images were available to Muslims.[22]

Ahmed has played with a number of the most renowned musicians of Andalusian musical styles in both Morocco and Spain, including some of the pioneering figures in the European early music movement who, from the late 1960s, began to study and attempt to recreate medieval Andalusian music. Some of the Spanish musicians who carried this project of historical re-creation forward—led by Eduardo and Gregorio Paniagua, Luís Delgado, and Begoña Olavide—had originally been inspired by listening to UNESCO recordings of Moroccan Andalusian music (Reynolds 2009, 185). This gave impetus to a series of collaborative efforts involving Spanish and North African musicians.[23] Many of the Spanish musicians ended up spending long periods in Morocco, especially Tétouan and Tangier, learning to play medieval Andalusian music through the lens provided by contemporary North Africa Andalusian traditions. With only the corpus of *muwashshahāt* at hand and with few surviving indications of what medieval Andalusi music sounded like or how it was to be performed, these musicians (as I mentioned above) had to distill the medieval tradition from its contemporary offshoots, the Moroccan being the closest. The result of this exchange, as Dwight Reynolds's work (2009) has explored, is a fusion of the principles and aesthetics of the European Early Music movement on the one hand and a living oral tradition on the other. Commenting on a more recent endeavor by these musicians to put to music the poetry of such medieval Andalusian figures as the mystic Ibn al-Arabi (d. 1240) and poet Ibn al-Khatib (d. 1375), Reynolds writes, "In all of these performances, the texts are authentically medieval, but the melodies are taken from modern Andalusian traditions from North Africa, and the aesthetic treatment is rooted in the ideas of the European Early Music movement, that is, in small ensembles rather than large orchestra and with use of reconstructions of period instruments, a fascinating hybrid based upon three different sources—and concepts—of 'authenticity'" (Reynolds 2009, 187). Here, a musical project founded on historicist assumptions emphasizing the discontinuity of a past practice from its contemporary heir (i.e., the European Early Music movement) is potentially rerouted by a tradition whose criteria of continuity and historical fidelity leave scope for processes of transformation and accretion (i.e., the Moroccan Andalusi musical tradition).

As I have stressed above, the new amalgamation that these musicians have forged is, of course, also enabled by and responsive to the market for world music, not to mention a range of new political and economic linkages uniting Spain with North Africa from the second half of the twentieth century. But the trans-Mediterranean impulses and aesthetic forms that have emerged as a result of this recuperative project have created solidarities and collaborative engagements that extend well beyond a calculus of economic advantage. Two of the leaders in the field of medieval Arabo-Andalusian musical traditions, Carlos Paniagua and Begoña Olavide, set up a music school to teach the tradition to poorer children from the casbah in Tangier, residing there for six years. Indeed, many of the musicians who have become interested and involved in Andalusi music have accommodated themselves to a life that straddles both sides of the Mediterranean.

While waiting for the photographer, I spoke with Ahmed about his encounters with some of these pioneering figures of the Andalusian music scene. "I remember when I first sat and played together with Luís Delgado," he began. "He knew the compositions very well and had great technical skills, but he had no sense of the *character* of the music. The character was missing from his playing. He was shocked the first time we played, as he saw he had to learn a new way to play" (conversation with the author, 2011). He demonstrated on the violin the contrast between Delgado's initial playing style and his own, emphasizing the colorations and textures specific to Andalusi music and their absence from Delgado's style.

Ahmed has become a committed advocate of Andalusi music and frequently performs in concerts organized by the Junta Andalusi. As with Javier, with whom he now plays, he has increasingly been drawn to perform pieces that combine Andalusi music and flamenco (a combination, as I mentioned, with which many musicians in the region now experiment). As opposed to Javier, Ahmed insists on the commonalities binding flamenco and Andalusi forms, and he again showed me on the violin some of the stylistic and tonal overlappings. He is particularly adamant about the need to teach Andalusi music in schools and has for a long while been working with other musicians and promoters of Andalusian culture to build a school in Spain that would offer instruction in the genre: "People often come up to me after a concert and want to know more about the music. Unfortunately, there are no institutions that teach about it. In Morocco, there are conservatories where one can learn all about the music, but here, in Andalusia itself, there are no institutions that support it. It is only through the individual efforts of people who care about it that it survives here" (conversation with the author, 2011).

As the oldest and most musically knowledgeable of the group, the others look to Ahmed for direction when needed. For many years now, he has been taking young Spaniards interested in Andalusi music under his wing, helping them to cultivate musical skills and sensibilities and establishing collaborative musical projects with some of them. Set right on the edge of the narrow medieval quarter of the Albayzín, where many North Africans now make a trade catering to tourists, the teahouse he runs with his brother provides a modest income.[24] His livelihood has been enabled by the cultural forms and expertise he has to offer, especially to tourists and nationalist promoters of Andalusian culture. That said, the trajectories he has followed—aesthetic, social, religious, geographic—map out a territory not simply of an Arab living in Europe but of an Arabic Europe, one whose historical possibility has been shaped by Andalucismo.

HEARING PLURALISM

Carmen sings with the group of Javier and Ahmed. She grew up in the nearby town of Motril, where she sang in a municipal choir that performed medieval *cantigas* (praise songs to the Virgin Mary) and other folk genres. Later on, she sang in a rock band. Carmen came to Granada to study art

history at the university, but when she discovered that there was little financial aid for art history students and far more for students of Arabic, she
decided to enroll in the Arabic program. It is there she met Javier, who invited her to join the Andalusi music group he and Ahmed were forming.
Although she had never sung Andalusi music, nor spoken or sung in Arabic, she soon found she liked it and continued with the group for a year.

Carmen attributes some her musical and political sensibilities to her father, who sang with her in the *cantigas* choir. A devout Catholic, according
to Carmen, her father belongs to the Catholic Action Workers Brotherhood
(Hermandad Obrera de Acción Católica [HOAC]), an association that promotes workers' rights and provides various forms of social assistance to
the needy. He is also a member of Motril Acoge (Motril Welcomes), a non-
governmental organization that offers assistance to immigrants and works
to promote respect for immigrant rights in the country. According to Carmen, her father's proimmigrant activism has led him to get to know and
establish friendships with some of the North African families now residing
in Motril. He and his wife are longtime members of the same local choral
group that Carmen sang with as a child, which performs works from the
thirteenth-century song repertory known as the *Cantigas de Santa Maria*.[25]

Until the early twentieth century, medieval scholars considered the
cantigas to be a direct offspring of French devotional songs. The dominant
narrative among medievalists at the time, as the Portuguese musicologist
Manuel Pedro Ferreira notes, was that "Paris was the undisputed center of
cultural activity and the sole origin of musical novelty and fashion" (Ferreira 2015, 1–2). In the 1920s this consensus view was challenged by the
Spanish Arabist Julián Ribera, the same scholar whose work had been piv-
otal to Blas Infante's thesis on the origins of flamenco. Ribera asserted, in
sharp contrast to the majority view, that the music of the *cantigas* was entirely Arabic. Ribera's claim was subsequently challenged by the priest and
Catholic nationalist Higinio Anglés, who in a 1943 essay insists on the Parisian basis of the *cantigas* and rejects outright the suggestion that the musical form owed anything whatsoever to Arabic traditions. Anglés was a disciple of Felipe Pedrell—whose argument on the Byzantine origins of *cante
jondo* I mentioned at the beginning of the chapter—and had also studied
with two leading musicologists in Germany, one of them a specialist in
medieval Parisian polyphony (Ferreira 2015). Much like the debate discussed above regarding the *kharja*, arguments within musicology about the
Arabic constituents of the *cantigas* have taken place in an institutional context highly ambivalent toward the presence of Arabic and Islamic elements
within European cultural forms.[26] Recent works on the *cantigas*, while taking issue with Ribera's claim for their origin as entirely Arabic, support the

view that at least the rhythmic structure of the songs is derived from Arabic musical traditions (see Ferreira 2015).

Though not a scholar on the topic, Carmen's father views the affinities between the *cantigas* and Arabo-Andalusi music as a pedagogical opportunity for promoting immigrant rights, and he has organized a number of public concerts where his choral group is joined by musicians performing Andalusi music. When I asked Carmen why her father thought such musical events important, she said, "It is to show that there is a mixture [*hay una mezcla*], that the two fit together here because they share so much. And this is true. Some of my friends ask why I hang out with Moroccans and people from North Africa. They have no interest in it. But now that I have gotten to know them, I see we have so many things in common, tastes, gestures, language" (conversation with author, March 2013). For both Carmen and her father, musical commonalities—the *fondo sonoro* left by the complex medieval sociology that characterized Mediterranean life— undergird an ethical stance against contemporary calls to harden the barriers between North Africa and Spain. The medieval hybridity of the *cantigas* sung in Motril or the Arabo-Andalusi *nubas* performed in Granada is reinscribed on the surface of social and political life today in the activities of association, sympathy, and friendship enacted by these two Andalusians.

MUSICAL LIFE

In the introduction to this chapter, I described as one of its primary goals an interrogation of sound and music as historical media. How do sounds, I wanted to know, give shape to the way past, present, and future hang together within the tradition of Andalucismo? In concluding this chapter, I want to return to this question by linking the preceding discussion of Andalusian sound and music to some of the broader theoretical foundations of the book. Let me start by briefly recalling an observation by W. E. B. Du Bois mentioned in the first chapter, one that bears directly on this topic. As I noted, in his autobiographical reflections Du Bois describes with fondness an African melody he learned as a boy from his grandmother. This song, he reflects, "traveled down to us and we sing it to our children, knowing as little as our fathers what its words may mean, but knowing well the meaning of its music" ([1988] 2007, 58). Pause for a moment on the final words of the sentence. What does "knowing well the meaning" of this melody mean for Du Bois? He does tell us emphatically that this song was his "one direct cultural connection" to the continent, to a place he was barely conscious of in youth but that over the course of his life gradually came to take on an immense significance for him, for how he understood himself and the history of which he was a part. This "knowing well," in other words, would seem to embrace, simultaneously, both the moments on his grandmother's knee and a lengthy process by which the meaning of that sonic connective tissue revealed itself through Du Bois's experience of racism in the United States. The meaning of this particular melody, he suggests, is bound up with his profound attachment to Africa; the melody is one essential, experientially dense component of this attachment. As I see it, Du Bois's reflection on this African melody warrants two reciprocal conclusions: on the one hand, as his encounter with "the race concept" accumulated across his life, the song revealed in ever greater depth its latent meaning, while on the other hand, as his life proceeded, the song increasingly lent its own musical gestures to new situations and events, inflecting or coloring the way Du Bois would come to experience them. The song, in short, resonated within diverse domains of his life, and those domains in turn resonated within the song.

Wittgenstein offers some comments on music that I believe are helpful in further elaborating Du Bois's reflections on the matter. In accord with his broader approach to philosophical issues, Wittgenstein rejected both formalist theories—which would identify music in terms of a set of essential properties and treat it as autonomous from other cultural domains—as well as expressivist ones—which aimed to ground musical meaning in the inner experiences of the listener (e.g., thoughts, images, kinesthetic sensations). Just as socially organized speech and behavior could not be understood according to the model of a "private language," so also music, as a social practice, had to be grasped through its public dimensions. Instead of offering a general theory about musical understanding, the philosopher emphasized the plurality of ways that any given musical form might relate to the broader cultural context from which it emerged. Commenting on the possible connections binding music to its outside, he notes,

Does the theme point to nothing beyond itself? Oh yes! But that means:—The impression it makes on me is connected with things in its surroundings—e.g. with the existence of the German language & its intonation, but that means with the whole field of our language games. If I say e.g.: it's as if here a conclusion were being drawn, or, as if here something were being confirmed, or, as if this were a reply to what came earlier,—then the way I understand it clearly presupposes familiarity with conclusions, confirmations, replies, etc. (Wittgenstein 1988, 59)

Notably, Wittgenstein is not suggesting here that the meaning of a musical theme can be found in the language uses that connect to it, as if one translated the other. Rather, a musical theme is inflected or colored by structured activities ("language games") that make up a form of life. As Béla Szabados highlights in his comments on this passage, for Wittgenstein a piece acquires meaning for us through the way it "resonates" with different aspects of our form of life: "The musical phrase is not about something—it does not picture some slice of the world—but it is borne out of a cultural tradition and can best be understood in its connections with the forms of life and associated language games of that tradition. Music is not alone, as formalists suggest; it resonates with the whole field of our language games—with our other musical and cultural practices" (Szabados 2014, 92). Importantly, there is no general principle underlying the connections between musical practices and other language games. Their connections, the resonances that bind them, correspond to the form of life that embraces them.

Wittgenstein's observations, as I understand them, do not pertain solely to musical meaning (which would presuppose music as an autonomous domain) but also concern the meaning of music within our lives, the ways in which our musical practices resonate across different arenas of daily existence. Such a resonance is not given, and indeed, Wittgenstein felt that much of contemporary music had little connection to modern forms of life. But his manner of inquiry, attending to patterns of felt connection between music and other practices, is particularly valuable in considering the place of flamenco and other musics within Andalucismo. As we have seen, the rhetorics and poetics of Andalucismo, as well as the listening practices the tradition promotes, seek to draw attention to the way these musical forms inhabit diverse arenas of Andalusian culture, politics, and history. Such discourses and practices are essential to the formation of historical sensibilities that open up the temporalities of Andalucismo, the meaningful connections between al-Andalus and present-day Andalusia. As a meaningful but nonreferential practice, music helps attune us to the embodied, "tonal" aspects of a given form of life, to life's noncoincidence with reason and language, a perspective shared both by Wittgenstein and the Romantics.

The terms of commonality that link Spain to the Middle East through the passageway of al-Andalus—Carmen's "tastes, gestures, language"—operate at the sensory level, a substrate of sonic correspondences and aesthetic affinities. In this chapter, I have approached this substrate through the figure of the *fondo sonoro*, a notion that conjoins two ideas, both a background of potentialities and a space of improvisation. There is an improvisatory dimension to Andalucismo, evident in Javier's account of the task of recovering and reworking Andalusi music in order to make it audible to a contemporary Spanish ear but also in the nomadic, volatile itineraries of many of the tradition's leading exponents.

Andalucismo attunes one to a musicality intrinsic to life, to the resonances of Andalusian music across the diverse moments of one's experience. By imbuing life with the musicality of flamenco, the tradition releases possibilities of thought and feeling foreclosed by the historicist discourses of nationalism. Admittedly, flamenco has itself often been incorporated within such nationalist discourse, and indeed, many practices of Andalusian origin (e.g., bullfighting) have come to stand as figures of Spanish identity. But flamenco also enfolds other histories than the conventional Spanish one, and it is these other histories that Andalucismo makes it possible for us to hear.

CHAPTER 4

The Universe from the Albayzín

In the final moment of Italo Calvino's *Invisible Cities*, Kublai Khan wonders despairingly whether the route traced by the succession of cities described to him by his interlocutor (the explorer Marco Polo) did not lead, "in ever narrowing circles," to the "infernal city"—a figure perhaps signaling Calvino's own despair over the dystopian direction of modern life. Marco Polo's response is as follows:

> The inferno of the living is not something that will be; if there is one, it is what is already here, the inferno where we live every day, that we form by being together. There are two ways to escape suffering it. The first is easy for many: accept the inferno and become such a part of it that you can no longer see it. The second is risky and demands constant vigilance and apprehension: seek and learn to recognize who and what, in the midst of the inferno, are not inferno, then make them endure, give them space. (Calvino 1974, 165)

While the first escape might be called "historicism," a mode of knowledge that naturalizes and hence legitimates the present, it is the second that interests me here: that "vigilance and apprehension" that does not flee from the dense reality of the spaces it surveys into the realm of fantasy but painstakingly seeks out and excavates valuable potentialities and forms that make up hidden (or not readily visible) dimensions of the present and "give[s] them space." These forms appear fantastical from the eschatological standpoint of "the inferno where we live every day," but they are, nonetheless, integral—if difficult to recognize—elements of everyday existence and essential to its possible redemption.

The city I am concerned with in this chapter, and for which I have invoked Marco Polo's reflection, is Granada. Nestled against the often snow-covered peaks of the Sierra Nevada, Granada is renowned for both its natural and architectural beauty, embodied most spectacularly in its Muslim-era monuments. The heart of the city is formed by two opposing hillsides, their descending slopes intersecting at the rumbling waters of the Darro river. On one of the hilltops above the river sits the vast complex of the Alhambra, Spain's most popular monument among tourists and a stunning accomplishment of medieval Muslim art and architecture. On the opposing hill ascends the neighborhood of the Albayzín, the city's one-time Muslim quarter, its winding cobblestone streets lined with houses oriented around interior gardens (called *carmenes*) reminiscent of those found in the old quarters of many cities in the Middle East (though most are early twentieth-century reconstructions). Few other cities in Europe exhibit in such spectacular fashion the lineaments of a medieval Mediterranean society prominently on display in its Islamic, Jewish, and Christian monuments. The city's configuration of architectural, aesthetic, and natural elements, sedimented into a unique historical mélange, has inspired writers, poets, and musicians for centuries, with Washington Irving's 1823 *Tales of the Alhambra* being perhaps the most well-known literary treatment. Indeed, there are few approaches to the city that do not pass through the Orientalist fantasies of countless writers, artists, and travel agents, an imaginary extended, like a thick gauze, over the various hotels and tourist attractions that form the backbone of its economy.

Yet beyond its status as a city of Orientalist dreams, packaged and served for touristic consumption, Granada has long served as an important catalyst for forms of engagement and reflection on the place of Islam and the Middle East within Spain and Europe. In any given year, the city hosts hundreds of cultural events and activities focused on both the Andalusian past and contemporary Muslim societies on topics ranging from music, art, and architecture to contemporary politics. Classes in the Arabic language, in Middle Eastern dance and music, and in Islamic art and calligraphy are available in multiple venues across the city, as are concerts and cultural events featuring Middle Eastern performers. Moreover, scholars, writers, and artists from the Middle East frequently come to the city to participate in conversations and colloquia organized by the many local associations dedicated to fostering scholarly exchange, intercultural dialogue, or simply an appreciation of ancient Muslim and Jewish cultural forms and their contemporary Middle Eastern kin. If the reverberations left by al-Andalus within Iberian society and culture had, from the sixteenth to the nineteenth centuries, found expression primarily within a literary idiom—for example, the *romancero* tradition, the novels of Cervantes and Pérez de Hita, the Romantic tales of the early 1800s—by the early twentieth century that echo was resonating across a range of scholarly discourses, with Granada increasingly positioned as a hub of trans-Mediterranean inquiry and aesthetic expression.

Over the first half of this chapter, I return to the lives of two Granadans who have appeared already at various junctures in the preceding pages and who had a decisive impact on the tradition of Andalucismo: the late nineteenth-century writer Ángel Ganivet and Spain's renowned poet Federico García Lorca. Captivated by their native city, both men dedicated themselves to understanding what they saw to be its distinct mystery and magic. Ascribing their own thought to the city itself, they looked both at Granada and through it, developing what each saw to be a uniquely Granadan perspective on the events of their time.[1] This perspective, decisively *andalucista*, entailed a poetic sensibility for their city's historical textures and particularly for the significance of al-Andalus in its composition. Each, if in different ways, took on himself the task identified by Marco Polo above of discerning the noninferno from the inferno by offering a distinctly Granadan diagnosis of the destructive forces of modernity. The complex urban world revealed through their explorations, in this sense, was only one possible Granada, "not that of today," as Ganivet put it, but "that which could and should be, but which may not ever be" (Ganivet [1896] 2003, 1). In the latter half of this chapter, I turn to present-day Granada in order to trace how the Granadan aesthetics of existence pioneered by Ganivet and Lorca continues to generate and sustain the tradition of Andalucismo—how, in other words, the warp of the Granadan cityscape disrupts our contemporary coordinates of political and aesthetic belonging.

A CITY OF RUINS

Born in Granada in 1865, Ángel Ganivet was one of the leading luminaries of the intellectual world of late nineteenth-century Spain. Writing in a period of great economic and political decline, one whose culmination was marked by Spain's loss of most of its colonial possessions at the conclusion of the Spanish-American War in 1898, Ganivet and his contemporaries— the "generation of '98"—dedicated much of their intellectual efforts to a diagnosis of the causes of Spanish weakness and decay. For a number of these thinkers, the pathway of renewal required an exhumation of a Spanish *Volksgeist*, a project that involved mining the country's past for models that could exemplify and animate a national spirit. In Ganivet's view, to unearth this core dimension of Spanish existence required an investigation into the anthropology of everyday life of the Spanish countryside and an attentiveness to the traces of earlier historical moments embedded within local practices, customs, and myths. His native Granada, a city that had "molded" him, initiating him into "the secret of its own spirit" (Ganivet 1896 [2003], 20), became the site of this investigation.[2]

Toward the conclusion of his brief life, Ganivet wrote a short story dedicated to his native city in which core aspects of his poetic vision appear. The story can be read as a meditation on ruin, on Granada as a chronotope of ruin, a conception that underlay Ganivet's assessment and interpretation of Spain's medieval heritage. The story reveals a sensibility for Granada's medieval legacy not as a relic of a bygone age but as a living feature of the city's existence, a sensibility that would make Ganivet's work a touchstone for later generations of *andalucistas.*

Set three thousand years in the future, "Las ruinas de Granada" (The ruins of Granada) speaks of a journey by a "poet" (*un poeta*) and a "wise man" (*un sabio*), who travel together to visit the remnants of Granada, destroyed by a volcano many centuries earlier.[3] For the wise man, embodiment of a scientific perspective, the destroyed city offers up the possibility of encountering a civilization frozen in time, the "petrification of life itself, as it then existed" (Ganivet 1899a, 206), much as the Alhambra is presented to tourists today. For the poet, in contrast, this "vision of the archaeologist" fails to discern the living memory or ideal embodied in the fragmented remains of the city. Once arrived at the site of the former city, the poet discovers among the ruins "not a petrification of life, but rather, another form of life, one for which mankind is no longer necessary, in which the idea lives and speaks in the air, inspired by the poetry that springs forth from the ruins" (206). The destroyed city lives on in the present, he finds, as a form of life whose "fecund experience" (*fecunda experiencia*) allows it to "explain great secrets" to those who will listen (205).

Ganivet's "Las ruinas" should be read in the context of the author's sustained critique of Enlightenment rationalism and the dystopian urban world that he saw as its outcome. In numerous writings, and most directly in his 1896 paean to his native city, *Granada la bella* ([1896] 2003), Ganivet complained bitterly of the subjection of the city to the "funesta simetría" (terrible symmetry) (25) of centralized state power and the concomitant destruction of the city's rich local traditions. In its unrelenting application of a commercial and utilitarian calculus to all matters of urban renewal, the modern capitalist system had, in his view, largely effaced the spiritual and historical foundations that underlay Granada's unique form of life. For Ganivet, as for many of the Romantic poets, the figure of the ruin stood as

a testament to the hubris and violence of modernity as well as its imper-
manence.

From beneath the ruins of this decimation, Ganivet—here in "Las
ruinas" and elsewhere in his writings—sought to uncover what he saw to
be the city's essential, "spiritual" character, one capable of withstanding the
destructive forces of modernization (figured in the story as a volcanic erup-
tion). This "other form of life" (*otra forma de vida*), bearer of an ancient
wisdom, had to be excavated from the sediments of history—sediments
formed by a process both natural and historical as allegorized by the ruin.
Indeed, Ganivet literalizes this merging of nature and history on the visible surface of the decimated city; whereas the wise man, upon surveying
the city from high above, finds only "the remains of the Moorish city," a
museum of its medieval past, the poet discerns in the ruins the shape of
a reclining human body, the figure's crossed hands formed by the fallen
cathedral, its head by the rubble of the Alhambra[4]—a chronotopic figure
(in death? asleep? dreaming?) that remains temporally ambiguous, both
the fragment of a distant past and the intact embodiment of a yet to be
achieved future still waiting to be born.[5]

As the poet sits by the Alhambran head a voice, as much the city's as
his own, begins to speak, or rather—this being Granada—sing. The melancholic song emerges, however, not from the mouth of the poet but from
an ebony box, called an *ideófono*, a device that sings when animated by the
user's thoughts and expressions. Here it seems that only with an instrument
made of African wood from across the Mediterranean, an instrument both
atavistic and futurist, can the poetry of Granada be released from its stony
entombment. This deus ex machina finds a parallel in Ganivet's insistence,
throughout his life, on the significance of the city's Muslim legacy for its
spiritual and aesthetic form of existence and for a political assessment of
Spain's relation to North Africa, as I discuss below.

The song produced by the *ideófono* speaks of ruination and death,
themes that will dominate the *andalucista* interpretation of the Alhambra.
The song begins

> How silently you sleep
> Towers of the Alhambra
> A dream of long centuries
> Slips along your walls
> You sleep, dreaming in death
> And death is far away
> Awaken, for already are drawing near
> The new lights of dawn

And a few stanzas later it closes

> A dream of long centuries
> Slips along your walls
> When it arrives to your foundations
> Your death will be near
> He who like you
> Long centuries were to dream
> And from her sleep will fall
> Into the shadows of nothingness
>   (Ganivet 1899a, 209)

This figure of the ruin highlighted in "Las ruinas de Granada," as the site of a poetic and historical excavation undertaken against the spiritual poverty of the age, will orient much of Ganivet's essayistic writing and shape his reflections on the Arabic and Islamic configuration of the city. While the story's iconography, and particularly the figure of the city in ruins, belongs to a well-established Romantic canon addressing the durability of nature in opposition to the ephemeral quality of human achievements (Hinterhäuser 1980; Rangel 2010), that "other form of life" inhabiting the city's stony remnants is uniquely Andalusian in the way it accommodates the irreducible heterogeneity of the historical layers that make up the urban palimpsest. Existing outside the homogenous, empty time of modernity as an ideal and imaginary space, this Granadan form of life that "lives and speaks in the air, inspired by the poetry that rises up from the ruins" (Ganivet 1899a, 206) is both historical and transcendent, rooted in the legacies of Muslim Iberia but also, in Ganivet's view, achieving a universal value.

As opposed to many of the *andalucistas* who would follow him, Ganivet was not a scholar, amateur or otherwise, of the history of al-Andalus, though his writings did establish an important precedent for a style of reflection on the Andalusian past as a formative dimension of the present. In many ways *Granada la bella*, a book that combines an exploration of the affective, sensuous contours of the city with a damning assessment of the transformations imposed on it in the name of modernization, can be considered the urtext of Andalucismo. Across his explorations, both in this work and elsewhere, Ganivet frequently hones in on the atmospheric qualities of the city. In an essay titled "El alma de las calles" (The spirit of the streets), for example, the account shifts from one Granadan street to the next, highlighting the distinct affective influence each exerts on passersby, the effect made by its width and curvilinear trajectory, the types of social and commercial activity most suitable given the mood it establishes, and

the tone created by churches, monuments, and other historical and architectural features (Ganivet 1899b). Moving across visual, aural, tactile and
visceral registers, Ganivet reveals the city not simply as an aesthetic composition but as a form of life, one characterized by its unique attitudes,
tastes, and styles of activity.

Anticipating an interpretation of Spanish history and identity today associated with the work of Américo Castro, Ganivet finds Granada's unique
form of life to be the result of a dynamic synthesis of diverse historical elements, among them, the Arabic and Islamic elements. This synthesis, however, does not result in a seamless fusion. Rather, the spirit of Granadan
existence celebrated in *Granada la bella*—one imperiled by the modernization of the city—embraces the so-called foreign elements via what Ganivet
calls "an extremely delicate work of assimilation" wherein they are trans-
formed and incorporated while never losing any degree of their alterity.[6]
El arábigo (the Arabic) appears throughout the narrative as an aspect of
Granadan aesthetics, architecture, philosophy, and character, but through
a language of identity that accommodates heterogeneity and difference.
His discussion of the significance of the Alhambra for Granada's tradition
of monumental architecture is characteristic: "As for our monumental
style, I doubt that it can be other than Arabic, not because it is ours, but for
the fact that it is on top of us and all around us" ([1896] 2003, 34). Ganivet
points to a city that is not identical to itself, that has been opened to the
outside by historical circumstance, specifically, the absorbing presence of
the Alhambra and other Muslim-era constructions. Instead of subsuming
this complexity under a single overarching form of identity—the terrible
symmetry of the modern nation-state—Ganivet's Granada embraces its
irreducible heterogeneity, the multiple genealogies, borrowings, amalga-
mations, and mimetic appropriations that contribute to its unique form.
In this fashion, and against the impulse toward purified forms of national
identity, Ganivet proposes the value of living with a complex and unsettling
inheritance.

A similar play of identity and difference appears in Ganivet's observations about Granada's domestic architecture:

> In architecture, we began with the realization that one cannot fight
> against reality; that however high we reached, we would always remain
> far below that which our land and sky afforded us. Artists of more imag-
> ination than we, the Arabs also did not struggle face to face, but rather
> hid in their houses, where they created an architecture of interiority. And
> thus, we also submit, and in this act of submission lies the soul of our
> art . . . our house (*carmen*) is a dove hidden in the forest, to use a phrase

consecrated by the poets, and our city residence, our antique house, was not a place of appearances, of much facade and little depth: it was a house of the patio. ([1896] 2003, 30)

The *carmenes* were originally constructed in the Albayzín during the Nasrid period of the fourteenth century. Etymologically, the word comes from the Arab term *karm*, or vineyard, in reference to the orchard or garden often enclosed within the *carmen*'s walls.[7] In the play of identities that Ganivet sets in motion here, his contemporary Granadans are seen to repeat the theologically defined act of the *carmen*'s former Muslim inhabitants: they "submit" (the literal meaning of Islam being "submission") to a reality ("a land and sky") that exceeds their capacities of knowledge and understanding and in doing so give birth, once again, to Granada's unique form of life and aesthetics.

Note here as well how the invocation of Islam within Ganivet's rhetoric works to dilute the impact of the Church on Granadan identity: the act of submission, a gesture inherited from Granada's Muslim ancestors, serves to anchor Granadan sensibilities in a relationship to a natural landscape ("land and sky"), and not in Spain's eternal Christian mission, as commonly found in the dominant narratives of Spanish identity. While Ganivet's ambivalence toward Christianity was not unique among his generation (Unamuno [1892] 2017, 361] at one point refers to himself as a "mystical atheist"),[8] his interpretation of Andalusia's Arabic and Islamic heritage as a prophylactic against the totalizing claims of what would later evolve into National Catholicism is one we have encountered among the *andalucistas* discussed in this book at numerous junctures. These include Rodríguez Ramos's interpretation of flamenco, with its Arab roots acting as an Andalusian barrier against a Madrid-centered Catholic power, or Ignacio Olagüe's positing of Muslim Iberia as an autochthonous development in the context of articulating a nationalist identity freed from the transnational encumbrance of Catholicism. A secular thread runs through the entire tradition of Andalucismo due to the potentially interruptive force of the Arabo-Islamic legacy on a would-be hegemonic Catholic identity centered in Madrid.

In short, while Ganivet is often read as another fin de siècle contributor to the project of defining an essential Spanish identity (*el genio español*), such an identity appears as more of an aspiration in his work than an accomplished fact, or as a desire endlessly deferred. He writes, "We have had, after all, only periods lacking a unity of character: a Hispano-Roman period, another Hispano-Visigoth, another Hispano-Arab. . . . But we have never had a purely Spanish period in which our spirit gave fruits in its own territory" (cited in Ochoa de Michelena 2007, 201). There is a melancholic tone pervading this claim but also an invitation to come to terms with historical complexity. The failure to achieve a "purely Spanish period," its repeated deferral, becomes in Ganivet's reading the source of the city's unique value and the basis of its universal significance.[9]

There is a gothic element in Ganivet's thought, evident in the way he conjoins an aspiration to unity and identity with the recognition of contingency and inescapable heterogeneity. In his exploration of Romantic challenges to the homogenizing and totalizing aspects of the modern political order, John Milbank draws on the example of a gothic cathedral, a figure whose irreducible complexity grounds a model of what he calls "complex space," one in sharp contrast to "the simple space of liberal modernity" (Milbank 1997, 272): "it is a building that can be endlessly added to, either extensively through new additions, or intensively through the filling in of detail. This condition embodies constant recognition of imperfection, of the fragmentary and therefore always-already ruined character of the gothic structure, which, as John Ruskin argued, expresses the Christian imperative of straining for the ultimate at the risk of thereby more comprehensively exhibiting one's finite and fallen insufficiency" (276). Constructed through a process that incorporates contingency, unforeseeable necessity—the unanticipated need to cut a window for the sake of extra light, Milbank mentions—the gothic cathedral is forged of "parts that escape the totalizing grasp of the whole" (276)—a description that resonates strongly with Ganivet's vision of the simultaneous "assimilation" and irreducible otherness (*"our* monumental style" that is also *"not ours"*) at the heart of Granadan aesthetics. Moreover, Ganivet's "gothicism" was not limited to the aesthetic realm but also shaped a political vision that highlighted the role of medieval institutions such as guilds and other free associations as a means to pluralize the sources of social power then being monopolized by state and market. This view was not the artifact of Romantic nostalgia, as some have suggested, but emerged from a concern for the relentless expansion of state power.

Much of Ganivet's reflection on Granada will center on the Alhambra, on the sadness emanating from its ancient walls.[10] Against the poetic tendencies of many of his contemporaries, Ganivet criticizes the popular perception, encouraged by Orientalist fashion, that exoticizes the Alhambra as a fantasy palace, one where only "lullabies of sensuality" are heard. The Muslim ruins, he suggests, have a more profound story to tell: one of greatness, certainly, but even more of sadness and death, of the calamitous demise of the city's previous inhabitants:

It is universally thought that the Alhambra is an Eden, an ethereal Moorish castle, where one lives in perpetual festivity. How can we understand that this castle was inspired by faith, one to be respected even if not shared, and was the theater of great sorrows, of sorrow of an agonizing domination? The destiny of greatness is to be misunderstood: there are still those who on visiting the Alhambra believe they hear the flattery and lullabies of sensuality, and don't feel the profound sadness that emanates from the deserted palace, abandoned by its builders, imprisoned in the impalpable threads woven by the spirit of destruction, that invisible spider whose feet are dreams. ([1896] 2003, 35)

For Ganivet this tragic demise, still echoing from the ruins of the Nasrid fortress that dominates the city, imparts a distinct mood to its forms of experience and thus to the poetry that expresses its unique form of life. This criticism of the then-reigning perceptual grid through which the Alhambra was interpreted as a place of "perpetual festivity" will leave a lasting imprint in the work of Lorca and other *andalucista* writers and artists.

The Alhambra emerged as a focal point of definition, as Barbara Fuchs has insightfully explored, soon after the fall of the city in the fifteenth century, as urgent questions about the status of Morisco and Muslim culture converged on the potential symbolism of the site. What would the palace come to stand for in the post-1492 context? To what past would it bear witness, and toward what future would it harken and gesture? As the campaign to erase traces of Muslim culture from language, art, custom, and architecture grew more intense in the years following the fall of Granada (a trend that was paralleled at that time by the increasing hostility to the Moriscos), questions about the significance and value of the Alhambra were posed and answered from various quarters (Fuchs 2009, 48–50). Francisco Núñez Muley, a Morisco advocate during the latter part of the sixteenth century, argued that the preservation of the Alhambra and other testaments to Muslim culture, in demonstrating the great achievements of the Andalusian Muslims, would only increase the stature and value of those who had conquered them. Fuchs reads Núñez Muley's intervention as an attempt to find a place for Muslim culture within the new Christian order in a context in which the status of the contemporary representatives of that cultural formation, the Moriscos, were facing the looming threat of total expulsion. From the contrasting point of view of Granada's new Christian rulers, the Alhambra was to bear witness not to the Muslim culture they had defeated but to their own triumph. The Alhambra was therefore one element within a broader cultural politics concerned with the implications of emergent notions of Spanish identity for the Moriscos.

For Ganivet, writing centuries later, it is no longer the status of the Moriscos as a living population facing the threat of expulsion that is at stake. Rather, it is the dead (Moriscos among their number) whose status is in danger, the long-extinguished inhabitants of the city whose ghostly presence is imperiled by the exoticization of the world they created and left behind. As in "Las ruinas," Ganivet identifies the Alhambra with decay and death, with the voices of the now entombed dead rising up from the stones to impart their eternal wisdom.

"Oriental" themes and architectural sites acquired a particular salience in the context of a variety of fin de siècle cultural and aesthetic movements, many of them critical of modernization (e.g., exoticism and the decadent movement). As the historian Lily Litvak has noted, "In Muslim architecture, in cities asleep under the sun of the desert, the late nineteenth-century found an imaginary coherence that went far beyond the poor patches [remiendos] of history" (1986, 70). In southern Spain, this fascination with representations of Islamic architecture and culture—as figures of "a silent and immobile substrate" (70)—when conjoined with the Orientalist notion of Muslim fatalism, helped to sustain an experience blending mal du siècle with a distinctly Andalusian sadness, a blend evident in Ganivet as well as Lorca (see García 2012, 241). Yet it was precisely this sadness—as both aesthetic and historical sensibility—that enabled Andalucismo's reassessment of the terms of Spanish identity.

While Ganivet's concern was with the dead, it embraced the living as well. In contrast to his better-known colleague and interlocutor Miguel de Unamuno, and to the mainstream of Spanish intellectual opinion among the generations that followed, Ganivet was a consistent critic of the notion of the superiority of European civilization.[11] Echoing Romantic critiques of the spiritual poverty of modern European society's utilitarian and materialist outlook, he frequently attacked what he saw as Spain's blind emulation of European models and encouraged his conationals to revive their own local traditions.[12] Moreover, his critique of European modernity also included a harsh judgment on its colonial enterprises. Having taken up a post as Spanish Vice Counsel in Antwerp, Belgium, in 1892, Ganivet had become increasingly interested in—and critical of—King Leopold's colonial occupation of the Congo, an occupation that in his view sought to hide its cruelty and purely exploitative motives under banners of heroism and philanthropy (Ginsberg 1985, 49). He soon came to see this ruthless utilitarianism as a feature characteristic of all of Europe's colonial practices, including Spain's. In his satirical novel, La conquista del Maya por el último *conquistador español: Pío Cid,* Ganivet (2019) dissects, with acerbic wit, the racism, brutality, and bald economic self-interest hiding behind Europe's civilizing mask.[13]

Although Ganivet expressed skepticism that any colonial enterprise could avoid degenerating into brutal forms of domination, elsewhere in his writings his views were more ambivalent (see González Alcantud 1997; Martín-Márquez 2008). Like many of the Spanish Africanists of his generation, Ganivet at times argued that Spain should at some point in the future seek to secure a colonial presence on the African continent both to revitalize Spanish political culture and, even more urgently, to respond to French colonial expansion in North Africa. In this, Ganivet anticipated many of the viewpoints we previously encountered in Gil Benumeya, including the notion that Spain was to be the pioneer of a more benign form of colonialism founded not on military, political, and economic domination but on shared interests within the framework of a broad Hispanic civilization (see Blinkhorn 1980, 15).[14] As I discussed in chapter 1, Spanish Africanists emphasized the historical linkages between Spain and North Africa as a justification for their own civilizing mission, a view Gil Benumeya sought to balance with his conviction that only with full independence could a lasting alliance be built across the Mediterranean. Ganivet's own statements on this topic were similarly ambivalent; enchanted in one moment by the idea of Spain reviving its North African legacy through colonial expansion, he evinced profound skepticism at other times about the desirability of any colonial enterprise. In both of these views we can discern the expression of a Granadan sensibility, the result of a practice of finding one's place in an unstable world of multiple and complex parentage.

Within Ganivet's Granada the Muslim features of the city are not relegated to the status of historical monuments, a petrified heritage to be nostalgically remembered. Nor are they simply a source of inspiration, a distant example to inspire later generations. Rather, disinterred from a frozen past though an act of imaginative recuperation, they are to be recognized as constitutive features of a sociability, aesthetics, and poetics that underlie a valued form of life.[15] They speak to the city's present—a European city whose spiritual and aesthetic contours are rooted in the non-European presence that inhabits and inflects it, a presence that leaves it disjointed from itself in such a way as to open up a space of critical reflection on European modernity and its colonial practices. Ganivet does not simply discover an ideal embedded in Granada's historical tapestry; his thinking emerges organically from the urban landscape of houses and monuments, hewing closely to the experience of the city, an ideal embedded as much in the city's heterogeneous artistic and architectural traditions as in the forms of collective habitation that those traditions have given rise to across the centuries. Guided by a poetic sensibility attuned to the constitutive force of Arabo-Islamic traditions and forms exerted on Granada, he elaborates a perspective that resisted the polarities that would counterpose Spain to the Middle East, a superior civilization to an inferior one. That such a perspective led Ganivet at times to affirm contradictory stances testifies to the challenge of thinking from the historical and geographic periphery of Europe.

LORCA'S ORIENT

In one of his most well-known comments on the city, first presented at a conference in 1926 honoring the baroque Granadan poet Pedro Soto de Rojas, Lorca identified the defining quality of Granadan aesthetic and architectural expression as "the aesthetic of the diminutive" (*la estética del diminutivo*): "The aesthetic of small things [*la estética de las cosas diminutas*] has been our most genuine fruit, the distinguishing note and the most delicate game of our artists" (from *Paraíso cerrado para muchos*, Lorca 1994, 263). The echoes of Ganivet here are pronounced. Distant from the sea and bordered by the Sierra Nevada mountains, Granada turns inward, Lorca says, "folds in on itself and uses the diminutive to gather its imagination." In its isolation, it cultivates the life of the interior, the intimate, the domestic. Preferring to view the surrounding landscape from his window rather than venture out in its midst, the Granadan willingly "makes his soul small and brings the world into his room" where he creates compact images, stories, and sculptures of great beauty.[16] The most characteristic site of this circumscribed, inward-facing world (here again, following Ganivet) is found in the *carmenes* of the Albayzín, with their small interior patios and gardens closed off to the outside. The paradigm of the aesthetic itself, however, lies in the arabesque figures of the Alhambra, a figural tradition, we are told, that "exerts an influence over all of the great artists of that land." Or, in an oft-cited statement, "The little palace of the Alhambra, a palace that the Andalusian imagination saw through backward binoculars, has always been the aesthetic core of the city" (Lorca 1994, 262).

Along the walls of the Alhambra, Lorca found what he took to be the key to the aesthetic unity of a form of life, one forged differently across time, as a response to the city's unique cultural and physical geography. In poetry, prose, letters to friends, and theatrical works, he explored the personality of the city in its many facets—the customs and character of its inhabitants, the textures, colors, and moods of its streets and houses, the many faces of its aesthetic and spiritual life. Following the sensuous contours of the city along their polysemous historical routes, Lorca was drawn continuously toward the manifold traditions embodied in the hybrid city, often to the Romani (*gitano*) contribution but also to the Arabo-Islamic. The Nasrid era builders of the inner chambers of the Alhambra and the *carmenes* of the Albayzín, the baroque poets of seventeenth-century Granada such as Soto de Rojas or the Granadan artists of Lorca's day revealed in their creations a unique philosophy of life—not simply Arabic or Spanish but Granadan—and hence an expression of that city's unique historical trajectory. For the poet, this Granada could never be entirely Western, as its poetic articulation required that he leave the West, explore and develop his own Granadan voice through an engagement with Arabic and Persian poetry.[17] The poetic cartography of Granada embraced the Middle East, much as later, in the works of Mahmoud Darwish, it would come to embrace Palestine.[18]

As I mentioned earlier, a central theme within Lorca's lyrical vision, one he saw to be at the heart of Granadan experience though also of much broader significance, was what he termed *la Pena Negra*, the Black Dread. In Lorca's rendition, *Pena Negra* connotes a kind of pain and anguish that defies definition in language. In describing Soledad Montoya, the *gitana* protagonist of his narrative poem *Romance de la Pena Negra* (*Ballad of the Black Dread*), Lorca notes that she "is the embodiment of unending Sorrow, of the black pain from which one can escape only by using a knife to open a deep wound in the left side. . . . It is a longing without object, a pronounced love for nothing, with the certainty that death (the endless concern of Andalusia) is breathing on the other side of the door" (Lorca 1997, 343–44). This fusion of love, anguish, and the presentiment of death finds its clearest expression for Lorca in the poetry of the *cante jondo*.

The *Pena Negra*, that most Andalusian of themes, also had a historical dimension for Lorca in the history of persecution and expulsion suffered by the Muslims, Jews, and *gitanos* of Iberia from the fifteenth to the seventeenth centuries. Lorca finds that this history of repression inflicted on Granadans of an earlier generation suffuses the gestures and attitudes of his contemporaries: in their reserve, their melancholy, their renunciation of action, their withdrawal into small enclosed spaces where they "hide in the interior of their houses and their landscape" (Lorca 1994, 264; cited in Martínez López 1989, 41), fertile ground of the aesthetics of the diminutive. Spanish literary historian Miguel Ángel García argues that Lorca's vision of "sad Granada," with its sorrowful Moors, made more so by their defeat, was integral to the poet's ambition to articulate a *Granadinismo universal*, a modernist aesthetic stance purified of Andalusia's folkloric baggage (García 2012, 284–85). What I want to emphasize here, however, is how Lorca's Andalusian sadness went hand in hand with an historical sensibility for Iberia's Muslim past as a lived inheritance, one that required study, exploration, and engagement for the sake of a Granadan modernity. An inheritor himself of Granada's painful history, Lorca interprets this inheritance in terms of an ethical sensibility toward the persecuted, an instinctual sympathy for the plight of the repressed. In an interview with Rudolfo Gil Benumeya following his return from a yearlong sojourn in New York, he suggests how this sensibility had opened him up to the plight of the African Americans he met in the United States: "I believe that being from Granada inclines me to a sympathetic understanding of the persecuted. Of the Gypsy, the Negro, the Jew . . . of the Morisco that we all carry inside" (cited in Laffranque 1954, 265).

Across a number of writings, Lorca will figure this history of persecution underlying the *Pena Negra* not as a concluded event but as an ongoing struggle: "The graves of the Catholic Kings have not prevented the half-moon from rising at times within the breast of the most refined children of Granada. The battle continues, obscure and without expression . . . without expression, no, for on the red hill of the city there are two palaces, both dead: the Alhambra and the Palace of Charles V, that sustain the duel to the death that beats in the conscience of the Granadan of today" (in *Impresiones: Santa Semana en Granada*, Lorca 1994, 23). This trope of an ongoing battle within the Spanish psyche founded on the conflict between Muslims and Christians will reappear in many different guises across twentieth-century Spanish literature and historiography, including, for example, in the works of Américo Castro and Juan Goytisolo. Pedro Martínez Montávez, a contemporary scholar who has dedicated much of his life to an exploration of Spain's Arabic inheritance, echoes Lorca's judgment on the eternal struggle within the Spanish soul: "To refer to the Hispano-Arabic . . . is to refer to a part of ourselves. To a part still obscure and buried, 'forgotten in its profundity,' as Adolfo Reyes recalled, whose reactualization will either be felt as agreeable or disagreeable, depending on the individual, her formation, sentiments and preferences, but that in no instance will be received with indifference; it will always agitate and disturb, certainly, our deepest existence, our supposed identity, producing an interior dialectic that is entirely unsettling" (Martínez Montávez 2011, 23). When viewed from this angle, a key dimension of Andalucismo appears as an exploration of the possibilities afforded by the dialectic of these two palaces on the hill above Granada, or by the hyphen conjoining Arabic and Hispanic, when the impulse to escape or overcome this disturbance is resisted.

The themes of loss and pain central to Lorca's poetic vision have a long history within Spain, one that includes Ganivet's fin de siècle sadness but also one that finds an earlier formative moment in the melancholic literature of the sixteenth and seventeenth centuries. A dominant trope within Spanish Golden Age literature, melancholy was viewed as a particularly Jewish disease, due both to the fact that most physicians at the time were assumed to be Jewish converts and because melancholy was understood to be symptomatic of a condition of exile, a condition often associated with Jews, having been expelled, most recently, from Spain in 1492 (see Labanyi 2004, 232–33). Roger Bartra has suggested that the persecution of Muslims and the attempts to eliminate their cultural practices also figured in the development of the sixteenth-century Spanish discourse on melancholy as a "border illness": "A sickness of displaced peoples, of migrants, associated with the fragile life of the people who suffered forced conversions and confronted the threat of huge reforms and mutations of the religious and moral principles that oriented them. . . . An illness that attacked those who lost something and have not yet found what they look for, and in this manner, a pain that affects the conquered as much as the conquerors" (Bartra 2000, 69). Spanish melancholy, Bartra argues, was grounded in the experience of loss associated with these expulsions and erasures, an experience of loss all the more intense for the fact of its denial, its banishment from consciousness.

This cultural trope would emerge again in the melancholic sentimentalism of early nineteenth-century Spanish Romantics, with their tales of impossible love often set in the medieval kingdoms of Muslim Iberia. According to the literary historian Jo Labanyi, Romantic love, by providing a model of a subject who willfully chooses to bind him or herself to an Other, the beloved, and does so in defiance of the conventions of birthright, allowed for the elaboration of a politically radical challenge to the existing order. Moreover, in foregrounding Morisco or mixed-race protagonists, these Romantic stories fashioned a model of society that embraced ethnic and cultural pluralism against the homogeneous and monocultural ideals of medieval society. "Melancholy," Labanyi concludes, "before it turned itself into the nostalgia of the 1840s—provided a way of opening oneself to the losses incurred in the past in order to propose an alternative to the present. . . . It keeps alive the hurt of the past as a motivating present" (Labanyi 2004, 241–42).

Both Ganivet and Lorca elaborate in different ways a sense of loss left by the traumatic erasure of medieval Andalusian society, and in doing so, they contribute to this Spanish—and highly Granadan—tradition of critical reflection on the present via the Andalusian past. For both, Andalusian melancholy engenders something different than nostalgia for an idealized and irretrievable past. Granada's medieval features inhabited the present of the city, the gestures of its people, its ruins an animate force even in their tenebrous stony silence. For both, coming to terms with those ruins, tracing the friction they exerted on the dominant traditions of Western identity is an essential condition for thinking through the problems of European modernity in Spain and beyond.

As I mentioned above, Lorca scholars have tended to view the poet's relation to Arab culture as superficial and folkloric and hence as inessential to the development of his own poetic voice. As with other Andalusian intellectuals of his generation, his "flirtations" with the East are seen to testify to the fact that he was not immune to the fascination that the Orient exerted on the imagination of the Spanish (and especially the Andalusians), but they indicate little more.[19] An early and authoritative statement of this view was propounded by the renowned Arabist Emilio García Gómez in what was to be a prologue to *Diván del Tamarit*, a collection of Lorca's poetry set to be published in 1934 but that only appeared some years after his 1936 death at the hands of Spanish fascists. In the *Diván*, Lorca explicitly modeled his poems on two classical Arabic poetic forms, the *casida* and the *ghazal*, employing verse structures and rhyme schemes characteristic of these forms. In his prologue to the collection, published years later in his book of personal reflections on Granada (*Silla del moro*), García Gómez downplays the formal and stylistic similarities of Lorca's poetry with Arabic and Arabic-Andalusi poetic genres, insisting, quite to the contrary, that the sublimity of the poet's work underscored its *lack of commonality* with Arabic poetic traditions. In a comment echoing a view widely shared among Orientalists at the time regarding the rigidity and superficiality of Arabic expressive genres,[20] García Gómez writes, "in general and fortunately, Lorca's poems depart from Arabic verse insomuch as they are not slaves to grammar, but, on the contrary, grammar is itself enslaved; the poems escape this pregongorian *gongorismo* in which everything is difficult, but cold and exact, and sparkles, in contrast, with vague intuitions, ineffable desires, unreachable sentiments" (García Gómez 1948, cited in Piras 1991, 174).[21] García Gómez's decisively negative judgment over a poetic tradition he had dedicated much of his life to exploring was not unusual within the ambit of early twentieth-century Orientalism, Spanish or otherwise (see Piras 1991). However, it is the vehemence with which he insists on the distance between the Spanish poet and the Arab poetic traditions he had explicitly engaged that I want to highlight, characteristic as it is of the dominant interpretive grid within Lorca scholarship. While not always as forthright, such pronouncements are common in a critical tradition of commentary on the poet and have served to autochthonize Lorca, to locate (and purify) the seeds of his originality and creativity within Spanish and European modernity, as a poetic voice that can stand for the historical experience of the Spanish people.[22] For many of his readers, Lorca's poetry may be characterized by an occasional Oriental flavor, a certain Oriental color, but it owes little to Arabic culture and poetry. For this, he is a *modern* poet, one whose creativity is unrestrained by the materialities of Arabic language or the legacies of Spain's Arabo-Islamic history.

THE SPOKEN ALHAMBRA

The lives of Ganivet and Lorca bear witness to a sensibility for the Arabo-Islamic warp of Granada. This sensibility worked on the borders between Spain, Europe, and the Middle East, giving aesthetic expression to historical legacies still integral to the city's lifeblood that were then being threatened by the petrifying force of folklorization. I was introduced to this Granadan sensibility, and to Lorca as an influential practitioner, by José Miguel Puerta Vílchez, a man whose own life, as I discuss below, bears witness to the ongoing development of this Andalusian tradition.[23] A professor at the University of Granada, Puerta Vílchez is one of Spain's leading scholars of Islamic art, having produced a number of groundbreaking works on medieval Islamic aesthetics and poetics, many of them focused specifically on the decorative art of the Alhambra. His scholarship has garnered him wide respect among Spanish Arabists and scholars of Islam, and his international reputation within the field of Islamic aesthetics is far reaching.[24]

At the same time, Puerta Vílchez speaks to the world of Spanish Arabism with a distinct Granadan inflection. The seeds of his *granadismo*, as he told me at our first meeting at a café in the heart of Granada, go back to his earliest youth. As a boy, he studied at a Catholic boarding school where among his teachers was the priest Enrique Iniesta Coullaut-Valera, a cofounder of an important center for the historical study of Andalusia. In the 1970s and 80s, Iniesta was involved in a number of initiatives aimed at promoting an appreciation for Andalusian culture. His primary intellectual contribution, however, has been as a curator to the legacy of Blas Infante, whose life and writings Iniesta documented across a number of biographical works and edited collections. Under Iniesta's guidance, Puerta Vílchez acquired a profound appreciation for the Arabic language as well as for Andalusian culture and history, one that would eventually lead him to the study of Islamic art. Iniesta also left him with a deep admiration for the life and accomplishments of Blas Infante, one that has remained with him up to the present.

Infante tends to be a polarizing figure within Spanish society, respected among many Andalusians for his progressive political vision and support for Andalusian culture but dismissed as little more than an ideologue of the nationalist movement by a wide swath of Spanish scholarly opinion. Infante's ideas about the Arab world and its relation to Andalusian culture are frequently denounced as figments of a Romantic imagination, a dilettante's collection of partial truths at the service of Andalusian nationalism. Thus, his forays into the Arabic language (without achieving mastery), his explorations of Islamic poetry and music (the work, many scholars say, of an enthusiast more than a scholar), his passional attachments to the Middle East, exemplified in such dramatic gestures as his 1924 visit to the tomb of al-Mu'tamid in Morocco (called a "traitorous act" by the press at the time)[25]—in these scenes from Infante's life most scholars will find little more than empty tokens of Romantic nationalism. Puerta Vílchez, in sharp contrast, judges these forays into the Middle East to be thoughtful responses of an Andalusian to the historical legacies of his homeland. The charge of dilettantism often leveled against Infante is, in other words, off the mark, a way of applying academic criteria to evaluate acts that can be better understood as the passional responses of an Andalusian for the place of his birth. The fact that Infante's nationalist vision was (in contrast to most other nationalist movements of his day) radically inclusivist and in direct opposition to the dominant ideas of racial purity of his day further bears witness to the value and singularity of his *andalucista* vision.[26]

Across Puerta Vílchez's work, one finds an insistence on disturbing the disciplinary imperative that would consign the value and meaning of an aesthetic object to its "historical context," forestalling any question of a more direct, unmediated relation to the present by placing it behind the screen of "history." During our early discussions in Granada, I would frequently find myself confused by what seemed to be unanticipated historical jumps in his thinking, as he shifted from medieval references to modern ones. Soon, however, I came to see such mobility as a central virtue of his aesthetic style. A few years back, as he recounted on one occasion, he had been invited by a colleague to contribute an article to an edited volume on the Alhambra. When the volume was assembled, he found to his chagrin that all of the other essays focused on "constructions of the Alhambra," its elaboration and representation within different historically anchored discursive regimes, while his essay was the only one that discussed "the actual motifs and stylistic elements of the Alhambra itself." Others had approached the palace as a text requiring a context but in doing so hadn't fully observed (and thus been moved by) key aspects of their object. Historicism, he suggests—the relegation of the Alhambra to one of its moments in historical time—is not adequate in itself to grasp the beauty and meaning of the monument.[27] Other perspectives are called for.

In this vein, during a private tour of the Alhambra he led for a group of visiting scholars from CSIC in Madrid that I also attended, Puerta Vílchez noted on a number of occasions how poetic verses inscribed on the interior walls of the fortress were still alive in the everyday expressions of people in various parts of the Middle East and that he had heard these very same verses spoken by people on a street in Beirut or Damascus. The temporality of the Alhambra, of the Andalusian world it expresses, escapes its enclosure behind the wall of 1492 to embrace the present of ordinary citizens within the Middle East. The more I got to know Puerta Vílchez, the more it became clear to me that such observations were born of a perspective both aesthetic and ethical, one with deep roots in the Andalucismo of Ganivet, Lorca, and Gil Benumeya. Upending the normative periodicities and geographies of art history, Puerta Vílchez approached the art and architecture of Granada in its lived relation to the societies of the Middle East, a relation covered over by the definitional imperatives of Spanish and European identity but nonetheless an essential and constitutive feature of the city.

Puerta Vílchez stresses the extent to which his own perspective on Islamic aesthetics is colored by the intimacy of his relation to the Middle East and the Arabic language: "I relate to the region more as an insider, a participant, whereas many Western scholars come to it from the outside" (conversation with author, July 10, 2011). He has returned to the area repeatedly and regularly since beginning his study of Arabic as a student, and he has developed many lasting friendships with Middle Eastern scholars. The lifelong struggles and privations many of these scholars have faced under the authoritarian regimes holding power throughout much of the region have given him a personal and intimate sense for the difficulties faced by people in these societies. Additionally, many members of his wife's family in Syria have suffered greatly in recent years with the country's seemingly interminable war. In short, there are few Europeans who in their intellectual and personal life are as much at home on one side of the Mediterranean as on the other or are as personally attuned to the plight of peoples on the southern and eastern shores as much as on the northern one. Within the ambit of this life, it could be said, the disciplinary commitments to upholding the borders between medieval Islamic aesthetics and contemporary artistic practices lose their moral force. Other ethical and passional demands impose themselves on the episteme.

This sense of being "an insider" to the region also owes much to language. Not only is Arabic the primary language of the scholarly and journalistic literature he reads, it is also the language of domestic life at home with his wife, Nairus, and their two daughters. And it is a language in which he writes and publishes, a practice extremely rare among European scholars. As with Lorca before him, Puerta Vílchez considers Arabic to be an essential part of the linguistic code of Granada, of the grammar of its form of life. "As an Arabic speaker," he tells me, "I feel in harmony with my surroundings here in Granada." Arabic attunes one to the composition of the city, equips one with the linguistic and affective skills needed to properly evaluate its aesthetic and historical complexity. His passion for the expressive virtues of the Arabic language very much informs his scholarship, one foregrounding a semiotic approach to Islamic architectural and decorative symbolism. In his frequent reference to this topic, one also senses the image of a language invested with an ethical potential that far exceeds the domain of the aesthetic. "When Spanish speakers from different parts of the world get together," he notes, "they rarely feel a sense of unity around the language, whereas when Arabic speakers from Sudan, Iraq, Lebanon meet, they often experience a connection between them due to the language" (conversation with the author, February 15, 2013). Arabic, he suggests, mediates a form of sociability wherein regional and national differences are more easily overcome than is the case with other languages. There are echoes of Gil Benumeya in these claims, his appreciation for the unifying power of Arabic. At an exhibition of Islamic calligraphy held in Madrid, Puerta Vílchez tells me on another occasion that sharp political and ideological rifts were offset by a sense of commonality born of a shared appreciation for a series of calligraphic figures inspired in the poetic and philosophical vision of the twelfth-century Andalusian mystic Ibn al-Arabi. In Spain—especially there—Arabic words can do things, create possibilities, diffuse conflict. In these reflections on the Arabic language, Puerta Vílchez invites us to reconsider the common assumption that those Andalusian nationalists or local converts to Islam who find themselves drawn to the Arabic language do so as part of a politics of identity and nothing more.

Of course, one could easily read these comments as continuous with the Romantic idealization of al-Andalus figured in the notion of *convivencia*, the idea of social and interconfessional harmony sometimes ascribed to medieval Iberian society. Yet something is lost here. In his personal and professional life, Puerta Vílchez experiences the impact of the structure of differential power and violence that characterizes the relationship between the West and the Middle East. This polarity, mobilized continuously to justify each new bombing campaign, drone attack, or denial of border entry, takes on a particularly acute form within the history of Spain, a country whose national mythology, as I have discussed above, foregrounds the defeat and elimination of Muslims and Jews as a defining moment. In this bipolar world—forged through the violent exclusion of Muslim and Jewish others, splintered into the civilized West and the chaotic and primitive Middle East, which must always be contained with violent force—to learn the Arabic language and come to appreciate the society it inhabits acquires a political and ethical value, one perhaps particularly evident to a person who regularly comes face-to-face with the sad consequences of this geopolitical order. In such a geopolitical context, the poetic and aesthetic values that Puerta Vílchez has dedicated himself to deciphering acquire a political—one could also say universal—valence: the sublime beauty of the Alhambra, its celebrated aesthetic powers, project a subversive and humanistic vision against the long history of Western domination. And it is from the vantage point of Granada—a city, like Benjamin's angel of history, facing backward as it moves ahead—that this decimation can be grasped as a singular historical event and where the possibility of its reversal can be imagined in the Arabic verses that line the walls of the Alhambra and that, as Puerta Vílchez highlighted in the guided tour I attended, are still spoken today in Amman, Beirut, and Ramallah. In this we recognize Puerta Vílchez as a successor to Ganivet and Lorca, both of whom found within the historical palimpsest of Granada a universal vision for their time, one lodged against some of modernity's most strident and deadly claims.

POETICS OF PLACE

The idea of al-Andalus as an "unfinished project"[28]—one with significant aesthetic, linguistic, and musical reverberations extending to the present—recurs throughout Puerta Vílchez's works and life. A presentation given in one of the salons of the Alhambra in 2011 exemplifies this *andalucista* orientation. More than an academic paper, the talk was an invitation to his audience to inhabit an *andalucista* imaginary, to follow a pathway of poetic affiliations and affective attachments held together by the figure of al-Andalus. Invited on the occasion to discuss the poetic traditions of Andalusia, Puerta Vílchez weaves a narrative in which each move toward contemporary Spain necessitates a return to medieval Iberia, each move into Spanish, a return to Arabic, the descent into Andalusian melancholy, a reflection on Palestinian loss. A small selection from his presentation will clarify.

Reciting a *qasida* in both Spanish and Arabic by the thirteenth-century Andalusian poet Abu al-Baqa' al-Rundi in which the poet mourns the loss of Muslim territories, Puerta Vílchez pauses to note that when he is in the

Middle East and happens to utter the poem's first lines, almost invariably his companions will continue on their own, so familiar is the poem among Arabic speakers (less so among the Spanish, he laments). Then, having situated the poem in its historical context, noted additions made to it after the author's death, and recited some of its mournful verses, he moves his focus to the town near Seville from which al-Rundi acquired his name, Ronda, while shifting to the early twentieth century. In 1918 in Ronda, he explains, an assembly of Andalusian notables was convened during which Blas Infante's design for the Andalusian flag was approved. This jump to the early years of the Andalusian nationalist movement, however, requires a simultaneous move backward to al-Andalus: the first mention of a flag of similar color, as Blas Infante noted in his supporting arguments, occurs in an eleventh-century poem by the Andalusian poet Abu al-Asbag Ibn Arqam. Reciting a stanza from this poem, Puerta Vílchez reminds his audience that Blas Infante, more than just a nationalist thinker, had a deep relation to the Arab and Muslim traditions of the province, and, thus, that an enlarged horizon of concern, one embracing the Middle East, was already present in the formative period of Andalucismo. Unfolding in rapid succession, these narrative shifts seem designed to disrupt his listeners' attachment to the linguistic, temporal, and geographic conventions of literary analysis (i.e., of European literary analysis), thereby introducing them to the poetic territory of Andalucismo.

As with Gil Benumeya and his concept of *Mediodía*, the geography of Puerta Vílchez's Andalucismo stretches well beyond Iberia to embrace the entire Middle East. Midway into his talk, he turns to a survey of twentieth-century Arab artists and poets who have drawn inspiration from Andalusian themes. As he proceeds, we find the poetic articulation of Andalusia increasingly merging with that of Palestine, a fusion explored and given symbolic expression by a long succession of Arab and Palestinian writers and poets. Among these, Puerta Vílchez first highlights a collaboration between the Palestinian artist Kamal Boullata and the Syrian poet Adonis — a project incorporating poetry in both Spanish and Arabic and set in an accordion book fashioned with motifs from the Alhambra — before turning to a work of poetry by Palestinian poet Mahmoud Darwish, for which Boullata contributed artwork. Upon visiting Granada in the early 1990s, Darwish published a collection of poems foregrounding themes and images from Andalusian history, particularly the experience of exile and loss suffered by the Muslims forced from the city in 1492 and subsequently expelled from Iberia in the early seventeenth century (Darwish 2004). Puerta Vílchez reads a stanza from one poem, "The Adam of Two Edens," in which Darwish invokes Lorca:

I am Adam of the two Edens
I who lost paradise twice.
So expel me slowly,
and kill me slowly,
under my olive tree,
with Lorca.

In the final moments of the talk, Puerta Vílchez returns to the lament for al-Andalus by al-Rundi with which he had begun: "Yesterday they were lords of their houses; Today they are, in a country of the faithless, slaves." Two images drawn from a collection of art and photography edited by Boullata accompany the reading, one of a destroyed house drawn by a Palestinian child, the other, a photograph of a Palestinian woman and her two children standing next to the rubble that had been her home, destroyed by the Israeli army.

Puerta Vílchez's talk carries a strong political message. Yet it would be inadequate to delimit it as the expression of a personal political opinion. More significantly, it is a discourse spoken from within the Alhambra and through it, from the purview afforded by the monument and the city in which it resides, a purview from which the historical expulsion of Muslims and Jews from Iberia and of Palestinians from Palestine today appear as successive moments of a single continuous event within the career of Europe, or, put differently, within the career of anti-Semitism within Europe. Europe's role in the creation of Israel, in defending and enabling the dispossession of the Palestinians at the hands of the Israeli army, in arming and fortifying the Israeli state to serve as a forward base for Euro-American interests in the region—while these policies and actions reflect a variety of different interests and political rationales, they also owe deeply to practices of religious and racial boundary-making integral to the political and theological constitution of Europe and for which 1492 stands as one early and decisive moment. What is at stake in Puerta Vílchez's discourse, in this light, is not (only) a political choice but a mode of historical attunement ("sensibilities of temporality," in Abeysekara's terms) that implicates or emplaces the subject within events and processes that may be unrecognizable for those who have not cultivated such an attunement. Recall that Gil Benumeya, who spent much of his career as an official within the Franco regime, began as an enthusiastic supporter of Jewish immigration to Palestine ("the renaissance of Semitism in the Levant"; Gil Benumeya [1928] 1996, 8) to later become an ardent critic of Israel's unrelenting and violent expropriation of Palestinian land. While Benumeya and Puerta Vílchez would no doubt be political adversaries on many issues, those differences emerge against a shared historical geography, what Gil Benumeya called the "universe seen from the Albayzín." In this universe, the relation between Andalusia and Palestine is not symbolic or an artifact of poetic invention; the linkages are deeply historical, ethical, and aesthetic, and they demand recognition.

GRANADA ABIERTA

Granada today is home to a vast number of associations and advocacy groups emphasizing the contemporary importance of Andalusia's Muslim and Jewish heritage and organized around a wide variety of social and political causes. One of these associations, the Ibn Tufayl Foundation for Arabic Studies (its primary offices are in the nearby city of Almería), was cofounded by Puerta Vílchez in 2003. His principal contribution to the foundation has been as editor of the *Enciclopedia de al-Andalus* (Encyclopedia of al-Andalus) (Delgado and Puerta Vílchez 2003), a massive effort involving dozens of scholars on both sides of the Mediterranean to create a compendium of all of the known poets, artists, and intellectuals of Andalusi origin. While the scope of the encyclopedia is entirely historical, it is also animated by a Borgesian ambition, an effort to harness that encyclopedic power to bring a world to life.[29]

Beyond such intellectual endeavors, there are also a variety of grassroots political movements that find inspiration for their own political perspectives in Granada's medieval heritage. One contemporary movement of this kind, the Manifesto 2 de Enero collective (the January 2nd Manifesto), is organized around a campaign to replace Granada's Catholic-nationalist festival celebrating the defeat of the city's Muslim rulers by Christian armies in 1492 with a festival emphasizing Andalusia's pluralist and liberal traditions: the interconfessional harmony, *convivencia*, of Jews, Muslims, and Christians during the Muslim period but also the liberal martyrs of the nineteenth and twentieth centuries from Mariana Pineda to Federico García Lorca, themselves inheritors of the lifeblood of this pluralist tradition (as Lorca himself asserted). For its organizers, this campaign is a vehicle for promoting and creating an open, tolerant, multicultural society in the city and Spain more broadly, and many of the group's activities focus on the policies and politics of immigration.

In the founding text of the Manifesto, written in 1995, the Christian conquest of the city is described as a lamentable act bringing about the destruction of a pluralist society: "The conquest of Granada brought about the ruin of the interconfessional harmony (*convivencia*) of the three religions, such that numerous neighbors of this city were persecuted because of their beliefs and customs. . . . Because of this, it is our view that the events of the annual celebration of the conquest do not contribute to consolidating sentiments of reconciliation and tolerance, sentiments necessary for any city aspiring to progress."[30] Since its formation, this collective has continually petitioned the city government to restrict the martial character and exclusivist message of the annual celebration and to introduce innovations highlighting the region's history of religious pluralism and cultural exchange. Expanding the scope of its activities in 2012 and changing its name to La Plataforma Granada Abierta (The Open Granada Platform), the group has gone on to stage various events at which poetry and fictional works are read aloud in Spanish, Arabic, and Hebrew, with Arabo-Andalusi music also being performed, often with the participation of North African writers, artists, and musicians. Signatories to the *Manifesto* include many prominent thinkers and artists from both Spain and abroad, among them José Saramago and Amin Maalouf, the Spanish writers Juan Goytisolo and Antonio Gala, Ian Gibson (a British scholar recognized internationally as the preeminent biographer of García Lorca), Pedro Martínez Montávez, and the celebrated Andalusian singer Carlos Cano (d. 2000). Puerta Vílchez also signed the petition when it was first brought forth. Although the signatories to the Manifesto include people of vastly different personal and professional commitments and trajectories, it is not difficult to identify a common thread linking many of them: a record of interest or concern for Middle Eastern societies and, in many cases, an effort to encourage recognition of their contribution to the formation of Spain and Europe.

Despite such international support for this movement, during my many visits to Spain, it was rare that I heard anyone express much appreciation for the Granada Abierta movement. For the majority of Spanish intellectuals, in my experience, the movement exemplifies the dangerous practice of fabricating historical accounts to serve ideological goals. When I spoke about the Manifesto movement with one of the Spanish Arabists at CSIC, she dismissed it as misguided: "Granadans consider themselves to be heirs—*and they are*—of the Castillian settlers of the Kingdom of Granada. The celebration of the damned Conquest Festival (*la Toma*) has nothing to do with xenophobia or racism. This is a theme that generates a lot of hubbub (*hace mucho ruido*) and will continue to do so." For this scholar, Granada Abierta wanted to "turn history into a political instrument," a dangerous strategy, she felt, whatever its goals. In her short retort, the political problem of a festival that celebrates the violent overcoming of a racial-religious Other as a foundational moment within Spanish national identity is resolved by reference to the historical accuracy of present-day Granadans' identification with the victors of that conflict. While the claim of the signatories to the *Manifesto* that they are recuperating their own historical traditions of interreligious cooperation is seen as an (illegitimate) political use of history, the ancient *Christian* roots of the contemporary identity of the Granadans is regarded as historical fact—with the celebration of their ancestors' victory viewed not as a political use of history but as a natural response to their historical identity, and as such, unsullied by xenophobia or racism. The deep Christian identity of Granada is invoked here to legitimate the popular sentiments of the city's Conquest Day revelers.

Most ordinary residents of Granada also see Granada Abierta and other such efforts as based on a fictive past. Indeed, it has become common today for Spaniards to hold together the two rather contradictory ideas that the *moros*, in some fashion, left a permanent imprint on Iberian soil *and* that the real history of Spain is to be found in an ideal that crystallized with Ferdinand and Isabella. This view was echoed by a Granadan friend of mine who complained, "they [the Granada Abierta movement] want to ignore our real history, that of our Catholic foundation," while then adding, as if it were a disclaimer, "plus, everyone knows that al-Andalus, Islam had great influence on Spain; look at its imprint in our language!" What is often called Spain's official narrative, that of its abiding Catholic identity founded in the event of the Reconquista, is reaffirmed despite the simultaneous recognition of the pervasive impact of the medieval Arab presence.

The success of the Granada Abierta movement has shifted over the years since the group was founded according to the respective fortunes of the city's various political parties. During the first five years, while the conservative Partido Popular was in power, the movement was met primarily with disdain, the then mayor of the city declaring, "let them put on the turban and go to Morocco!" While the group had more success in the early 2000s when a coalition of liberal and leftist parties ran the city government, many of the changes introduced into the celebration during those years were subsequently rescinded as conservative politicians returned to power in 2004. Today, right-wing, Catholic-nationalist groups have become a common presence at the *Toma* festival, carrying banners announcing fealty to the anti-immigrant stance they find represented in the figures of Ferdinand and Isabel.

Granada Abierta is Andalucismo as liberal multiculturalism. In my conversations with one of the founders of the movement, Francisco Vigueras, I encountered a familiar journey of self-discovery, one guided by the texts of Andalucismo from Blas Infante and Américo Castro, to Ignacio Olagüe, Federico García Lorca, and Antonio Manuel Rodríguez Ramos, always accompanied along the way by sounds of flamenco echoing from one shore of the Mediterranean to the other. Vigueras's vision of al-Andalus is one of perfect *convivencia*: "The poet-king al-Mu'tamid was as Sevillian as Antonio Machado; the philosopher Averroes, as much a son of Córdoba as Seneca; and King Boabdil (the last Moorish ruler, who surrendered to the Spanish), no less Granadan than our Federico García Lorca. . . . In these times, when xenophobia has returned to the old continent, it is useful to remember that Andalusia was much more than beaches, sun, bulls, and subsidies; that while Europe wrapped itself in shadows, and agitated itself with the phantom of the Inquisition, al-Andalus knew how to share, to exchange, to create."[31]

For over twenty years, Vigueras has worked within Granada Abierta and other associations to counter the xenophobia and intolerance he considers inherent in contemporary Andalusian cultural forms and public life through an ongoing effort to give public recognition to the region's rich cultural legacy. Much of this work has focused on the plight of immigrants from Africa, providing direct assistance to those in need and mobilizing support to change Spain's restrictive immigration policies. The Granada Abierta collective awards an annual prize—called the Granada Abierta a la Tolerancia (Granada Open to Tolerance) prize—a prize usually given to groups that offer aid to immigrants seeking to cross the straits. As described in 2002 on the occasion of presenting the award to the maritime Red Cross of the city of Tarifa for their work in rescuing and treating immigrants who risk their lives crossing the Straits of Gibraltar to come to Europe, the prize "marks a different way of celebrating the date of the conquest of Granada, the moment in which an entire community was expelled from its land in al-Andalus, and that now, 500 years later, has the right to return in peace and be received as they deserve, not by throwing up a new wall where many already encounter their deaths."[32]

This is a sad Granadan tale, one that "rises up from the ruins" of the city, Ganivet might tell us. The story of a people who accomplished wondrous things but were then brought painfully to their knees and forced into exile and who today are still drowning by the thousands in the sea off the coast. And it is a story of another people left scarred by their own acts of violence. Yet perhaps from Granada, the sad tale concludes, from the "many secrets" Ganivet hears rising from its stones, there lies a possibility of righting the deep injustice so many have suffered, of removing the walls that prevented people from being able "to share, to exchange, to create." This story, one told differently by each generation of *andalucistas*, colonialists and anticolonialists alike, can rightly be called a founding myth of Andalucismo, as González Alcantud (2014) has perceptively argued.[33]

Vigueras and other nonacademics like him who invoke an idealized image of al-Andalus in their political work tend to draw the scorn of many scholars who view their claims as a dangerous distortion of historical truth. I find this impulse to dismiss such claims for their lack of historical rigor to be misguided. *Andalucistas* like Vigueras, as I see it, are autodidacts of their own history, people who, moved by stories of the Andalusian landscape, by the monuments and ruins that surround them, have taken it on themselves to read and explore a past to which they feel powerfully drawn. "A group of people," in Emilio González Ferrín's words, "trying to understand their land and history" (personal communication with the author, February 2016). They do so not as professional historians but as ordinary people attempting to confront and respond to the challenges they face in their lives personally, politically, and otherwise. This embeddedness in life does not vitiate their attempts to deepen their understanding of the past. It does, however, condition the kind of knowledge they cultivate and the place it will occupy in relation to other aspects of their lives. In this, they are much like ordinary practitioners of a religious tradition who may only have a rudimentary understanding of religious doctrine, who may even misunderstand some aspects of it, but who nonetheless do their best to live a religiously informed life. For some of the inhabitants of Granada, for Ganivet and Lorca, for Puerta Vílchez and Vigueras, this is a life of "vigilance and apprehension," one which strives to keep open the lost legacies of the city in order to "make them endure, give them space," as Calvino advised.

Conclusion

In writing this book, as I noted at the outset, I have walked along a thin edge, summoning the powers of Orientalism and Romanticism while attempting to avoid the pitfalls they present, their "sterile fantasies." As a reader, you will probably have reached some conclusion as to whether or not I have succeeded in this attempt. My approach to this material has been guided by the conviction that one cannot get a sense of the stakes of Andalucismo, of the meaning of its claims, without entering its literary and aesthetic world, that the tradition can be best understood, in other words, less through the powers of description than those of enactment. The result may appear to some as partisan, but it is so only in the sense that I take the claims of the tradition seriously and draw on its own affective resources to communicate why. These claims, I have sought to show, are not abstract statements of fact about the Iberian past, such as those proffered by the discipline of history, but ways of inhabiting a complex inheritance. The connections binding al-Andalus and Europe (or for that matter, Palestine and Andalusia) demand more than dispassionate explanation, or rather, they ask of us—subjects, in one way or another, of Euro-America—far more than such an academic treatment can provide. A language capable of doing justice to these connections requires more dimensions of our thinking and emotion, of our lives, than can be found within the narrow confines of the academy.

The Andalusians whose lives I have explored in this book find themselves inhabited by a medieval past, a past that makes them unrecognizable to themselves within the normative languages of identity and belonging. The *andalucista* tradition these men and women sustain and extend, more than a set of ideas or statements of fact, is an attempt to make sense of this predicament, to speak and act sanely and thoughtfully from within the space illuminated by such a past. In my analysis of this tradition, I have eschewed a common line of inquiry that construes the past to be a manipulable resource for projects of self-construction, though such projects are an undeniable aspect of modern political life. Instead, I have foregrounded

an approach to history that starts with a recognition of a certain recalci-
trance of the past to manipulation, the way our lives, in other words, are
always already inscribed within a particular articulation of past, present,
and future, and that hence, our experience necessarily has a temporal dimension. Insomuch as this positioning within and across time is not simply
conceptual but vital, our experience of it will not necessarily find satisfac-
tion in a detached, intellectual response. This is what I take Wittgenstein
to have meant when he noted that a "hypothetical explanation" may leave
us unsatisfied when the object we are seeking to explain makes a deep impression on us, when it moves, captivates, or disturbs us. For Wittgenstein,
such impressions could only be explained up to a certain point, as they ultimately were aspects of our "forms of life."

Andalucismo teaches us that parallel to the history we feel ourselves to
be a part of, there is another, in the shadows, that is also in some way ours.
The more we start to notice it, discover its signs and sounds, the more we
come to recognize our place within it; our location—geographic, political, even religious—shifts as we accommodate to these new historical surroundings. What the *andalucistas* eventually come to achieve through this
process of exploration is not a more enlightened political standpoint but a
perspective from which new political questions and answers become available or from which certain old ones lose their purchase and necessity. Andalucismo thus deforms the horizon of our thinking.

Not just our thinking. The tradition diagnoses and occupies a tear in
the fabric of Europe, in the ontology of Europe. The notion of a "counter-
history," therefore, pulls us in the wrong direction, collapsing the tradition to the status of a competing narrative, which is only one of its aspects.
A better entrée to Andalucismo is found in Borges's "Garden of Forking
Paths," a story whose denouement pivots on the coexistence of multiple
times, "diverging, converging, and parallel times." In the labyrinth/novel
described in this story, to follow a course of action does not eliminate other
possible scenarios; an action not taken still occurs but in a time that has
branched off from the first and now runs parallel to it. At some point in
the future, circumstances may lead these two times to again converge, as
occurs toward the end of Borges's story. Borges's vision—in which one
time may branch off from another, remain distant from it for a long period,
and then reconnect at some later point—seems particularly germane to the
case of Andalucismo, itself a story of three fates or times, at times diverging, at times brought together: one anchored in al-Andalus, another born
of its elimination, and a third a time of exile, of the refugee.

Importantly, the account of this tradition that I have offered here is in no
way meant to stand as a general endorsement for projects of historical recu-

peration. The claim that one is recuperating a lost, buried, or distorted past is today ubiquitous and is attached to the full spectrum of political projects. As Foucault noted in his reference to this style of historical reflection, one he called "a counterhistory of races," although it emerged in the context of a revolutionary critique of state sovereignty, it was soon repurposed to serve and amplify the power of the state. From a discourse on race struggle, on the suppression and effacement of one race by the tyrannical force of another, it shifted to become a claim about the necessity of the sovereign state as the sole agency capable of securing and protecting the racial purity of the nation (Foucault 2003, 181–83). For many observers, contemporary projects that assign value to a distant past should be viewed with suspicion; they betray real history for the sake of ideology, a betrayal for which such terms as *nostalgia*, *Romanticism*, or the *invention of tradition* offer a diagnosis. In this book, I have largely avoided this terminology for reasons that I hope are clear. My argument is that Andalucismo deserves our attention not only for the way it brings to light a past left in darkness but because the horizons of thought and life it opens may be crucial to the task of finding our way beyond the stubborn polarities that continue to threaten our collective existence.

∴

I want to conclude these reflections by recalling a literary device that has made its appearance more than once across these pages: the mirror. For many observers of the tradition, Andalucismo is founded, first and foremost, on a "play of mirrors": what *andalucistas* discover, it is said, when they look across the Mediterranean, or back to medieval Iberia, is their own ideas and values, a reflection of their own desires and fantasies. I have criticized this solipsistic reading of the tradition (one that at times claims inspiration in a reading of Edward Said's *Orientalism*) for failing to recognize how Andalucismo disturbs the reflecting waters of European identity and exerts a friction on the political, aesthetic, and historiographical discourses of Spain and Europe. Here at the end, however, I want to bring the mirror back again, to recruit it for a different use than that of confirming what one already knows or already is.

"Mirror therapy" is a technique sometimes administered to amputees who are experiencing phantom limb pain. A mirror is positioned along the vertical axis of the body such that the intact limb is on one side with the residual stump on the other. When the patient looks in the mirror on the side of the good limb, the reflected image of the good limb will appear as if it were the one that was lost. Thus, when the patient moves an intact arm, it will appear as if she is controlling both the still remaining arm and the phantom one. Through use of this visual feedback, some patients are able to overcome pain, for example, by learning to unclench a phantom fist that had been frozen in a painful position.

A recent film titled *Reflecting Memory* (*Réfléchir la mémoire*) (2016), by the French Algerian artist Kader Attia, takes the practice of mirror therapy for amputees as a starting point for a wider reflection on the experience of loss, not only in its physical and psychological dimensions but in its social and historical ones as well. Like severed limbs, buried or silenced pasts can become sites of "phantom pain," pain lodged in histories denied reality by the present epistemic regime. The Armenian genocide and the Caribbean slave trade are two of many examples mentioned during the film. Attia's film invites us to think about historical narrative as a kind of mirror therapy, as a practice through which a certain coordination of the fragmented (collective) body can be achieved and unrecognizable experiences of pain be given a home. At one juncture in the film, the art historian Huey Copeland comments on the fact that some historians of Caribbean slavery have used photographs of Jamaican laborers, taken after emancipation, as a substitute for images of slaves, given the paucity of photographic evidence at the time. He notes, "Those scholars use that image to represent slavery. So there is this sense of, 'we need something, even if it's not historically accurate, to sort of fill in this imagistic void, to let us picture what it was.'" In other words, an image, even an imperfect one, may be of use in finding a way to live sanely within the shadows of a painful history. There may be much at stake, we could say, in the game of "playing with mirrors."

Reflecting Memory is about living in the aftermath of radical loss, about finding a way to recognize, and hence mourn, that loss, and through this process reacquire a new kind of integrity and mobility. The process achieves its therapeutic goals via a staged encounter with an image—of a lost limb, or a lost past—that is simultaneously an act of recuperation and an act of letting go: the clenched fist, the phantom pain, the historical trauma, can finally be released. This vision of the transformative work of the mirror speaks to the tradition of Andalucismo that I have explored in this book, a tradition founded on a diagnosis of an injury—an amputation of memory—in the historical ontology of Spain and Europe. That amputation has severely constricted our ethical and political imagination, the *andalucistas* tell us, a myopia that finds expression across history in acts of xenophobia and racism. Such an injury cannot be healed by a practice of historical representation alone but requires a broader reattunement of our senses and hence, a form of historical reflection and engagement adequate to this task. The sensory powers of music, literature, art, and architecture are needed. It is only through a delicate historical labor of attunement and assimilation that al-Andalus can be reconnected to Andalusia, to Spain, and to Europe.

Acknowledgments

I am grateful to the Carnegie Foundation and the American Council of Learned Societies for the financial support they provided me while I undertook this project. In addition, I want to thank some of the people who generously read and commented on the work at different moments in its evolution: Hussein Agrama, Gil Anidjar, Talal Asad, Donald Moore, Maria José de Abreu, Seth Kimmel, Jacob Liming, Aaron Eldridge, Basit Iqbal, James Monroe, Dianne Elise, Elena Arigita, Alessandra Ciucci, and Birgit Meyer. I also want to express my profound gratitude to the Spanish scholars and musicians who guided me along the way: Jose Antonio Gonzalez-Alcantud, Jose Miguel Puerta Vílchez, Mercedes García-Arenal, Maribel Fierro, Javier Roson, Emilio González Ferrín, Bernabe Lopez, Ali Keeler, Aristotles Moreno, Francisco Vigueras, Antonio Miguel Rodríguez Ramos, Lola Ferre, Fernando Rodríguez Mediano, Vicente Marti Tormo, and Meli Salinas Martin. I am grateful as well for the generosity and insight of Rosa Norton, who edited a version of this manuscript, and for perceptive comments offered by two anonymous reviewers.

Notes

1. Throughout this book, I use the term *Andalucismo* to indicate a much wider phenomenon than a nationalist movement, though nationalism is one of the strains in which this tradition appears.

2. Although Andalucismo has since its inception in the late nineteenth century involved a concern for both the Muslims and Jews of medieval Iberia, this book focuses primarily on the tradition's relationship to Muslim Spain. This choice reflects the very different status assigned to Judaism as opposed to Islam within contemporary Spanish and European culture and political thought. Today, inquiries into the legacies of al-Andalus are deeply entwined with debates about the status and desirability of Muslim immigrants in Spain and Europe. In contrast, parallel debates concerning the Jewish inhabitants of Europe are rare despite the long and brutal history of anti-Semitism on the continent.

3. *Al-Andalus* is the Arabic term used by Muslims from the early eighth century to describe the parts of the Iberian Peninsula under Muslim sovereignty. At its greatest geographic extension, this included much of the peninsula and small parts of what is now southern France. Up until the latter part of the eleventh century, al-Andalus remained under the authority of a series of Umayyad rulers, though with increasing autonomy from the Umayyad Caliphate based in Damascus. The Umayyads were subsequently displaced first by the Almoravids (1086–1147) and then by the Almohads (1147–1212), both political dynasties of North African (Berber) origin. By the mid-thirteenth century, the only remaining Muslim kingdom in Iberia was the Emirate of Granada, ruled by the Nasrid dynasty until its final defeat in 1492.

4. On the contemporary status of the descendants of the exiled Andalusians now residing in Morocco, see Bahrami (1995, 2000) and Calderwood (2018).

5. Responding to an assertion by Harold Bloom that "Muslim Andalusians" nowhere still exist, Gil Anidjar throws into question the sensory epistemology that secures this judgment: "One may wonder whether Bloom is equipped with the apparatus (visual, linguistic, and whatnot) that would enable him to recognize such Muslims (But why only Muslims? And against which horizons?). Or what he thinks about all of the Muslims (and non-Muslims) who today are prevented, by means of elevated walls, visa requirements and hyper-militarized police forces, from entering the very geography of al-Andalus" (Anidjar 2008, 196).

6. On the history of the Moriscos, see García-Arenal (1996), Vincent (2006), and Harvey (2006).

7. A discussion of the career of the Jesuit priest Juan Andrés, an early exponent of this view (often referred to as the "Arab thesis") can be found in Dainotto (2006).

8. On "the generation of '98,'" as these intellectuals came to be referred, see Laín Entralgo (1971), Molina (1968), Sánchez Dueñas (2010).

9. Seminal contributions to the history of Spanish Arabism and Orientalism are those by Monroe (1970) and López García (1990, 2012).

10. Useful discussions of Andalusian nationalism include Moreno Alonso (1986), Cortés Peña (1994), Domínguez Ortiz (1983), and González de Molina and Sevilla Guzmán (1987).

11. On Spanish Africanism, see Calderwood (2018), Velasco de Castro (2014), López García (2012), and Aragón Reyes (2013). Spanish Arabists, with a few exceptions, tended to remain aloof from Africanism, their concerns largely limited to Spain's "internal Orient," the Muslim kingdoms of medieval Iberia.

12. While Castro wrote many works on Spanish literary traditions, the most important statement of his broader vision of the Muslim and Jewish contributions to Spain is found in his *España en su historia* (translated as *The Structure of Spanish History*), first published in 1948. See chapter 2 for a discussion of contemporary anxieties that Castro's work continues to evoke among historians.

13. While the cult of "pure blood" (*limpieza de sangre*) promoted in part by the Holy Inquisition in sixteenth-century Spain affected the lives of many, it also was met with criticism and opposition in many parts of the peninsula. As Henry Kamen notes, "The vision of a Spain agonizing under the impact of *limpieza* is erroneous, and also unreliable as a tool of analysis. *Limpieza* played an identifiable role in determined parts of the peninsula, at determined times. But it had a restricted impact, was often scorned by the social and intellectual elite, and did not have much effect among the mass of the population" (Kamen 1996, 27). As opposed to many scholars of this period, Castro was well aware that early-modern Spain included highly contradictory impulses toward both repression and tolerance.

14. Important discussions of Castro's work include Laín Entralgo (1971), Armistead (1988, 1997), and Goytisolo (2003).

15. An objection might be raised at this point that there is no singular object corresponding to the designation *Europe*, that the term actually disguises the real heterogeneity of countries, histories, and cultures that display none of the unity and integrity implied by the singularizing notion of Europe—especially in this moment when the project of economic coordination—the European Union—seems to be unraveling. Which Europe? As invoked by whom? What should be noted, however, is how commonly one encounters, whether in popular, journalistic, or academic writing, the notion of Europe as the site of a shared civilization, one typically defined by a heritage that stretches from ancient Greece and the Roman Empire to Christianity, the Protestant Reformation, and on to the Enlightenment and the Industrial Revolution. In recent decades, it has also become common for Europeans to view themselves as the inheritors of a Judeo-Christian civilization. Although not everyone in Europe inhabits that space equally (Roma, for example, are only marginally embraced by the term) and the boundaries of that space are constantly in flux (the place of Russia, Turkey, and the now autonomous republics of the former Soviet Union have all shifted considerably in recent decades), the notion, nonetheless, exerts a force in debates about who properly

fits within the European continent. This genealogy exists uncomfortably, indeed necessarily precludes, that traced by Andalucismo.

16. As Talal Asad has noted, the barrier that secures medieval Spain's externality to the civilizational processes that constitute Europe involves two rhetorical moves. "First," he writes, "by denying that it has an essence of its own, 'Islam' can be represented as a carrier civilization that helped to bring important elements into Europe from outside, material and intellectual elements that were only contingently connected to Islam. Then, to this carrier civilization is attributed an essence: an ingrained hostility to all non-Muslims. That attribution constitutes Islam as Europe's primary alter. This alleged antagonism to Christians then becomes crucial to the formation of European identity. In this, as in other historical narratives of Europe, this oppositional role gives 'Islam' a quasi-civilizational identity. One aspect of the identity of Islamic civilization is that it represents an early attempt to destroy Europe's civilization from outside, another is that it signifies the corrupting moral environment that Europe must continuously struggle to overcome from within" (Asad 2003, 168–69).

17. On the marginality of Arabic within the field of medieval studies, see Menocal (1987, chap. 1).

18. The claim that Islam has had little impact on the formation of Europe has been made with renewed insistence in recent years in the context of a growing European anxiety about Muslim immigrants to the continent. Note, for example, the sense of vindication and relief expressed by reviewers (in Le Monde and Le Figaro) of Sylvain Gouguenheim's book on what the author deems is an exaggerated emphasis regarding an Islamic contribution to Europe. "Mr. Gouguenheim wasn't afraid to remind us that there was a medieval Christian crucible, a fruit of the heritage of Athens and Jerusalem," while "Islam hardly proposed its knowledge to Westerners. All in all, and contrary to what has been repeated in a crescendo since the 1960s, European culture in its history and development shouldn't be owing a whole lot to Islam. In any case, nothing essential" (John Vinocur, "Europe's Debt to Islam Given a Skeptical Look," New York Times, April 28, 2008, https://www.nytimes.com/2008/04/28/world/europe/28iht-politicus.2.12398698.html).

19. One highly influential statement of this point is found in Edward Said's touchstone study, Orientalism (1978), where he argues that key aspects of Europe's own self-understanding were constructed on a principle of differentiation opposing a Muslim Orient to a Christian Europe.

20. From as early as the sixteenth century, Mastnak argues, Europe begins to replace Christendom as a term of collective identity and action in anti-Muslim polemical writing.

21. The Spanish historian Mercedes García-Arenal has highlighted the similarities between seventeenth-century discourses on Iberia's Muslim population and those taking place today: "It is striking how present-day reactions to this presence [of Muslims], and the ways they are formulated in the press—asking whether Muslims can be Europeans, whether they are always Muslims first and foremost, whether they can be assimilated or not, whether they are going to alter fundamentally the host societies to which they migrate, whether their religious beliefs are compatible with western cultural and political values, whether they profess a 'civilizational hatred' of Europeans, and so on— bear a striking resemblance to the discussions and emotions engendered in sixteenth-century Spain and which reached a peak around the expulsion of the early 1600s. For then, as now, the debate hinged on the possibility and desirability of assimilation,

and above all particularly on the same fundamental question: can they become us?" (García-Arenal 2009, 891).

22. Among the most vociferous and influential exponents in Spain today of the idea that Islam is incompatible with European values are Vidal Manzanares (2005, 2009), Fanjul (2000, 2004), and Rodríguez Magda (2006).

23. Although Menocal was Cuban by birth and taught for many years at Yale University, her work on medieval and early-modern Iberian literature and her enthusiasm for the heterogeneous culture that produced it made her an important reference within the archive of *andalucista* writings.

24. The Romantics' engagement with Islam is explored in works by Almond (2009) and Einboden (2014).

25. In a footnote, Nirenberg suggests that Menocal's arguments suggesting that medieval Muslims made a decisive contribution to European culture rely on "pre-Foucauldian genealogical methodologies generally associated with colonialism" (Nirenberg 2008, 20). To clarify this claim, he offers the following comparison: "What Arabist today would claim that, because the mid-twentieth-century Arabic poets who broke the monopoly of classical metrical forms and rhyme schemes did so under the influence of Shakespeare and Shelley (e.g., Nazik al-Malaika), contemporary Arabic poetry is therefore European?" (Nirenberg 2008, 20). Yet Menocal's argument is not that Europe is "Islamic." Her claim is simply that aesthetic, philosophical, and medical traditions practiced by medieval Muslims were part of the world from which those traditions we now identify as "European" emerged. Nirenberg's misreading of this point would seem to reflect a discomfort with identities that cannot be called wholly one thing, whether wholly European or wholly Arabic.

26. In my own reading of the *andalucista* tradition, I view idealization as a risk, a pitfall into which practitioners of this tradition have frequently fallen, but not a defining feature of the enterprise itself. Moreover, it is worth noting that many of the most celebrated "achievements of Europe" (say, the music of Beethoven or Mozart) are themselves the product of a small elite and in no way representative—in a statistical sense—of a broader European culture. Yet the musical works of these composers can be heralded as one of the finest achievements of European culture without any worry that one has, therefore, replaced the reality of this culture with an idealized image.

27. Said (1978) provides ample evidence of the pervasiveness of such disparaging or disdainful attitudes within Orientalist writing. See Almond (2009) for a useful survey of the complex but ultimately negative assessment of Islam prevalent among the German Romantics.

28. The greater value attributed to studies of Greek culture is due, I would argue, to the place of that culture within the teleology of European identity.

29. As the literary scholar Ryan Szpiech has insightfully observed, "In the same sense that *convivencia* has represented an attractive, albeit simplistic, model for some medievalists faced with what were perceived as dangerous tendencies towards uniform models of Eurocentric westernness, so it has come to represent for other philologists and historians a dangerous imprecision that runs the risk of resurrecting the ideologies of nationalism and propagandistic historiography" (Szpiech 2013, 151).

30. The Black Legend (*Leyenda Negra*) refers to a style of anti-Spanish historical writing produced by rival European nations beginning in the late sixteenth century and characterized by a highly disparaging view of the country, emphasizing its decadence, repressiveness, and brutality. Such literature epitomizes what had been Spain's long-

standing denigration by its European neighbors, its forced exile from the story of European progress, only overcome with the end of the Franco regime in the mid-1970s.

31. The following observation by the Greek anthropologist Nadia Seremetakis highlights the problem with such a dismissive stance: "Thus the modernist critic would look at Greek society and dismiss any residues and incongruities emanating from the pre-modern as both Romantic and invented. In both cases, static impositions of the polarity authentic/inauthentic led to the dismissal of important discontinuous cultural systems and sensibilities that have been repositioned within the modern as nonsynchronous elements" (Seremetakis 1994, 17).

32. To give but one example, the arguments of Johann Georg Hamann, an eighteenth-century scholar whose critique of Kant had a decisive impact on the formation of the Romantic movement, anticipate many aspects of Ludwig Wittgenstein's view on the inseparability of linguistic meaning from the context of the traditions wherein words are actually used. In a passage that has strong echoes of Wittgenstein's critique of a particular style of philosophical inquiry, Hamann writes, "For me the question is not so much What is reason? as What is language? It is here I suspect the basis of all paralogisms and antinomies can be found which are ascribed to reason: it comes from words being held to be concepts, and concepts to be the things themselves" (Hamann 1965, 264–65). Hamann's emphasis on the importance of tradition, and on the "priority of the sensual over the intellectual" (Green 1996, 300), left a lasting imprint on the leading intellectuals of the Romantic movement and, indirectly, on the *andalucistas* who, beginning in the late nineteenth century, built on and extended that movement within their own context.

33. In a useful 2009 discussion of the Spanish commemoration of the 1609 expulsion of the Moriscos, the Spanish scholar Elena Arigita (2018) calls attention to the way public events were orchestrated precisely to affirm the irrelevance of the expulsion to present-day Spain. Referring to a statement by the Peruvian writer Mario Vargas Llosa that "the injustices of the past cannot and should not be selected according to the needs of the present," Arigita responds, "And where should we establish the divide between memory and history, on the one hand, and politics on the other? Rather than defining domains and creating strict separations, we need to approach these issues from a genealogical perspective to understand the mechanisms of exclusion, inclusion and reconfiguration inherent in memory politics with regard to their relationship with historical narratives (and more precisely, with historical nation-state centered narratives)" (Arigita 2018, 9).

34. See David Scott's insightful discussion of the epistemological and political challenges that attend scholarly attempts to assert the reality of an Afro-Caribbean literary tradition. Scott's concern is that scholars who aim to challenge the dominant Eurocentric reading of this tradition (his examples run from Herskovitz to Gilroy) have generally felt compelled to occupy the same epistemological terrain as their Eurocentric opponents, a terrain defined by the discourses of anthropology and rationalist historiography. In contrast to this approach, he proposes "a vocabulary that attempts to free black diaspora criticism from the seeming need for the guarantee of an authoritative Outside: call it Anthropology" (Scott 1999, 127).

35. A recently published collection of essays edited by da Col and Palmié (2020) offers a number of thoughtful and original discussions of Wittgenstein's "Remarks on Frazer." See, in particular, the contributions by Palmié, Lambek, Das, and Puett.

36. In his unpublished thesis, Carlo Germeshuys (2009) offers a perceptive reading

of these passages from Wittgenstein and their importance for understanding the view of history found in the literary works of the German writer W. G. Sebald.

37. Many authors have addressed the persistence of the Andalusian past though the figure of haunting, the ghostlike return of a repressed or excluded past. While such a concept resonates with some of the writings of Andalucismo, the approach to this tradition I elaborate here does not start from the assumption, implicit in much of this literature, that it is a failure of historical closure, or the repression of the past that accounts for its weight in the present. What worries me about such a view is the implication that often accompanies it, namely, that a tie to the past is something that might be exorcised. See my comments on this issue in Charles Hirschkind, interview by Mahshid Zandi and Khalidah Ali, University of Toronto, January 18, 2019, https:// entangledworlds.utoronto.ca/index.php/interview-with-charles-hirschkind/.

38. Michael Lambek points to this predicament in his discussion of Sakalava concepts of historicity. In his elegant formulation, "Sakalava do not so much discover the past or the truth as it discovers them" (Lambek 2016, 336). Lambek's analytically subtle and ethnographically rich analysis of Sakalava historicity can be found across a number of essays and most extensively in his book *The Weight of the Past* (2002).

39. In his famous essay "Theses on the Philosophy of History," Walter Benjamin describes these processes by which past and present enter into meaningful relation in terms of a "constellation," a unique pattern that the historian may reveal and animate: "Historicism contents itself with establishing a causal nexus among various moments in history. But no state of affairs having causal significance is for that very reason historical. It became historical posthumously, as it were, through events that may be separated from it by thousands of years. The historian who proceeds from this consideration ceases to tell the sequence of events like the beads of a rosary. He grasps the constellation into which his own era has entered, along with a very specific earlier one. Thus, he establishes a conception of the present as newness shot through with splinters of messianic time" (Benjamin 1968, 263).

40. Charles Stewart has written elegantly on the "affective resonance" that brings events from different historical moments into productive alignment, establishing patterns of analogy and correspondence. See Stewart (2013, 2017) as well as the essay co-written with Stephan Palmié (2016). See also Yael Navaro-Yashin (2009).

41. Américo Castro makes a similar observation in regard to the historiography of Spain: "Those who do not have in advance a kindred feeling for the historical deeds of a people will not accept as valuable what was achieved by that people, no matter how high we may heap praises thereon. Unless it finds in the reader an adequate receptivity for a certain kind of values, the history of a people may glance off his sensibility, just as Shakespeare's works did off the spirit of a number of eighteenth century rationalists" (Castro 1954, 32).

42. Ganivet discusses the importance of Ribot and Janet for his own assessment of nineteenth-century Spain in *Cartas finlandesas* (Finish Letters) (Ganivet 1906, 162–72).

43. In a fascinating study of the legacies of Aristotle's philosophy of perception, the literary scholar Daniel Heller-Roazen (2007) situates the ideas of Ribot and Janet within a longer tradition of philosophical and psychological thinking founded on Aristotle's notion of the synthetic or common sense (*sensus communis*). Commenting on the "depersonalization phenomena" studied by these French scholars, Heller-Roazen notes, "Cartesian consciousness, too, now appears in a new form, at once verified and

carried to an extreme. With the discovery of those 'doubting' people who do not feel that they feel and do not feel that they even are, one may at last point to subjects who reason, in purity, without sensing that they do so; one may indicate the incontrovertible evidence of cogitating beings who think that they exist even—or especially—when they cannot be said, with any rigor, to sense it" (Heller-Roazen 2007, 287).

44. Ribot and Janet very much anticipated many of the observations made today by scholars working on affect. Janet, for example, followed Maine de Biran in defining "affection" as "that which remains of a complete sensation after one has removed all individual personality" (Heller-Roazen 2007, 281). From this perspective, "affect theory" can be read as both diagnosis and symptom of modernity.

45. A useful discussion of Ganivet's unique idealist perspective is found in Robles Egea (1997, esp. 213–14).

46. In his essay "The Storyteller" (1969), Benjamin used the disappearance of the practice of storytelling to highlight the loss of the sensory substrate on which experience depended and its replacement by abstract forms of knowledge ("information"). Within the sensorially dense practice of storytelling—grounded in a coordination of hand and eye—collective experience acquired its authority and communicability. The conditions of this art were decisively lost, Benjamin suggests, with the advent of modernity, as authoritative knowledges were divested of their grounding in the sensory condition of daily life.

47. In "The Storyteller" Benjamin also refers to Don Quixote to highlight the evacuation of experience qua wisdom that he identifies as a characteristic of the novel genre (Benjamin 1968, 87–88).

48. Castro wrote extensively on the figure of the Morisco in Cervantes's work. See in particular his *El pensamiento de Cervantes y otros estudios cervantinos* (2002).

49. On the importance of historiography in Cervantes, see Cascardi (1997) and Quinn (2013).

50. Admittedly, among the characters that populate Don Quixote, there are both Muslims and Moriscos. My reference to an "absent subject" is meant in this light to highlight the way the text stages the embattled status of the Muslim/Morisco population, anticipating their imminent disappearance. There are numerous studies of the figures of Muslims and Moriscos in Don Quixote. Among those who take up the theme I address here, see Fuchs (2003), Brownlee (2005), Johnson (2000), and Menocal (2002). Fastrup (2012) offers a challenge to this interpretive trend, arguing that Cervantes's texts provide the possibility of a more ambiguous stance in relation to the forms of state power then being consolidated.

51. Rogozen-Soltar's (2017) recent ethnographic study of Granada bears out this impression.

CHAPTER ONE

1. Tétouan (or Tetuán, in Spanish) was capital of the Spanish Protectorate in Morocco from 1912 to 1956.

2. Rodolfo Gil Benumeya, "Cuadro esquema de los diversos campos de acción del pensamiento 'joven marroquí' y posición de las distintas zonas concéntricas del problema indígena en relación con los problemas generales del Islam," Ministerio de Educación, Cultura y Deporte, Archivo General de la Administración, Fondo Ministerio de la Presidencia del Gobierno, caja 81/10199, 3.

3. Today, scholars of the region frequently refer (dismissively) to visions of Middle

Eastern resurgence such as Gil Benumeya's as *Arabophilic*, a term used to indicate a perceived overidentification with Arabs, Islam, and the Middle East found among some of their brethren. The term, however, often conceals more than it reveals, diagnosing a problematic attachment but not explaining why that attachment merits a skeptical assessment while others—say a felt connection with Europe or Spain—do not. Substituting a psychological origin for a political and historical one, the diagnosis forestalls a deeper exploration into the claims of Andalucismo: in this case, its unique political vision of a resurgent Mediterranean society.

4. As the historian Montserrat Huguet Santos notes in regard to Gil Benumeya's Africanist perspective, Spain was envisioned in the role of mediator more than as an occupier: "The role of Spain in regard to the Moroccans and Arabs of the Middle East and the Americas could only be as a continental bridge between these societies and Europe. This thesis emphasized the defense of a pan-Arab movement based in a desire for political union among the peoples of Arab culture" (Huguet Santos 1999, 39).

5. This is not to say that Gil Benumeya's work was devoid of the paternalism expressed by most other Europeans for Europe's colonial subjects; his stipulation, in the comments I began with, that the young Moroccans will discover their political destiny only "once they begin to think for themselves" makes this clear.

6. *Mediodía*, literally "middle of the day," is the Spanish equivalent of the French *midi* and the Italian *mezzogiorno*.

7. The Albayzín is the name of the old Muslim quarter of the city of Granada. "The Universe Seen from the Albayzín" is the subtitle of Gil Benumeya's book *Ni oriente, ni occidente* (Neither Orient nor Occident, 1928).

8. I borrow this phrase from Brian Massumi (2002, 183).

9. In *Colonial al-Andalus* (2018) Eric Calderwood provides perhaps the most thoroughly researched and rigorously argued example of this approach, highlighting Gil Benumeya's various contributions to the Spanish colonial enterprise in Morocco. While I find his assessment of Andalucismo in terms of its political utility ultimately too reductive an approach to this complex tradition, I have benefitted greatly from his broad historical grasp of early twentieth-century Spain and Morocco.

10. My approach, in this sense, does not invoke Spanish Orientalism as an explanatory lens through which to interpret the texts of Andalucismo but, on the contrary, takes the tradition of Andalucismo as necessary for a reassessment of Orientalism.

11. Useful readings of Gil Benumeya's career are found in González Alcantud (1996), Calderwood (2014a, 2018), and Vagni (2016).

12. Abd Allah Ibn Umayya was the brother of Muhammad ibn Umayya, known in Spanish as Abén Humeya (or by his adopted Christian name, Hernando de Válor y Córdoba), a renowned Morisco leader who led the increasingly persecuted "New Christians" in the Alpujarras Rebellion (1568–1570). On the history of the Moriscos, see Domínguez Ortiz and Vincent (1993) and Fletcher (2001).

13. On the history of Spanish colonial ambitions in North Africa see Parra Monserrat (2012a, 2012b), Aragón Reyes (2013), Casals i Meseguer (2006), Mateo Dieste (2012), and Martin-Márquez (2008).

14. Spanish Africanism's discourse of fraternal bonds between Spain and Morocco has its early and influential articulation in the works of Joaquín Costa, an important contributor to late nineteenth-century Spanish intellectual and political life. Thus, in a speech given in 1884, Costa argued, "In the Middle Ages, Morocco accomplished its

providential destiny of founding a civilization on our Peninsula, and now, in the modern age, Spain has the providential mission to promote civilization in Morocco" (cited in Velasco de Castro 2014, 217).

15. Notably, a strong current within twentieth-century scholarship on Iberia's medieval past has been dedicated to overcoming this contradiction by arguing that the Iberian Muslims, or at least the cultural forms they produced, were essentially Spanish or, as Asín Palacio would argue, essentially Catholic.

16. Antonio Martín de la Escalera, an editor in chief of the Africanist journal *Revista de Tropas Coloniales* (edited at one point by Franco himself), in which Gil Benumeya's writings were frequently published, wrote in 1933, "No other state is as free of imperialist pretensions as Spain, nor finds its self-interest as far from this ambition. All of our possibilities in Africa are perfectly compatible with the freedom and independence of the Moroccan people. More than this: Morocco and Spain have many common interests" (cited by Cordero Torres 1956, 24).

17. In *Neither Orient, nor Occident: The Universe Seen from Albayzín*, a publication that appeared just shortly after *Mediodía*, the editors refer to the earlier publication with the subtitle, "Introduction to the Study of Contemporary Arabic Spain" ("España árabe actual").

18. Gil Benumeya's status as representative of an occupying power was not as significant a barrier to these relationships as one might imagine. At the time, many of the nationalist leaders saw a partial convergence between the interests of the Protectorate and those of the nationalist movement itself, particularly in regard to the necessity of modernization for the region's political, educational, and economic institutions. On this convergence, see Calderwood (2018), González Alcantud (1996), Vagni (2016), Jensen (2005), and Aragón Reyes (2013).

19. On Bennuna's contribution to the Moroccan nationalist movement, see essays by González González (2013) and Sánchez Arroyo (2013).

20. Many of these writings on the Arab Awakening (*Nahda*) and its relation, historical and contemporary, to Spain, appeared in the Africanist journals *Cuaderno de Estudios Africanos y Orientales*, *Revista de Tropas Coloniales*, and *Africa*.

21. To deepen and extend linkages between Spain and the Middle East and to help Spain secure a role in relation to transformations taking part in the region, Gil Benumeya participated in the founding of the Hispano-Islamic Association in Madrid in 1932. This association included among its members a number of key activists within the independence movements taking place in the Middle East: Chekib Arslan, a Lebanese follower of the reform movement initiated by Jamal al-Din al-Afghani and Muhammad Abduh and an important proponent of pan-Islamism; the Moroccan independence leaders Bennuna, Torres, and Allal al-Fassi; as well as Habib Bourguiba, who would eventually become the first prime minister of Tunisia. This association served not only as a forum for political exchange and discussion but also aimed to promote commercial relations between Spain and the Middle East.

22. Beyond his association with what were considered "Arabophilic" positions, Gil Benumeya was also a contributor to various "philosephardic" initiatives and publications, among them *La Gaceta Literaria*, a journal of art and culture founded in 1927 and aligned with nationalist currents. Philosephardic views were not uncommon among proponents of Spanish fascism, and contributors to *La Gaceta* frequently wrote in support of Sephardic movements in Morocco and the Balkans while also calling

attention to historic contributions by Sephardic Jews to medieval Spain. On early twentieth-century philosephardic views in Spain, see Calderwood (2018) and Álvarez Chilada (2002).

23. On the career of the term *Semite* and its relation to Orientalism, colonialism, and the constitution of Europe, see Anidjar's pioneering work, *Semites: Race, Religion, Literature* (2008).

24. As Huguet Santos has observed, "Without denying that Spain had a natural right to belong to Europe, Rodolfo Gil Benumeya rejected the legitimacy of exploiting the Hispanic-Mediterranean ties of friendship for the sake of Western interests, thus expressing a veiled disapproval of the regime's utilitarian approach to Mediterraneanism" (Huguet Santos 1999, 45).

25. Gil Grimau follows his father in defending an anticolonialist reading of this text: "*Marruecos andaluz* is certainly a visceral and Africanist work, but it reflects, not the colonialist rhetoric of the time, but the convictions of its author who himself was not a colonialist. And the proof that neither he nor his work were colonialist can be seen in the repercussion I mentioned earlier that took place, not among the Spanish, but the Moroccans, specifically among the Moroccan nationalists who liberated their country, for many of whom this book was, and is, a primary reference" (Gil Grimau 1996, 24).

26. The letter in which this comment is found was sent to the Moroccan nationalist leader Balafrej. See Rodolfo Gil Benumeya Grimau, "Sobre la diáspora ya la ocultación morisca dentro de su patria: Hechos y recuerdos por vía verbal," WebIslam, April 18, 2006, http://www.webislam.com/articulos/28896-sobre_la_diaspora_y_la_ocultacion _moriscas_dentro_de_su_patria_hechos_y_recuerdo.html.

27. Mateo Dieste describes one practice used to promote the *hermandad* discourse among Moroccans: "During the Protectorate, for example, trips were organized for 'indigenous leaders' or 'Berber girls' (Álvarez Salamanca 1926) to visit Granada's Alhambra palace, a perfect device for demonstrating the ideology of Hispano-Moroccan brotherhood" (Mateo Dieste 2003, 242–43).

28. This "indifference" noted by the bishop also found expression in sexual relations (including marriages), between Moroccans and Spaniards, especially between Moroccan men and Spanish women. According to the Franciscan jurist García Barriuso, in Tangiers it was common to see Spanish women accompanied by Moroccan men who, in his view, "follow their religion in a very relaxed manner" (cited in Mateo Dieste 2012, 253). Although these liaisons were highly discouraged by the colonial administration—to the point of being prohibited by the fascist regime—they took place with considerable frequency (Nerín i Abad 1998, 116–20). This pattern of sexual relations between Indigenous men and colonial women stood in sharp contrast to earlier Spanish colonial practices in the New World where Spanish women, guarantors of the purity of Spanish blood, were strictly forbidden from associating with the "inferior" races in the colonies (see Stolcke 1992).

29. Paralelo 36 Andalucía defines its own political orientation as a combination of "Andalucismo, environmentalism, feminism, radical democracy, and the social left." The group describes its choice of name as follows: "The imaginary line that traverses the strip of water that both separates and unites the economic and political hemispheres of the planet." From "¿Qué es Paralelo 36 Andalucía?" Paralelo 36 Andalucía: Espacio de Pensamiento y Cooperación Política, http://www.paralelo36andalucia.com /que-es-paralelo-36-andalucia/.

30. The notion of a "third Spain" has also been elaborated by scholars outside the

ambit of Andalucismo. Rodríguez Ramos's employment of the term, however, owes greatly to the work of the historian Emilio González Ferrín, whose scholarship I discuss in chapter 2.

31. Useful discussions of this conflict over the ownership of the Mezquita-Catedral can be found in Arigita (2013), Boll (2017), Calderwood (2015), Rosa and Jover Báez (2017), and Astor, Burchardt, Griera (2019).

32. Interview with Manuel Nieto Cumplido, "'Todo lo original de la Mequita supera lo musulmán, es Mediterráneo," *El Día de Córdoba*, January 27, 2008, http://www .eldiadecordoba.es/cordoba/original-Mezquita-supera-musulman-Mediterraneo_0 _117288876.html.

33. An official brochure for the monument from 2014 describes the Islamic aspects of the edifice as "an ostentatious display of power, though . . . not very original" (Cathedral of Córdoba n.d.). In chapter 2 I discuss a common trope within the historiography of medieval Iberia whereby Islam is identified as a "carrier society," one that enabled the transmission of the Greek philosophical heritage to Renaissance Europe but that contributed little of its own. Nieto Cumplido's argument partakes of this same discourse.

34. This claim is disputed by some of Spain's leading archaeologists (see, e.g., Fernando Arce-Sainz 2015), though it continues to be upheld in much of the literature, including the monument's Wikipedia site.

35. The legibility of this "canonical and liturgical expression" to the law owes, in part, to two twentieth-century amendments to Spanish property law. First, Article 206 of the Law for the Inscription of Titles (Ley Hipotecaria), promulgated during the Franco regime, extended to the Church the right to claim ownership of properties under its administration that lacked prior official title. In accord with the National Catholic ideology of the fascist regime, the law explicitly draws a parallel between the property rights of the Catholic Church and those of the state. Second, in 1998 the right-wing government of José María Aznar removed a legal stipulation that had prevented the Church from owning properties designated for cultic practice—defined as "public property"—thereby opening the way for the Church to register as its own sites of worship such as the Mezquita-Catedral.

36. On the emergence and development of the notion of the Reconquista, see García Sanjuán (2013, 2016), Ríos Saloma (2011), and García Fitz (2009).

37. Original quotation from the Carlist magazine *Pelayos* (December 27, 1936, 147) published during the civil war. Reproduced in Otero (2000, 142).

38. Hashim Cabrera, "A propósito de la tristeza de Don Manuel Nieto Cumplido," WebIslam, January 16, 2006, https://www.webislam.com/noticias/45200-a_proposito _de_la_tristeza_de_don_manuel_nieto_cumplido.html.

39. "Aznar Defends Pope's Remarks," *Gulf News*, September 25, 2006, https:// gulfnews.com/news/europe/spain/aznar-defends-pope-s-remarks-1.256520.

40. Notably, while Gomá Lanzón does register some discomfort with the adequacy of the notion of Reconquista (preceded initially by *so-called* and with added scare quotes), these grammatical hedges are shortly abandoned. As noted in other sections of the book, I differ from Gomá Lanzón's move to render a relationship to the past suspicious by default, as only ever an anachronism. Javier Gomá Lanzón, "Libre y con compromiso," *El País*, February 21, 2016, http://elpais.com/elpais/2016/02/19/opinion /1455892924_603940.html.

41. As of publication, their petition had garnered close to four hundred thousand signatures.

42. For a discussion of this effort and of other recent initiatives to recognize the historical wrongs visited on the Moriscos, see Arigita (2018).

43. *El País*, June 11, 2015.

CHAPTER TWO

1. Particularly useful discussions of the *convivencia* polemic are found in Szpiech (2013), Ray (2005), and Soifer (2009).

2. In the early years of the twentieth century, the term acquired a technical use within the field of scientific linguistics. For Américo Castro's development of the term, see his two classic texts on Spanish history, *España en su historia: Cristianos, moros y judíos* (1948) and *La realidad histórica de España* (1954).

3. In his speech in Cairo in 2008, President Barack Obama gestured to this notion (without using the term itself) in his reference to Andalusia's "proud tradition of tolerance." See Hirschkind (2009) for a discussion of Obama's speech.

4. On the history of Spanish Arabism, see López García (1990, 2011), and Monroe (1970).

5. As Miguel Asín Palacios and Emilio García Gómez, the leading Arabists of the early twentieth century, wrote in their "Preliminary note" to the first edition of the journal *al-Andalus*, "For us, Arabic studies are an intimate and endearing necessity, given that . . . they are entwined with many pages from our history and reveal valuable features of our literature, our thought, and our art; they enter our language and, perhaps, more or less, our life" (cited in López García 1990, 5).

6. Szpiech traces the imprint of Vico's thought on both Erich Auerbach and Castro, including his basic and well-known dictum *verum ipsum factum* (that which is true is the same as that which is made), or as Szpiech glosses, "the task of the scholar is to seek the true in a human context, in human things, not in nature or metaphysics" (Szpiech 2013, 142).

7. Carmelo López-Arias, "El CSIC es el mayor logro alcanzado por laicos católicos en el desarrollo científico del siglo XX," *Religión en Libertad*, July 30, 2014. A comment in the left-wing newspaper *El País* offered this sarcastic rejoinder: "Let's celebrate 1939, the year in which science was swept out of Spain, the year in which it had to become Catholic like everyone else. A miracle." Jorge M. Reverte, "Aniversarios," *El País*, September 4, 2014, https://elpais.com/elpais/2014/09/03/opinion/1409732798_975176.html.

8. "Consejo Superior de Investigaciones Científicas," Wikipedia (Spanish language), https://es.wikipedia.org/wiki/Consejo_Superior_de_Investigaciones_Cient%C3%ADficas.

9. As Gil Anidjar has persuasively argued, the religious and political exclusion of Islam and Judaism from the civilizational space of Europe—their assignment to the status of "enemies" within that project—created the theological-political basis for Europe's own self-definition (Anidjar 2008).

10. González Ferrín, paper presented at the annual meeting of the American Comparative Literature Association, Cambridge, Massachusetts, March 17–20, 2016.

11. García-Arenal, a colleague and collaborator of Rodríguez Mediano's at CSIC, attributes this decline of ideological pressures on the discipline of history to Spain no longer having to defend its European identity. It is an interesting paradox that only by achieving what Rodríguez Mediano calls the "illusion of identity"—that is, its identity

as a European nation—can Spain acquire the ability to grasp its own history dispassionately and thus, objectively.

12. Jacques Rancière notes among the historians of the Annales School a tendency to disqualify the words used by the medieval societies they described, an effect achieved by means of territorializing their words and actions such that they might be interpreted as expressions of the geological and geographic parameters of their lives: "All speech production can be represented as the exact expression of what gives it a place, of its own legitimacy. Thus, the discourse of the book, as utopian or heterodox as it appears, is always interpretable as a *doxa*, as the expression of a *topos*" (Rancière 1994, 67).

13. See, for example, Davis (2008), Heng (2018), and, in the Iberian context, Menocal (2002) and Fuchs (2009).

14. Again, Constantin Fasolt's discussion of the ideological functions of the discipline of history highlights this point: "History calms the mind. It has a soothing function. It issues safe-conducts to passengers through time by drawing a firm line between the present and the past: that was then, and this is now. What was then is past—dead and gone. It happened, that much is true. But now it can no longer pose a threat, nor can it help in any way" (Fasolt 2005, 5).

15. See, for example, García Sanjuán (2013). Numerous authors have insinuated that despite González Ferrín's long-standing support for leftist causes, he is a Falangist in disguise. Much of the campaign against him (though not all, by any means) has been waged by the Department of Jewish and Islamic Studies at CSIC in Madrid.

16. This view of the spread of Islam as a historical interruption is sometimes called the "Pirenne thesis" after Henri Pirenne, the early twentieth-century Belgian historian who popularized this account.

17. A similar critique of the norms of historical periodization is found in Fowden (2014).

18. González Ferrín's work has received a far warmer reception outside of Spain than within it, and particularly in North America, for reasons that Szpiech (discussed above) makes clear.

19. In developing his notion of a third Spain, González Ferrín builds on the work of García Cárcel (2003, 2014) and Abellán (2005) as well as the Erasmus scholar Bataillon (1966).

20. See Enenkel (2013) for a useful discussion of Erasmus's irenic vision.

21. Barbara Fuchs's exploration of the highly ambivalent relation that sixteenth-century Spaniards had to the Muslim culture they so vehemently attempted to negate has interesting parallels to Ferrín's account of an alternative Iberian genealogy. On ceremonial occasions, she notes, it was common that participants would adorn themselves in "Moorish" attire. Such usages of Andalusian Muslim style, Fuchs suggests, could be and have been interpreted as "ethnic cross-dressing"—a practice of staging Otherness as a means to fabricate, by counterposition, a Spanish national identity. However, while this is clearly one feature of the practice, the identification with Muslim dress is far more contradictory than this suggests. For in many instances, Fuchs observes, "Moorish style" was not fetishized or marked as "Other" in any way but was simply made to represent Spanishness, much as was Mudejar art. In other words, it was through such a self-Orientalizing gesture that, paradoxically, Spain constructed certain elements of its own identity in the sixteenth century. As Fuchs concludes, "whether embraced or

stigmatized, Moorishness becomes an essential component in the construction of national identity. The process is not one of simple othering but a more complex negotiation between past and present, intra- and extra-European pressures, and fictive identities crafted both at home and abroad" (Fuchs 2007, 97). This double gesture whereby styles associated with Muslim practice are both denigrated and celebrated, expunged and embodied, points to a far more complicated relationship than that which we see today in the simultaneous enthusiasm for the Noble Moor coupled with an often racist discourse on the Arab immigrant.

22. For a discussion of this aspect of the Quixote, see Mancing (1981).

23. In a recent article, the historian Seth Kimmel locates a sixteenth-century Spanish secular not in an Erasmist skepticism of Church dogma but in the disciplinary strategies of inquisitorial discipline itself. He notes, "to demarcate and police the shifting boundaries of Christianity was to theorize a new and problematic civic space of cultural diversity. The exigencies of inquisition produced a counter-intuitive peninsular logic of secularization" (Kimmel 2013, 289–90). See my reference to this argument in chapter 1.

24. The 1974 Spanish version is titled *La revolución islámica en Occidente*.

25. Among Giménez Caballero's classmates at the university was Américo Castro. Politically opposed, they overlapped in their shared concern for the historical bases of Spanish identity.

26. See García Sanjuán (2013, 75–77). García Sanjuán also interprets Blas Infante to be an early exponent of this current.

27. Some of the greatest accomplishments in this field in the 1930s and 40s were achieved by scholars working under the auspices of the Franco regime who were faced with institutional pressures to construct a coherent nationalist history for Spain. I briefly mention two well-known examples. The first, Emilio García Gómez, was one of the foremost Arabists of his day and founder in 1932 of the Department of Semitic Studies at the University of Granada. Together with the Orientalist Samuel Miklos Stern, García Gómez is widely credited with having discovered the Arabic origins of the *muwashshah*, a medieval Andalusian poetic form (see chap. 3). Yet despite this discovery, García Gómez continued to classify and describe many *kharja* (the concluding verses of the *muwashshah* that were written in a different lexical register) under the rubric of Romance poetry, a decision many have seen as reflecting a political imperative to root the origin of Spanish literature in a recognizably "European" tradition. García Gómez's mentor, the Catholic priest and scholar of Arabic Miguel Asín Palacios's work demonstrates a different but not uncommon solution to the problem of Islam's foreign origin. Asín Palacios argued that Islam as practiced in the Iberian context was in actuality Christian, or rather, a current of Christianity in which a number of doctrinal errors had accumulated over the years.

28. See Dainotto (2006) for an extended discussion of Juan Andrés and the development of the Arabist theory.

29. Dainotto, borrowing, in part, from Menocal (1985), claims that "the Arabist Theory 'first ceases to be discussed and then becomes altogether taboo' in the second part of the nineteenth century, when 'a European sense of self emerged . . . which was the height of the colonialist period, and the prevailing attitudes precluded, consciously or sub-consciously, any possibility of 'indebtedness' to the Arabic world. . . . It would have been inconceivable or very difficult for most Europeans to imagine, let alone ex-

plore or defend, a view of the 'European' as being culturally subservient to the 'Arab'" (Dainotto 2007, 130).

30. García Sanjuán points out that both negationisms—that which denies the Holocaust and that which denies that Muslim armies conquered Iberia—have fascist origins, the latter in the figure of Ignacio Olagüe (García Sanjuán 2013, 70).

31. In my discussions with Ferrín, he acknowledged the seriousness of García Sanjuán's historical challenge, one he found useful for further honing and refining his own perspective.

32. It is worth stressing here both the paucity of evidence on which this debate hinges (according to González Ferrín, the conflicting views in this particular debate devolve almost entirely on the interpretation of two coins) and the fact that most of the historical accounts of the arrival of Islam in Iberia were written more than a century after the event and therefore very much from the standpoint of the ideological interests of those latter writers.

33. García Sanjuán has written extensively (and critically) on the development of Reconquista ideology within Spanish nationalist discourse. See, for example, his essay "Rejecting al-Andalus, Exalting the Reconquista: Historical Memory in Contemporary Spain" (García Sanjuán 2016).

34. Web comment in response to Kenneth Baxter Wolf, "La conquista islámica: *Negacionar* el negacionismo," *La Revista de Libros,* June 9, 2014, http://www.revistadelibros.com/articulos/la-conquista-islamica.

35. Immanuel Kant's comments on Spain represent an eighteenth-century contribution to this tradition of reflection: "The Spaniard's bad side is that he does not learn from foreigners; that he does not travel in order to get acquainted with other nations; that he is centuries behind in the sciences. He resists any reform; he is proud of not having to work; he is of a romantic quality of spirit, as the bullfight shows; he is cruel, as the former auto-da-fé shows; and he displays in his taste an origin that is partly non-European" ([1797] 1996, 231–32).

36. Web comment in response to Kenneth Baxter Wolf, "La conquista islámica."

37. Flesler locates this contemporary anxiety within a much longer history going back to the "Reconquista": "What has remained a constant since the eleventh century, when the Roman Christian rite was imposed over the Mozarabic one, is the idea that what separates Spain from Europe is this religious, racial, cultural, and, later, economic difference that had its origin in Spain's 'impure' contact with Africa and Islam. From this perspective, full European membership, in its different historical manifestations, seems the solution to get rid of this 'impurity.' Even for thinkers who embrace this 'difference,' there is an understanding that the norm to which Spain should aspire is Europe, and that the connections with Africa and Islam, as opposites of that desired model, should be severed once they are not politically useful anymore" (Flesler 2008b, 21).

38. See, for example, Rivero (1999, 127). In *Disorientations,* Susan Martin-Márquez describes a conference that took place the same year on "the three cultures" of Spain in which topics of cultural exchange were discussed and critiqued. As she notes, the volume that emerged from this conference, titled *The Three Cultures,* "implicitly affirms the identity of Spain with Christianity by excluding consideration of religious plurality in the Muslim dominated areas of the Iberian peninsula, while European values and the Roman-Gothic tradition are characterized as of greater significance than the transi-

tory Islamic influences. Somewhat paradoxically, this project also functions to resignify the 'three cultures' moniker, as the papers appear in Spanish, Catalan, and English in a gesture in favor of '*convivencia* and understanding among different cultures and societies in Europe and the world,' in the words of the Director of the Academy, Gonzalo Anes Alvarez. The languages selected reveal exactly how that world is circumscribed" (Martin-Márquez 2008, 320).

39. Flesler describes the disturbance to the Spanish psyche engendered by the reappearance of the "Moor" in the guise of the Moroccan immigrant in Spain. She notes, "not only is the Moroccan immigrant the contemporary embodiment of a terrifying historical ghost [i.e., Iberia's eighth-century conquerors], but also a reminder of Spain's own Oriental self, and, as such, the return of the repressed. Moroccans are the one group most directly implicated in the question of Spanish identity in relationship to Africa, and, therefore, in the question of Spain's status as a Western, European nation, becoming, in the Spanish collective imaginary, the embodiment of everything there is to fear from their history" (Flesler 2008a, 116).

CHAPTER THREE

1. Falla's personal library included a number of collections of North African musical scores, including that of Edmond-Nathan Yafil, *Répertoire de musique arabe et maure* (1904) and Alexis Chottin, *Airs populaires recueillis a Fès, Hespéris: Archives Berbères* (1924). For a discussion of Falla's personal musical archive, see Michael Christoforidis (1999).

2. Falla's views on the Arab contribution to Spanish music are discussed in Hess (2001, 174–75), Harper (2005, 96–98).

3. The distinction between *cante jondo* and flamenco is not a rigorous one. *Cante jondo* is often identified as one of three varieties of flamenco. Another popular understanding of this distinction can be traced back in large part to García Lorca who considered *cante jondo* as a more authentic and serious genre, with flamenco as its popularized and trivialized cousin.

4. Notably, Américo Castro turns repeatedly to sonic metaphors ("echo," "reverberation") in order to figure the presence of the medieval within the modern.

5. When I asked Cruces Roldán to give me a more specific example of a sonorous foundation, she added, "In flamenco we exploit microtonalities, though of course on the guitar, because it is a fretted instrument, we can't make them. The Oud, without frets, can play quarter notes; so we recognize the kind of moves they make, especially as they also make use of the Dorian scale."

6. In his superb study on Andalusi musical forms, Jonathan Shannon (2015) foregrounds the concept of nostalgia in his analysis in order to highlight the modern roots of Andalucismo's orientation to the past. While I find his book to be a rich and insightful treatment of this tradition, I am not persuaded that Andalucismo is best illuminated through a normative modernist vocabulary, especially if we are to grasp some of the ways that tradition unsettles that vocabulary. For an insightful critique of the concept of nostalgia, see Naqvi (2007).

7. To be clear, I am not interested here in a historical defense of the claim that Spain's musical traditions are genealogically linked to Middle Eastern poetic and musical forms, a claim that, in rough outline, few would dispute today (though the relevance and political status of the claim remain fraught topics). Rather, I want to explore practices and sensibilities that such historical entwinements make possible, practices

partially enabled by, but not reducible to, the geographic and temporal coordinates that regulate heritage and tradition within global culture.

8. A few years later, in 1928, Infante helped organize a tribute to al-Mu'tamid in the poet's native city of Silves in Portugal. The event was canceled, however, after a number of journalists from Lisbon began publishing stories in the press accusing Infante of being an "Islamita" and conspiring to plant a crescent on top of the cathedral of the town. See Infante (1931, 84).

9. A useful discussion of Infante's Moroccan visit and the impact it had on his thought can be found in González-Alcantud (2014, 88–90).

10. Along the way to completing the project, Infante studied music at the Conservatory of Seville and took classes in Arabic in the city's Muslim palace, the Alcázar of Seville, from a Syrian instructor.

11. In developing his thesis on the origins of flamenco, Infante was profoundly influenced by the work of the Spanish Arabist Julián Ribera.

12. The Arabist Serafín Fanjul, a vociferous defender of the view that the Arab contribution to Spain—past as well as present—was definitively negative, invokes an ethnological stance to reject Infante's thesis of a Morisco-*gitano* fusion, arguing that the "impermeability of two groups so fixedly endogamous created an obstacle to any contact beyond trade, mockery, story-telling" (Fanjul 2004, 115).

13. On these debates within the field of flamenco studies, see Bäcker (2005), Washabaugh (2012), Paetzold (2009). For many of these scholars—insomuch as most phenomenologies of hearing emphasize the distance and discontinuity between perceiving subject and perceived object—music and the listening practices it occasions have offered a key site from which to grasp the phantom presence of the Muslim past in its elusive materiality, as an echo that perdures despite the seeming disappearance of its source. Matthew Machin-Autenrieth's *Flamenco, Regionalism, and Musical Heritage in Southern Spain* (2019), provides a particularly useful examination of the shifting significance of flamenco within both regional and national political discourses.

14. Many scholars have a more agnostic view, emphasizing the obstacles that beset any such inquiry into the history of flamenco. As one writer puts it, "Is flamenco a genre reminiscent of the Arab world that occupied the Peninsula, even of the Asian or Indian worlds? We say positively yes. But in no greater extent than other musical expressions in Spain, located in places where the historical presence for centuries on end of Arab communities was confirmed; positively yes, but in degrees hard to estimate when compared with other powerful and attractive influences to musical creation as those of the Jewish communities" (Labajo 1997).

15. See Miguel Ángel García (2012) for a discussion of the theme of Andalusian melancholy and Lorca's contribution to the genre.

16. Very little is written about the career of Aziz Balouch. One of the few sources on Balouch I have found is an unpublished paper by Stephen Fa presented in Pakistan a few years ago and which the author generously shared with me.

17. On the aesthetics, politics, and economics of the world music industry, see Erlmann (1996) and Feld (2000).

18. On contemporary varieties of Andalusi music in both Spain and the Middle East, see Shannon (2015), Reynolds (2009), and Glasser (2016). Both Shannon (2015) and Goldstein (2017) provide wonderfully rich accounts of Granada's Andalusi music scene.

19. On conversion to Islam in post-Franco Spain, see Bahrami (1998) and Rogozen-Soltar (2017).

20. The fact that the *kharjas* were formed by an amalgamation of Arabic and Romance—not just the use of one's form for the other's content but also the intertwining of lexical elements and grammatical forms from the two languages—meant that their interpretation required the collaboration of scholars across disciplinary divisions. As James Monroe, an important contributor to this interpretive effort, put it, "Little can be gained from pitting Arabists against Romanists. A serious study of *muwashshah* poetry requires that one be an Arabist, a Hebraist, a Romanist and much else besides (musical expertise and literary competence are essential)" (cited in Mallette 2010, 174).

21. Mikaela Rogozen-Soltar provides a rich and fascinating exploration of similar, seemingly contradictory aspects of Andalucismo in her recent book *Spain Unmoored: Migration, Conversion, and the Politics of Islam* (2017).

22. Another commonplace within immigrant narratives, as I was told by Javier and Ahmed, is that, upon arriving in Andalusia, Muslims from North Africa begin to take their religious commitments much more seriously than they had previously done, attending mosque regularly, praying, and giving alms.

23. The founding event in this series of collaborations took place in the late 1960s when Gregorio Paniagua and his group *Atrium Musicae* (specializing in the Troubadour tradition), spent two weeks with Abd al-Sadiq Shikara's ensemble from Tétouan, living and playing music together in the late fifteenth-century Iglesia Colegiata de Covarrubias (Reynolds 2009, 185).

24. A number of recent ethnographic works have examined the tension that Arabs in Granada experience in the tourist trade, where they are simultaneously appreciated as lending authentic Middle Eastern color to the place and disparaged for intruding on the pristine beauty of the historic city. An ethnographically rich and nuanced treatment of this theme is found in Rogozen-Soltar (2017), though a dissertation by Rosón Lorente (2008b) also provides an excellent account of some of these dynamics.

25. The *cantigas* are one of the largest collections of medieval poems with associated musical notation still in existence. Sung in medieval Galician-Portuguese, they were commissioned by the Castilian King Alfonso X (1221–1284) during the last two decades of his life.

26. A review of Anglés's writings from 1947 mentions Ribera's essay on the *cantigas* as "an extreme case of incompetence and blundering" and suggests that what Ribera took to be "'Arabic' rhythms . . . are suspiciously similar to those of the polka and the gallop" (Apel 1947, 57).

CHAPTER FOUR

1. Their approach to the city of Granada shows an affinity with Walter Benjamin's reflections on the phenomenology of the modern cities of Naples and Paris, among others. For Benjamin, the historical material of urban life—objects, streets, monuments, gestures—gave expression to a philosophy, to a critical vision of the present. The task of the historian-sociologist, as Benjamin saw it, was to excavate the philosophical ideas expressed in the object world of the city, ideas concealed by the myth of progress and the geopolitical order which that myth sustained. Benjamin's critique of historicism intersects with the ideas of Ganivet and Lorca at many points, though it is the way this critical stance leads them outside the aesthetic boundaries of Spain and Europe that most interests me here.

2. He defined his approach to this investigation, as I noted in the introduction, in the aesthetic register of late nineteenth-century Romanticism: "to see, hear, smell,

taste, and even touch—that is, to live—is my exclusive method" (Ganivet [1896] 2003, 19).

3. Useful readings of this story can be found in Ginsberg (1985) and Sánchez-Alarcos (2015).

4. The image of Granada as a human body composed of rubble carries a strong echo of Percy Shelley's Ozymandias, a figure whose own stony voice similarly bears witness to the hubris of civilization.

5. As the Italian historian Loretta Frattale observes in her comments on *Granada la bella*, "Ganivet projects his Granadan ideal toward 'another present,' a parallel time without chronological or topological ties, a time *only possible* . . . in the interior of this space-time dimension without limits, or with only nuanced and confused limits, that polemically makes present times and places of the past and future, Ganivet animates a community formed 'not only by the living, but by those who died and those who will be born,' a world, therefore, set apart from history, that travels from the temporal to the eternal" (Frattale 1997, 67–68).

6. Ganivet compares the labor of creative elaboration necessary to implant such forms within the lived experience of Spanish society to the activity of bees. Certain Spanish artists emerge in his text as exemplars of this process of "delicate assimilation," among them, the painter Mariano Fortuny: "The Spanish artist who, by temperament, was drawn to Arabic traditions and who suffered more than anyone the influence of our environment, Fortuny, did not limit himself to the appropriation of exterior forms, but rather, infused them with a psychological depth that brought them to life" (Ganivet [1896] 2003, 21).

7. Between the late eighteenth and early twentieth centuries, many of these were rebuilt in the Romantic style dominant at the time.

8. Ganivet's disdain for Spain's contemporary institutional fabric extended to the Catholic Church. As for his clear spiritual passion, he defines it at one point as a "negative mysticism" (Ramsden 1974, 171).

9. In another section of *Granada*, Ganivet argues that the Spanish soul was in its essence mystical and individualist, forged from Senecan stoicism and developed through Christianity. This spiritual formation, however, turns out to have been profoundly marked by the influence of *el arábigo*, the Arab element: "the mystic is the Spaniard, and Granadans are the most mystical of all the Spanish, for our Christian lineage but even more for our Arabic lineage" ([1896] 2003, 17). This core of Spain, its mystical heart, in other words, has required Arabic culture and religiosity to become, in his words, "more refined and pure" (17). I would also note, in relation to what might be called an anti-Catholic current within Andalucismo, how reference to *el arábigo* here serves once again to inflect and limit the Christian element.

10. "If there is anything more beautiful than life," the poet exclaims, "it is the bitterness and disenchantment that existence leaves behind" (Ganivet 1899a, 205).

11. Ganivet's strongest statement of this point is found in his *Idearium español* (1897).

12. Ganivet's antimodernism has led scholars to identity him as a conservative voice within the intellectual circuits of late nineteenth-century Spain and, for some, as a contributor to what eventually became Spanish fascism.

13. A useful discussion of this novel in relation to Ganivet's shifting political views is found in González Alcantud (1997).

14. Ganivet's views on the possibilities of territorial expansion afforded by Spain's historical relation to North Africa stressed the unique "understanding" of the south,

one he saw embodied not only in Spain's Orientalist tradition but in the Reconquista itself: "Granada is the center from which our greatest orientalists have arisen and where we find preserved the strongest attachment to the politics symbolized in the testament of the Catholic Monarch, Isabel" (Ganivet and Unamuno [1912] 1998, 173).

15. As Frattale notes, Ganivet articulates a chronotype that "enacts a convergence, in an emblematic contraposition between a 'here' and a 'beyond,' elements of real experience (history, the quotidian, technology, commerce, urbanism, and industry) and reflection (ideas, dreams, art, values, and myths)" (Frattale 1997, 68).

16. González Alcantud identifies Ganivet and Lorca's aesthetic of the small, the hidden, and the interior as one manifestation of a modernist rendering of Mediterranean cities as sites of mystery and secrecy, an interpretation encouraged by local elites (González Alcantud 2014, 202–7). As he notes, in Granada, the *carmen* became the paradigmatic example of this aesthetic.

17. Within Lorca scholarship, the poet's engagement with Arabic poetry and culture has been largely downplayed or viewed as a superficial dalliance. There is considerable evidence, however, of Lorca's sustained interest in traditions of Islamic poetry. Pina Rosa Piras, summarizing the result of her exploration of Lorca's engagement with "Islamic culture," asserts that rather than a passing fancy discovered late in his life, "one finds a passion, an attention, that it would be correct to posit as a constitutive and continuous part of the multiple components of Lorca's poetics" (Piras 1991, 175).

18. See, in particular, Mahmoud Darwish's (2004) collection *Aḥada 'Ashara Kawkaban.*

19. Lorca's interest in traditions of Islamic poetry began very early in his career. His first publication—written under a pseudonym when he was nineteen years old—was an article titled "Commentary on Omar Khayyam," which appeared in 1917 in a journal of the faculty of arts at the University of Granada (see Gibson 1986). Lorca submitted the piece under the name Abu Abdallah, the Arabic for "Boabdil," the last Muslim ruler of Granada, forced to abandon the city by the armies of the Catholic monarchs Ferdinand and Isabella in 1492. Among the books found in Lorca's personal library is a copy of the *Rubáiyát* of Omar Khayyam purchased by the poet in 1917 and with the poet's extensive handwritten notes written in the margins.

20. A brief overview of some of this nineteenth-century literature is found in Starrett (1995, 954–59).

21. Luís de Góngora y Argote, from whom the derogatory term *gongorismo* is derived, was a seventeenth-century Spanish poet whose poetic style is characterized by great syntactical complexity and an exaggerated use of metaphor.

22. Brian Morris (1997), in his otherwise superb analysis of Lorca's "lyrical landscapes," enacts a variant of this procedure in his description of the *Diván* as "a tribute to Mozarabic poetry." Mozarabic refers to the Iberian Christians who lived under Muslim rule while maintaining their own Christian faith. Lorca's European spirit is thereby secured by reading his venture into Arabic poetic genres as a tribute to Christianity.

23. Puerta Vílchez emphasized to me the impact Lorca had made on him, particularly the discovery that Lorca, as a Granadan, felt powerfully drawn to Arabic and Persian poetry, much as Puerta Vílchez himself was drawn to Arabic literature, art, and architecture. Although he has explored Lorca's relation to the Islamic world in a number of public talks, his audiences, he tells me, remain skeptical—as if the discovery that a part of the poet belonged to the Middle East was felt to weaken or complicate his audience's own passional embrace of him, their exclusive claim on him.

24. As the art historian Olga Bush notes: "The work of José Miguel Puerta Vílchez stands apart. . . . His monographs are seminal works in the field of medieval Andalusian studies" (Bush 2009, 142).

25. A few years later, right-wing forces allied with Franco also found Infante to be a "traitor to the nation" and executed him in August of 1936, a few days before Lorca's own execution.

26. As Martin-Márquez observes, "The Andalusian nationalist project that was shaped in accordance with Infante's inclusive vision differed radically from the policies of racist exclusions advocated by other nationalists in Spain. . . . The Andalusian electoral program of 1931 would go so far as to state that 'in Andalusia there are no foreigners'" (Martin-Márquez 2008, 49).

27. A number of Spanish scholars I met acknowledged the unique perspective that Puerta Vílchez brought to the study of Islamic aesthetics. Rosa Isabel Martínez Lillo, a scholar of Arabic literature, told me during our conversation, "Most scholars working on al-Andalus understand the past as past and don't relate to it though the present. That is, they don't allow concerns in the present to enliven their thinking on the past. Puerta Vílchez is one of the few exceptions" (February 10, 2014)

28. In "Futures of al-Andalus" (Anidjar 2006), Gil Anidjar explores one possible interpretation of this figure of al-Andalus as an unfinished project.

29. The Ibn Tufayl Foundation declares its mission to be spreading "knowledge of the language, literature, and history of the Arab World in the Spanish context, with special attention for al-Andalus, as the site of encounter of the Arabo-Islamic civilization with the West" (http://ibntufayl.org/la-fundacion/).

30. "Manifesto 2 de Enero 1995," *Ideal* (Granada), January 2, 1995, 1.

31. Speech by Francisco Vigueras given in the Plaza Mariana Pineda, Granada, January 2, 2007.

32. J. E. Gómez, "Premio a la tolerancia como replica a la fiesta de la toma," *Ideal* (Granada), December 29, 2002.

33. González Alcantud has emphasized the value of an anthropological notion of myth for elucidating many of the current discourses on the Andalusian past. The term works within his writings as a rejoinder to those who dismiss the works of Andalucismo as pure fiction.

Bibliography

Abellán, José Luis. 2005. *El erasmismo español*. Madrid: Espasa-Calpe.

Abeysekara, Ananda. 2019. "Protestant Buddhism and 'Influence': The Temporality of a Concept." *Qui parle* 28 (1): 1–75.

Agamben, Giorgio. 1993. *Infancy and History: Essays on the Destruction of Experience*. Translated by Liz Heron. London: Verso.

———. 2018. *What Is Philosophy?* Translated by Lorenzo Chiaso. Stanford: Stanford University Press.

Almond, Ian. 2009. *History of Islam in German Thought*. London: Routledge.

Álvarez Chillida, Gonzalo. 2002. *El antisemitismo en España: La imagen del judío, 1812–2002*. Madrid: Marcel Pons.

Anglés, Higinio. 1943. *La música de las Cantigas de Santa María del rey Alfonso el Sabio*. Barcelona: Biblioteca Central.

Anidjar, Gil. 2003. *The Jew, the Arab: A History of the Enemy*. Stanford, CA: Stanford University Press.

———. 2006. "Futures of al-Andalus." *Journal of Spanish Cultural Studies* 7 (3): 225–39.

———. 2008. *Semites: Race, Religion, Literature*. Stanford, CA: Stanford University Press.

Apel, Willi. 1947. "Recent Musicological Publications in Spain and Portugal." *Notes* 5 (1): 57–61.

Aragón Reyes, Manuel, ed. 2013. *El protectorado español en Marruecos: La historia trancendida*. "Introducción," 1:23–31. Bilbao: Iberdrola.

Arce Sainz, Fernando. 2015. "La supuesta basílica de San Vicente en Córdoba: De mito histórico a obstinación historiográfica." *Al-Qantara* 36, no. 1 (January–June): 11–44.

Arigita, Elena. 2013. "The 'Cordoba Paradigm': Memory and Silence around Europe's Islamic Past." In *Islam and the Politics of Culture in Europe: Memory, Aesthetics, Art*, edited by F. Peter, S. Dornhof, and E. Arigita, 21–40. Bielefeld: Transcript, 2013.

———. 2018. "Narratives on the Margins of History: Memory and the Commemoration of the Moriscos." *Journal of North African Studies* 24 (1): 134–51.

Armistead, Samuel G. 1988. "Américo Castro in Morocco: The Origins of a Theory." In *Américo Castro: The Impact of His Thought*, edited by Ronald E. Surtz, Jaime Ferran, and Daniel P. Testa, 73–82. Madison, WI: Hispanic Seminary of Medieval Studies.

———. 1997. "Américo Castro in the United States: 1937–1969." *Hispania* 80, no. 2 (May): 271–74.

Asad, Muhammad. (1954) 1982. *The Road to Mecca*. 2nd ed. Lahore: Islamic Book Service.

Asad, Talal. 2003. *Formations of the Secular: Christianity, Islam, Modernity.* Stanford, CA: Stanford University Press.

Astor, Avi, Marian Burchardt, and Mar Griera. 2019. "Polarization and the Limits of Politicization: Cordoba's Mosque-Cathedral and the Limits of Cultural Heritage." *Qualitative Sociology* 42 (3): 337–60.

Bäcker, Rolf. 2005. "Lo decisivo fue la mezcla y esa mezcla sólo ocurrió en Andalucía: Algunas reflexiones acerca de la identidad andaluza en el discurso flamencológico." *Nassarre: Revista Aragonesa de Musicología* 21:109–20.

Bahrami, Beebe. 1995. "The Persistence of the Andalusian Identity in Rabat, Morocco." PhD diss., University of Pennsylvania.

———. 1998. "A Door to Paradise: Converts, the New Age, Islam, and the Past in Granada, Spain." *City and Society* 10 (1): 121–32.

———. 2000. "Al-Andalus and Memory: The Past and Being Present among Hispano-Moroccan Andalusians from Rabat." In *Charting Memory: Recalling Medieval Spain,* edited by Stacy N. Beckwith, 111–43. New York: Garland.

Balouch, Aziz. 1968. *Spanish* cante jondo *and Its Origin in Sindhi Music.* Hyderabad: Mehran Arts Council.

Barreñada, Isaías. 2006. "Alliance of Civilizations, Spanish Public Diplomacy and Cosmopolitan Proposal." *Mediterranean Politics* 11 (1): 99–104.

Bartra, Roger. 2000. "Arabs, Jews, and the Enigma of Spanish Imperial Melancholy." *Discourse* 22 (3): 64–72.

Bataillon, Marcel. 1966. *Erasmo y España: Estudios sobre la historia espiritual del siglo XVI.* Translated by Antonio Alatorre. 2nd ed. México: Fondo de Cultura Económica.

Benjamin, Walter. 1968. *Illuminations: Essays and Reflections.* Edited by Hannah Arendt. Translated by Harry Zohn. New York: Schocken.

Blinkhorn, Martin. 1980. "Spain: The 'Spanish Problem' and the Imperial Myth." *Journal of Contemporary History* 15 (1): 5–25.

Boll, Jessica R. 2017. "Irony Made Manifest: Cultural Contention and Córdoba's Mosque-Cathedral." *Journal of Cultural Geography* 34 (3): 275–302.

Brownlee, Marina S. 2005. "Zoraida's White Hand and Cervantes' Rewriting of History." *Bulletin of Hispanic Studies* 82:569–86.

Buresi, Pascal. 2009. "Al-Andalus entre Orient et Occident: L'invention des origines." In *Al-Andalus / España. Historiografías en contraste, siglos XVII–XXI,* edited by Manuela Marín, 119–29. Madrid: Casa de Velázquez.

Bush, Olga. 2009. "The Writing on the Wall: Reading the Decoration of the Alhambra." *Muqarnas* 26 (1):119–47.

Calado Olivo, Silvia. 2013. "Aziz Balouch, the Reincarnation of Ziryab." Flamenco World. Last modified January 23, 2013 (accessed July 10, 2014; no longer posted). http://www.flamenco-world.com/magazine/about/aziz_balouch/balouch.htm

Calderwood, Eric. 2014a. "'In Andalucía, There Are No Foreigners': Andalucismo from Transperipheral Critique to Colonial Apology." *Journal of Spanish Cultural Studies* 15 (4): 399–417.

———. 2014b. "The Invention of al-Andalus: Discovering the Past and Creating the Present in Granada's Islamic Tourism Sites." *Journal of North African Studies* 19 (1): 27–55.

———. 2015. "The Reconquista of the Mosque of Cordoba." *Foreign Affairs,* April 10.

———. 2018. *Colonial al-Andalus: Spain and the Invention of Modern Moroccan Culture.* Cambridge, MA: Belknap Press of Harvard University Press.

Calvino, Italo. 1974. *Invisible Cities.* Translated by William Weaver. New York: Harcourt Brace Jovanovich.

Carrasco Urgoiti, María Soledad. 1989. *El moro de Granada en la literatura europea (del siglo XV–XX).* Estudio preliminar de Juan Martínez Ruiz. Granada: Universidad de Granada.

———. 2005. *Vidas fronterizas en las letras españoles.* Barcelona: Bellaterra.

Casals i Meseguer, Xavier. 2006. "Franco 'El Africano.'" *Journal of Spanish Cultural Studies* 7 (3): 207–24.

Cascardi, Anthony J. 1997. *Ideologies of History in the Spanish Golden Age.* Philadelphia: University of Pennsylvania Press.

Castro, Américo. 1948. *España en su historia: Cristianos, moros y judíos.* Buenos Aires: Editorial Losada.

———. 1954. *La realidad histórica de España.* México: Editorial Porrúa.

———. 1956. Dos ensayos: Descripción, narración, historiografía; Discrepancias y mal. Mexico City: Editorial Porrúa.

———. 1961. *De la Edad Conflictiva.* Madrid: Editorial Taurus.

———. 1967. *Iberoamérica, su historia y su cultura.* Edited by Raymond S. Willis and Frederic Ernst. New York: Holt, Rinehart and Winston.

———. 2002. *El pensamiento de Cervantes y otros estudios cervantinos.* Madrid: Editorial Trotta.

Christoforidis, Michael. 1999. "A Composer's Annotations to His Personal Library: An Introduction to the Manuel de Falla Collection." *Context: Journal of Music Research*, no. 17 (Winter): 33–68.

Chottin, Alexis. 1924. *Airs populaires recueillis a Fès, Hespéris: Archives Berbères.* Paris: Émile Larose.

Cordero Torres, José María. 1955. "El Mediterráneo, nexo de colaboración hispano-árabe." *Cuadernos de estudios arabes* 31:9–26.

———. 1956. "El pensamiento español sobre Marruecos: Problemas nuevos, criterios perennes." *Cuadernos de estudios africanos* 35:9–40.

Córtes Peña, Antonio Luis. 1994. "El último nacionalismo: Andalucía y su historia." *Manuscrits* 12:213–44.

Cruces Roldán, Cristina. 2003. *El flamenco y la música andalusí: Argumentos para un encuentro.* Barcelona: Ediciones Carena.

———. 2008. "El aplauso difícil: Sobre la 'autenticidad,' el 'Nuevo Flamenco' y la negación del Padre Jondo." *Comunicación y Música* 2:167–210.

Dainotto, Roberto M. 2000. *Place in Literature: Regions, Cultures, Communities.* Ithaca, NY: Cornell University Press.

———. 2006. "The Discreet Charm of the Arabist Theory: Juan Andrés, Historicism, and the De-Centering of Montesquieu's Europe." *European History Quarterly* 36 (1): 7–29.

———. 2007. *Europe (in Theory).* Durham, NC: Duke University Press.

Darwish, Mahmoud. 2004. *Aḥada 'Ashara Kawkaban* [Eleven planets]. Casablanca: Dār Tūbqāl lil-Nashr.

Davis, Kathleen. 2008. *Periodization and Sovereignty: How Ideas of Feudalism and Secularization Govern the Politics of Time.* Philadelphia: University of Pennsylvania Press.

Delgado, J. Lirola, and J. M. Puerta Vílchez, eds. 2003. *Enciclopedia de al-Andalus: Diccionario de autores y obras Andalusíes*. Vol. 1, A–Ibn B. Granada: Legado Andalusí.

Diamond, Cora. 2003. "The Difficulty of Reality and the Difficulty of Philosophy." *Partial Answers: Journal of Literature and the History of Ideas* 1, no. 2 (June): 1–26.

Domínguez Ortiz, Antonio. 1983. *Andalucía, ayer y hoy*. Barcelona: Planeta.

Domínguez Ortiz, Antonio, and Bernard Vincent. 1993. *Historia de los moriscos: Vida y tragedia de una minoría*. Madrid: Alianza Editorial.

Du Bois, W. E. B. (1988) 2007. *Dusk of Dawn: An Essay toward an Autobiography of a Race Concept*. Oxford: Oxford University Press.

Einboden, Jeffrey. 2014. *Islam and Romanticism: Muslim Currents from Goethe to Emerson*. London: Oneworld.

Enenkel, Karl A. E., ed. 2013. *The Reception of Erasmus in the Early Modern Age*. Boston: Brill.

Erlmann, Veit. 1996. "The Aesthetics of the Global Imagination: Reflections on World Music in the 1990s." *Public Culture* 8:467–87.

Falla, Manuel de. 1950. *Escritos sobre música y músicos*. Edited by Federico Sopeña Ibanez. Buenos Aires: Espasa-Calpe.

Fanjul, Serafín. 2000. "Al-Ándalus contra España: La forja de un mito." Mexico City: Siglo Veintuno.

———. 2004. *La quimera de al-Andalus*. Madrid: Siglo XXI.

———. 2014. "La catedral de Córdoba como pretexto." *Religión en Libertad*, December 12. https://www.religionenlibertad.com/el-prestigioso-arabista-serafin-fanjul-denuncia-la-operacion-politica-contra-la-39259.htm.

Farmer, Henry George. 1925. "Clues for the Arabian Influence on European Musical Theory." *Journal of the Royal Asiatic Society of Great Britain and Ireland* 1 (January): 61–80.

Fasolt, Constantin. 2005. "The Limits of History in Brief." *Historically Speaking* 6, no. 5 (May/June): 5–10.

Fastrup, Anne. 2012. "Cross-Cultural Movement in the Name of Honour: Renegades, Honour and State in Miguel de Cervantes' Barbary Plays." *Bulletin of Spanish Studies* 89 (3): 347–67.

Feld, Steven. 2000. "A Sweet Lullaby for World Music." *Public Culture* 12, no. 1: 145–71.

Ferreira, Manuel Pedro. 2015. "Rhythmic paradigms in the *Cantigas de Santa Maria*: French versus Arabic Precedent." *Plainsong and Medieval Music* 24 (1): 1–24.

Fierro, Maribel. 2009. "Al-Andalus en el pensamiento fascista español: La *Revolución islámica en Occidente* de Ignacio Olagüe." In *Al-Andalus/España. Historiografías en contraste, siglos XVII–XXI*, edited by Manuela Marín, 325–49. Madrid: Casa de Velázquez.

Flesler, Daniela. 2008a. "Contemporary Moroccan Immigration and Its Ghosts." In *In the Light of Medieval Spain: Islam, the West, and the Relevance of the Past*, edited by Simon R. Doubleday and David Coleman, 115–32. New York: Palgrave Macmillan.

———. 2008b. *The Return of the Moor*. West Lafayette, IN: Purdue University Press.

Fletcher, Richard. 2001. *Moorish Spain*. London: Phoenix.

Foucault, Michel. 2003. *Society Must be Defended: Lectures at the Collège de France, 1975–1976*. New York: Picador Press.

Fowden, Garth. 2014. *Before and After Muhammad: The First Millennium Refocused*. Princeton, NJ: Princeton University Press.

Frattale, Loretta. 1997. "Perspectivas ganivetianas sobre Granada: Variaciones sobre un cronotipo." *RILCE* 13 (2): 57–72.

Fuchs, Barbara. 2003. *Passing for Spain: Cervantes and the Fictions of Identity.* Urbana: University of Illinois Press.

———. 2007. "The Spanish Race." In *Rereading the Black Legend: The Discourses of Racism in the Renaissance Empires,* edited by Margaret Greer, Walter Mignolo, and Maureen Quilligan, 88–97. Chicago: University of Chicago Press.

———. 2009. *Exotic Nation: Maurophilia and the Construction of Early Modern Spain.* Philadelphia: University of Pennsylvania Press.

Ganivet, Ángel. (1896) 2003. *Granada la bella.* Helsingfors: J. C. Frenckell é Hijo.

———. 1897. *Idearium español.* Granada: Lit. Vda. e Hijos de Sabatel.

———. 1899a. "Las ruinas de Granada." In *Libro de Granada,* 205–13. Granada: P. V. Sabatel.

———. 1899b. "El alma de las calles." In *Libro de Granada,* 107–12. Granada: P. V. Sabatel.

———. 1906. *Cartas finlandesas.* Granada: Defensor de Granada.

———. 2019. *La conquista del Maya por el último conquistador español: Pio Cid.* Madrid: Verbum.

Ganivet, Ángel, and Miguel de Unamuno. (1912) 1998. *El porvenir de España.* Granada: Diputación de Granada.

García, Miguel Ángel. 2012. *Melancolía vertebrada: La tristeza andaluza del modernismo a la vanguardia.* Barcelona: Anthropos Editorial.

García-Arenal, Mercedes. 1996. *Los moriscos.* Granada: Universidad de Granada.

———. 2007. "La conquista islámica y el uso político de la historia." *Revista de Libros* 1 (March). https://www.revistadelibros.com/articulo_imprimible.php?art=2996&t=articulos.

———. 2009. "Religious Dissent and Minorities: The Morisco Age." *Journal of Modern History* 81, no. 4 (December): 888–920.

García Cárcel, Ricardo. 2003. *Felipe V y los españoles: Una visión periférica del problema de España.* Barcelona: Nuevas Ediciones de Bolsillo.

———. 2014. "La memoria histórica sobre la expulsión de los moriscos." *eHumanista/Conversos* 2:120–32.

García Fitz, Francisco. 2009. "La Reconquista: Un estado de la cuestión." *Clío & Crímen,* no. 6, 142–215.

García Gómez, Emilio. 1948. *Silla del moro, y nuevas escenas andaluzas.* Madrid: Revista de Occidente.

García Sanjuán, Alejandro. 2013. *La conquista islámica de la Península Ibérica y la tergiversación del pasado: Del catastrofismo al negacionismo.* Madrid: Marcial Pons.

———. 2016. "Rejecting al-Andalus, Exalting the Reconquista: Historical Memory in Contemporary Spain." *Journal of Medieval Iberian Studies* 10 (1): 127–45.

Germeshuys, Carlo. 2009. "Towards a 'Living Connection with the Past': Ludwig Wittgenstein and the Representation of History in W.G. Sebald's *Austerlitz.*" PhD diss., Cape Town University.

Gibson, Ian. 1986. "Un probable artículo de Lorca sobre Omar Jayyam." *Cuadernos Hispanoamericanos* 433/434:37–42.

Gil Benumeya, Roldofo. 1926. "Los tres puntos fundamentales de nuestra futura política indígena." *África: Revista de tropas coloniales* (September): 211.

———. (1928) 1996. *Ni oriente, ni occidente: El universo visto desde el Albayzín.* Facsimile of the first edition. Madrid: Comparía Ibero-Americana de Publicaciones.

———. 1929. "Hacia una España mayor: Otra vez el andalucismo." *África: Revista de tropas coloniales* (April): 90.

———. 1929. *Mediodía: Introducción a la historia andaluza.* Madrid: Compañía Ibero-Americana de Publicaciones.

———. 1931. "Granada y la enseñanza hispano-árabe." *África: Revista de Tropas Coloniales* (August): 163–65.

———. 1939. "Sobre las líneas generales de las relaciones hispano-árabes en su evolución actual." *Cuaderno de Estudios Africanos y Orientales* 32:39, CAO_032_039.

———. 1942. *Marruecos andaluz.* Madrid: Vicesecretaría de Educación Popular.

———. 1956. "Egipto ante Europa, Israel y Mundo Árabe." *Revista de Política Internacional* 26 (April–June): 81–87.

Gil Grimau, Rodolfo. 1988. "Corrientes ideológicas internas en el africanismo español." *Actas del Congreso Internacional El Estrecho de Gibraltar* 3:277–85. Madrid: Universidad Nacional de Educación a Distancia.

———. 1996. "Un prólogo sobre la vida y actitud de Rodolfo Gil Benumeya." In *Ni oriente, ni occidente: El universo visto desde el Albayzín,* 7–43. Facsimile of the first edition. Granada: Universidad de Granada.

Ginsberg, Judith. 1985. *Ángel Ganivet.* Suffolk: Tamesis, 1985.

Glasser, Jonathan. 2016. *The Lost Paradise: Andalusi Music in Urban North Africa.* Chicago: University of Chicago Press.

Goldstein, Ian. 2017. "Experiencing Musical Connection: Sonic Interventions in Mediterranean Social Memory." PhD diss., University of California, Berkeley.

González Alcantud, José Antonio. 1992. "Andalucía: Invención del país y realidad etnográfica." *Historia y fuente oral* 8:7–24.

———. 1996. "El ensayo en el país de la poesía: Rodolfo Gil Benumeya y el andalucismo africanista." In *Ni Oriente, Ni Occidente: El universo visto desde el Albayzín,* 45–96. Granada: Universidad de Granada.

———. 1997. "Ángel Ganivet ante el debate sobre los modos de colonización: A propósito del conquista del reino de Maya por Pio Cid." *RILCE* 13 (2): 75–96.

———. 2014. *El mito de al Ándalus: Orígenes y actualidad de una idea cultural.* Córdoba: Almuzara.

González de Molina, Manuel, and Eduardo Sevilla Guzmán. 1987. "En los orígenes del nacionalismo andaluz: Reflexiones en torno al proceso fallido de socialización del andalucismo histórico." *REIS: Revista Española de Investigaciones Sociológicas* 40 (October–December): 73–95.

González Ferrín, Emilio. (2006) 2016. *Historia general de Al Ándalus: Europa entre Oriente y Occidente.* 4th ed. Córdoba: Almuzara.

———. 2008 "La tercera España: El alma morisca." http://www.ilya.it/chrono/pages/terceraespannasp.html.

———. 2014a. "Francisco Márquez Villanueva y la Historiología de Américo Castro." *eHumanista Conversos* 2:175–88.

———. 2014b. "Sobre al-Andalus, el islam, la conquista." *Revista de libros,* July 28.

———. 2015. "La antigüedad tardía islámica: Crítica al concepto de conquista." In *Frontera inferior de al-Andalus,* edited by Bruno Franco Moreno, Miguel Alba, and Santiago Feijoo, 2:29–52. Mérida: Mérida Consorcio Ciudad monumental histórico-artísca y arqueológica.

———. 2016. "The Conceptual Conquest: Ideological Need of an Artifactual Early Islam." Paper presented at the annual meeting of the American Comparative Literature Association, Cambridge, MA, March 17–20.

———. 2018. *Cuando fuimos árabes.* Córdoba: Almuzara.

González González, Irene. 2013. "Educación, cultura y ejército: Aliados de la política colonial en el Norte de Marruecos." In *El protectorado español en Marruecos: La historia transcendida,* edited by Manuel Aragón Reyes, 1:341–61. Bilbao: Iberdrola.

Goytisolo, Juan. 2003. "Américo Castro en la España actual." In *Américo Castro y la revisión de la memoria (El Islam en España),* edited by Eduardo Subirats, 23–37. Madrid: Ediciones Libertarias.

Green, Garrett. 1996. "Modern Culture Comes of Age: Hamann versus Kant on the Root Metaphor of Enlightenment." In *What Is Enlightenment? Eighteenth-Century Answers and Twentieth-Century Questions,* edited by James Schmidt, 291–305. Berkeley: University of California Press.

Habermas, Jürgen. 2006. *Time of Transitions.* Cambridge: Polity.

Hamann, Johann Georg. 1965. *Briefwechsel.* Vol. 5. Edited by Arthur Henkel. Frankfurt: Insel.

Handley, Sharon. 1996. "Federico García Lorca and the 98 Generation: The 'Andalucismo' Debate." *Anales de la literatura española contemporánea.* 21 (1/2): 41–58.

Harper, Nancy Lee. 2005. *Manuel de Falla: His Life and Music.* Lanham, MD: Scarecrow.

Harvey, L. P. 2006. *Muslims in Spain, 1500 to 1614.* Chicago: University of Chicago Press.

Hayot, Eric. 2009. *The Hypothetical Mandarin.* Oxford: Oxford University Press.

Heller-Roazen, Daniel. 2007. *The Inner Touch: Archaeology of a Sensation.* Cambridge: Zone Books.

Heng, Geraldine. 2018. *The Invention of Race in the European Middle Ages.* Cambridge: Cambridge University Press.

Hess, Carol A. 2001. *Manuel de Falla and Modernism in Spain, 1898–1936.* Chicago: University of Chicago Press.

Hinterhäuser, Hans. 1980. "'Ciudades muertas,' fin de siglo." In *Figuras y Mitos,* 41–66. Madrid: Taurus.

Hirschkind, Charles. 2009. "Obama on Palestine: What New Beginning?" *Immanent Frame,* June 9. https://tif.ssrc.org/2009/06/09/obama-on-palestine-what-new-beginning/.

Huguet Santos, Montserrat. 1999. "Africanismo y política exterior española en el franquismo." In *Al-Andalus: Una identidad compartida; Arte, ideología y enseñanza en el protectorado español en Marruecos,* edited by Federico Castro Morales, 31–55. Madrid: BOE.

Infante, Blas. 1931. *La verdad sobre el complot de tablada y el estado libre de Andalucía.* Seville: Álvarez y Zambrano.

———. 1980. *Orígenes de lo flamenco y secreto del cante jondo (1929–1933).* Seville: Junta de Andalucía Consejería de Cultura.

———. 1989. *AAN: Los inéditos de Blas Infante.* Edited by Eduardo Iniesta. Seville: Blas Infante Foundation.

———. 2008. *Andalucía: Teoría y Fundamento Político.* Edited by Manuel Pimentel and Antonio Manuel. Córdoba: Almuzara.

Iniesta Coullaut-Valera, Enrique. 2001. "Al-Andalus en Blas Infante" WebIslam, October 10. http://www.webislam.com/articulos/25802alandalus_en_blas_infante.html.

Irving, Washington. 1869. *The Alhambra*. New York: Putnam.

Jensen, Geoffrey. 2005. "The Peculiarities of 'Spanish Morocco': Imperial Ideology and Economic Development." *Mediterranean Historical Review* 20 (1): 81–102.

Johnson, Carroll B. 2000. *Cervantes and the Material World*. Champaign: University of Illinois Press.

Kamen, Henry. 1996. "Limpieza and the Ghost of Américo Castro: Racism as a Tool of Literary Analysis." *Hispanic Review* 64 (1): 19–29.

Kant, Immanuel. (1797) 1996. *Anthropology from a Pragmatic Point of View*. Translated by Victor Lyle Dowdell. Carbondale: Southern Illinois University Press.

Kimmel, Seth. 2013. "'In the Choir with the Clerics': Secularism in the Age of Inquisition." *Comparative Literature* 65 (3): 285–305.

Labajo, Joaquina. 1997. "How Musicological and Ethnomusicological is Spanish Flamenco?" *TRANS: Revista transcultural de música*. http://www.sibetrans.com/trans/articulo/314/how-musicological-and-ethnomusicological-is-spanish-flamenco.

Labanyi, Jo. 2004. "Love, Politics and the Making of the Modern European Subject: Spanish Romanticism and the Arab World." *Hispanic Research Journal* 5 (3): 229–43.

Laffranque, Marie. 1954. "Federico García Lorca: Nouveaux textes en prose." *Bulletin Hispanique* 56 (3): 260–300.

Laín Entralgo, Pedro, ed. 1971. *Estudios sobre la obra de Américo Castro*. Madrid: Taurus.

Lambek, Michael. 2002. *The Weight of the Past: Living with History in Mahajanga, Madagascar*. London: Palgrave Macmillan.

———. 2016. "On Being Present to History: Historicity and Brigand Spirits in Madagascar." *HAU: Journal of Ethnographic Theory* 6, no. 1 (Summer): 317–41.

Larmore, Charles. 1996. *The Romantic Legacy*. New York: Columbia University Press.

Litvak, Lily. 1986. *El sendero del tigre: Exotismo en la literature española de finales de siglo XIX, 1880–1913*. Madrid: Taurus.

López Enamorado, María Dolores. 1998. "La mirada del otro: La visión del africanismo español (el Gil Benumeya de los años veinte)." In *Relaciones interétnicas y multiculturalidad en el Mediterráneo Occidental*, edited by Elías Zamora Acosta and Pedro Maya Álvarez, 261–78. Melilla: V Centenario de Melilla.

López García, Bernabé. 1990. "Arabismo y orientalismo en España: Radiografía y diagnóstico de un gremio escaso y apartizado." *Awraq* 11:35–69.

———. 2011. *Orientalismo e ideología colonial en el arabismo español (1840–1917)*. Granada: Universidad de Granada.

———. 2012. "Los españoles en Tánger." *Awraq* 5/6:1–46.

Lorca, Federico García. 1994. *Obras*, vol. 4, *Prosa, 1*. Edited by Miguel García-Posada. Madrid: Akal.

———. 1997. *Obras completas*. Vol. 3. Edited by Miguel García-Posada. Galaxia Gutenberg.

———. 2012. *Poesía completa*. Edited by Miguel García-Posada. New York: Vintage Español.

Machin-Autenrieth, Matthew. 2019. *Flamenco, Regionalism, and Musical Heritage in Southern Spain*. New York: Routledge.

Mallette, Karla. 2010. *European Modernity and the Arab Mediterranean: Toward a New Philology and a Counter-Orientalism*. Philadelphia: University of Pennsylvania Press.

Mancing, Howard. 1981. "Cidi Hamete Benengeli vs. Miguel de Cervantes: The Metafictional Dialectic of *Don Quijote*." *Cervantes: Bulletin of the Cervantes Society of America* 1 (1/2): 63–81.

Manzano Moreno, Eduardo. 2009. "Repensar el legado histórico de la españa musulmana." In *Musulmanes en España: guía de referencia*, 64–73. Madrid: Casa Árabe.

Marín, Manuela. 1998. "L'art de vivre d'Al-Andalus a-t-il vraiment existé?" *Le monde arabe danls la recherche scientifique*, no. 9, 53–59.

Martínez López, Emilio. 1989. "Federico García Lorca, poeta granadino." Introduction to *Granada, paraíso cerrado y otras páginas granadinas*, by Federico García Lorca, 15–69. Edited by Enrique Martínez López. Granada: Miguel Sánchez.

Martínez Montávez, Pedro. 2011. *Significado y símbolo de al-Andalus*. Madrid: Cantarabia Editorial.

Martin-Márquez, Susan. 2008. *Disorientations: Spanish Colonialism in Africa and the Performance of Identity*. New Haven, CT: Yale University Press.

Massumi, Brian. 2002. *Parables of the Virtual: Movement, Affect, Sensation*. Durham, NC: Duke University Press.

Mastnak, Tomaž. 2003. "Europe and the Muslims: The Permanent Crusade?" In *The New Crusades: Constructing the Muslim Enemy*, edited by Emran Qureshi and Michael A. Sells. New York: Columbia University Press.

Mateo Dieste, Josep Lluís. 2003. "'Pourquoi tu ne m'écris plus?': Les rapports mixtes et les frontières sociales dans le Protectorat espagnol au Maroc." *Hawwa: Journal of Women of the Middle East and the Islamic World* 1 (2): 241–68.

———. 2012. "Una hermandad en tensión: Ideología colonial, barreras e intersecciones hispano-marroquí en el protectorado." *Awraq* 5/6: 79–96.

Menocal, María Rosa. 1985. "Pride and Prejudice in Medieval Studies: European and Oriental." *Hispanic Review* 53, no. 1 (Winter): 61–78.

———. 1987. *The Arabic Role in Medieval Literary History: A Forgotten Heritage*. Philadelphia: University of Pennsylvania Press.

———. 2002. *The Ornament of the World: How Muslims, Jews, and Christians Created a Culture of Tolerance in Medieval Spain*. Boston: Little, Brown.

Mignolo, Walter D. 2007. "What Does the Black Legend Have to Do with Race?" In *Rereading the Black Legend: The Discourses of Religious and Racial Difference in the Renaissance Empires*, edited by Margaret R. Greer, Walter D. Mignolo, and Maureen Quilligan, 312–24. Chicago: University of Chicago Press.

Milbank, John. 1977. *The Word Made Strange*. Oxford: Blackwell.

Molina, Antonio F. 1968. *La generación del 98*. Barcelona: Editorial Labor.

Monroe, James T. 1970. *Islam and the Arabs in Spanish Scholarship: Sixteenth Century to the Present*. Leiden: E. J. Brill.

Moreno Alonso, Manuel. 1986. "El nacionalismo andaluz." In *Actas del III Congreso de profesores-investigadores*, 363–78. Huelva: Asociación Andaluza de Profesores Hespérides.

Morris, C. Brian. 1997. *Son of Andalusia: The Lyrical Landscapes of Federico García Lorca*. Nashville: Vanderbilt University Press.

Mulhall, Stephen. 2012. "Realism, Modernism and the Realistic Spirit: Diamond's Inheritance of Wittgenstein, Early and Late." *Nordic Wittgenstein Review* 1 (1): 7–33.

Naqvi, Nauman. 2007. "The Nostalgic Subject: A Genealogy of the 'Critique of Nostalgia.'" CIRSDIG-Working Paper no. 23, Messina, Italy.

Navarro, Josep María, ed. 1997. *El Islam en las aulas: Contenidos, silencios, enseñanza*. Barcelona: Icaria Antrazyt.

Navaro-Yashin, Yael. 2009. "Affective Spaces, Melancholic Objects: Ruination and the

Production of Anthropological Knowledge." *Journal of the Royal Anthropological Institute* 15 (1): 1–18.

Nerín i Abad, Gustau. 1998. *Guinea Ecuatorial, historia en negro y blanco: Hombres blanco y mujeres negras en Guinea Ecuatorial (1943–1968)*. Barcelona: Ediciones Penínsulas.

Nirenberg, David. 2008. "Islam and the West: Two Dialectical Fantasies." *Journal of Religion in Europe* 1:1–33.

Nogué, Joan. 1999. "Las sociedades geográficas y otras asociaciones en la acción colonial española en Marruecos." In *España en Marruecos (1912–1956)*, edited by Joan Nogué and José Luis Villanova, 183–224. Lleida: Editorial Milenio.

Ochoa de Michelena, Francisco Javier. 2007. "La europeización de España desde la cultura y las categorías del juicio: reflexiones en torno a Ganivet, Unamuno y Ortega." *Revista Castellano-Manchega de Ciencias Sociales* 8:193–213.

Otero, Luis. 2000. *Flechas y pelayos: moral y estilo de los niños franquistas que soñaban imperios*. Madrid: EDAF.

Paetzold, Christopher. 2009. "Singing Beneath the Alhambra: The North African and Arabic Past and Present in Contemporary Andalusian Music." *Journal of Spanish Cultural Studies* 10 (2): 207–23.

Palmié, Stephan, and Giovanni da Col, eds. 2020. *The Mythology in Our Language: Remarks on Frazer's* Golden Bough. Chicago: Hau Books.

Parra Monserrat, David. 2012a. "La narrativa del africanismo franquista: Génesis y prácticas socio-educativas." Doctoral thesis, Universitat de Valencia.

———. 2012b. "¿Reescribir la 'historia patria'? Diversas visiones de España del africanismo franquista." In *La nación de los españoles: Discursos y prácticas del nacionalismo español en la época contemporánea*, edited by Ismael Saz and Ferran Archilés, 225–41. Valencia: Publicaciones de la Universidad de Valencia.

Pedrell, Felipe. 1900. *Cancionero musical popular español*. Vol. 1. Valls: Eduardo Castells.

Piras, Pina Rosa. 1991. "La 'precoce' cultura islámica di Federico García Lorca." In *Dai modernismi alle avanguardie*, edited by Carla Prestigiacomo and Maria Caterina Ruta, 173–80. Palermo: Flaccovio.

Puerta Vílchez, José Miguel. 2011. "al-Ándalus and the Arab World." Paper presented at the congress "Al-Andalus y el mundo árabe (711–2011): Visiones desde el arabismo," Granada, Spain, September 22–23.

Quinn, Mary B. 2013. *The Moor and the Novel: Narrating Absence in Early Modern Spain*. New York: Palgrave Macmillan.

Ramsden, Herbert. 1974. "The Spanish 'Generation of 1898': A Reinterpretation." *Bulletin of the John Rylands Library* 57 (1): 167–95.

Rancière, Jacques. 1994. *The Names of History: On the Poetics of Knowledge*. Translated by Hassan Melehy. Minneapolis: University of Minnesota Press.

Rangel, Cecilia Enjuto. 2010. *Cities in Ruins: The Politics of Modern Poetics*. West Lafayette, IN: Purdue University Press.

Ray, Jonathan. 2005. "Beyond Tolerance and Persecution: Reassessing Our Approach to Medieval Convivencia." *Jewish Social Studies*, n.s., 11, no. 2 (Winter): 1–18.

Redding, Paul. 1987. "Anthropology as Ritual: Wittgenstein's Reading of Frazer's *The Golden Bough*." *Metaphilosophy* 18 (3/4): 253–69.

Reina, Carmen. 2014. "La Iglesia inscribió la Mezquita-Catedral a su nombre sin tener 'título escrito de dominio.'" *Andalucía*, February 27. https://www.eldiario.es/andalucia/Iglesia-inscribio-Mezquita-escrito-dominio_0_233427308.html.

Reynolds, Dwight. 2009. "New Directions in the Study of Medieval Andalusi Music." *Journal of Medieval Iberian Studies* 1 (1): 37–51.

———. 2010. "The Re-Creation of Medieval Arabo-Andalusian Music in Modern Performance." *Al-Masaq* 21 (2): 175–89.

Ríos Saloma, Martín F. 2011. *La reconquista: Una construcción historiográfica (siglos XVI–XIX)*. Barcelona: Marcial Pons.

Rivero, Isabel. 1999. *Síntesis de historia de España*. Madrid: Globo.

Robles Egea, Antonio. 1997. "El neoidealismo y la rebelión de Ángel Ganivet contra el positivismo: Sobre Alfred Fouillee y la teoría de las ideas." *RILCE* 13 (2): 201–21.

Rodríguez Magda, Rosa María. 2006. *La España convertida al Islam*. Barcelona: Áltera.

Rodríguez Mediano, Fernando. 2011. "Al-Andalus, España y la inexistencia de las culturas." *Revista de Occidente* 362/63 (July/August): 75–95.

Rodríguez Ramos, Antonio Manuel. 2010. *La huella morisca: El Al Ándalus que llevamos dentro*. Córdoba: Almuzara.

———. 2013. "Apuntes jurídicos sobre la titularidad pública de la Mezquita Catedral de Córdoba." *SecretOlivo: Cultura Andaluza Contemporánea*, April. https://secretolivo.com/index.php/2013/04/25/informe-mezquita/.

Rogozen-Soltar, Mikaela. 2017. *Spain Unmoored: Migration, Conversion, and the Politics of Islam*. Indianapolis: Indiana University Press.

Rosa, Brian, and Jaime Jover Báez. 2017. "Contested Urban Heritage: Discourses of Meaning and Ownership of the Mosque-Cathedral of Cordoba, Spain." *Journal of Urban Cultural Studies* 4 (1/2): 127–54.

Rosón Lorente, Javier. 2008a. "Cultura oral y patrimonio inmaterial en el barrio de Albaycín, Granada: Una aplicación del modelo de catalogación en el marco del proyecto Mediterranean Voices." In *El patrimonio cultural inmaterial: definición y sistemas de catalogación*, 211–46. Murcia: Servicio de Patrimonio Histórico.

———. 2008b. "¿El Retorno de Tariq? Comunidades etnorreligiosas en el Albayzín granadino." Doctoral thesis, University of Granada.

Sáenz, Pilar G. 1997. "Castro, Americo." In *Encyclopedia of the Essay*, edited by Tracy Chevallier, 161–63. London: Fitzroy Dearborn.

Said, Edward W. 1978. *Orientalism*. New York: Vintage.

Sánchez-Alarcos, Raúl Fernández. 2015. "Las ruinas de Granada (ensueño), un relato insólito de Ángel Ganivet." In *Espejismos de la realidad: Percepciones de lo insólito en la literatura española (siglos XIX–XXI)*, edited by Natalia Álvarez Méndez and Ana Abello Verano, 109–16. León: Universidad de León.

Sánchez-Albornoz, Claudio. 1975. *Spain, a Historical Enigma*. Madrid: Fundación Universitaria Española.

Sánchez Arroyo, Germán. 2013. "Socialización y enseñanzas: Recuerdos personales; La religión, ¿huella del Protectorado?" In *El Protectorado español en Marruecos: La historia transcendida*, edited by Manuel Aragón Reyes, 1:393–413. Bilbao: Iberdrola.

Sánchez Dueñas, Blas. 2010. *Andalucía y la generación del 98*. Granada: Caja General de Ahorros.

Sant Cassia, Paul. 2000. "Exoticizing Discoveries and Extraordinary Experiences: 'Traditional' Music, Modernity, and Nostalgia in Malta and Other Mediterranean Societies." *Ethnomusicology* 44 (2): 281–301.

Scott, David. 1999. *Refashioning Futures: Criticism after Postcoloniality*. Princeton, NJ: Princeton University Press.

Seremetakis, Nadia, ed. 1994. *The Senses Still: Perception and Memory as Material Culture in Modernity.* Boulder, CO: Westview.

Shannon, Jonathan Holt. 2015. *Performing al-Andalus: Music and Nostalgia across the Mediterranean.* Indianapolis: Indiana University Press.

Soifer Irish, Maya. 2009. "Beyond Convivencia: Critical Reflections on the Historiography of Interfaith Relations in Christian Spain." *Journal of Medieval Iberian Studies* 1 (1): 19–35.

Starrett, Gregory. 1995. "The Hexis of Interpretation: Islam and the Body in the Egyptian Popular School." *American Ethnologist* 22 (4): 953–69.

Steingress, Gerhard. 1993. *Sociología del cante flamenco.* Jerez: Centro Andaluz de Flamenco.

———. 2002. "El flamenco como patrimonio cultural o una construcción artificial más de la identidad andaluza." *Revista Andaluza de Ciencias Sociales* 1:43–64.

———. 2005. "La hibridación transcultural como clave de formación del nuevo flamenco (aspectos histórico- sociológicos, analíticos y comparativos)." *Música Oral del Sur* 6:119–52.

Stewart, Charles. 2013. "Dreaming and Historical Consciousness." *Historically Speaking* 14 (1): 28–30.

———. 2017. "Uncanny History: Temporal Topology in the Post-Ottoman World." *Social Analysis* 61:129–42.

Stewart, Charles, and Stephan Palmié. 2016. "Introduction: For an Anthropology of History." *HAU: Journal of Ethnographic Theory* 6 (1): 207–36.

Stolcke, Verena. 1992. "¿Es el sexo para el género como la raza para la etnicidad?" *Mientras tanto,* no. 48, 87–112.

Subirats, Eduardo. 2003. *Américo Castro y la revisión de la memoria: El Islam en España.* Madrid: Libertarias.

Szabados, Béla. 2014. *Wittgenstein as Philosophical Tone-Poet: Philosophy and Music in Dialogue.* Amsterdam: Rodopi.

Szpiech, Ryan. 2013. "The Convivencia Wars: Decoding Historiography's Polemic with Philology." In *A Sea of Languages: Rethinking the Arabic Role in Medieval Literary History,* edited by Suzanne Conklin Akbari and Karla Mallette, 135–61. Toronto: University of Toronto Press.

Talbayev, Edwige Tamalet. 2017. *The Transcontinental Maghreb: Francophone Literature across the Mediterranean.* New York: Fordham University Press.

Unamuno, Miguel de. (1892) 2017. *Epistolario I (1880–1899).* Salamanca: Ediciones Universidad de Salamanca.

Vagni, Juan José. 2016. "Escenarios periféricos y perspectivas que se reflejan: España, el mundo árabe y América Latina en la mirada de Rodolfo Gil Benumeya." *Revista de Estudios Internacionales Mediterráneos* 21 (December): 59–72.

Velasco de Castro, Rocío. 2014. "La imagen del 'moro' en la formulación e instrumentalización del africanismo franquista." *Hispania* 74, no. 246 (January–April): 205–36.

Vidal Manzanares, César. 2005. *España frente al islam: De Mahoma a Ben Laden.* Madrid: La esfera de los libros.

———. 2009. *Historia de España.* Barcelona: Planeta.

Vincent, Bernard. 2006. *El río morisco.* Translated by Antonio Luís Cortés Peña. Granada: Universidad de Granada.

Washabaugh, William. 1995. "Ironies in the History of Flamenco." *Theory Culture Society* 12:133–55.

———. 2012. *Flamenco Music and National Identity in Spain: Music and Memory*. Farnham: Ashgate.

Wittgenstein, Ludwig. (1931) 1993. "Remarks on Frazer's *Golden Bough*." In *Philosophical Occasions: 1912–1951*, edited by James Klagge and Alfred Nordmann. Indianapolis, IN: Hackett.

———. 1973. *Philosophical Investigations*. 3rd ed. Translated by G. E. M. Anscombe. Englewood Cliffs, NJ: Prentice Hall.

———. 1998. *Culture and Value*. Edited by Georg Henrik von Wright. Oxford: Blackwell.

Wolf, Kenneth Baxter. 2014. "La conquista islámica: Negacionar el negacionismo." Review of *La conquista islámica de la península ibérica y la tergiversación del pasado: del catastrofismo al negacionismo*, by Alejandro García Sanjuán. *Revista de libros*, June 9.

Yafil, Edmond-Nathan. 1904. *Répertoire de musique arabe et maure*. Edited by Jules Rouanet. Alger: Yafil & Seror.

Index

Made in the USA
Coppell, TX
24 January 2023

11629695R10118